Language and Learning in Early Childhood

Edited by
ALAN DAVIES

HEINEMANN
LONDON
in association with
SSRC and SCRE

Heinemann Educational Books Ltd
LONDON EDINBURGH MELBOURNE AUCKLAND TORONTO
SINGAPORE HONG KONG KUALA LUMPUR
IBADAN NAIROBI JOHANNESBURG
LUSAKA NEW DELHI KINGSTON

ISBN 0 435 10191 9

The report *Research on Spoken Language in the Primary
School* (Part 3 of this volume) was originally prepared
for the Scottish Education Department and
financed by the department under SED grant no.
914.860. It is reproduced here in full with only
minor changes made necessary by its inclusion in
this volume. Thanks are due to the Scottish
Education Department for permission to publish
the report.

Set in Baskerville

Published by
Heinemann Educational Books Ltd
48 Charles Street, London W1X 8AH
Printed in Great Britain by
Butler & Tanner Ltd, Frome and London

Contents

Contents

Foreword

The Educational Research Board of the Social Science Research Council is sponsoring a series of research seminars on the topic of language and learning, in collaboration with a committee chaired by Dr W. B. Dockrell. At the first meeting in January 1973, the papers concentrated primarily on the theoretical aspects of the topic and they have been published under the title *Problems of Language and Learning*.

For its second meeting (Leeds, 1974), the seminar discussed a group of original papers on language and learning in early childhood, which have a consciously practical slant and are based on empirical studies. They follow logically from the consideration of fundamental issues in the previous volume. We hope that they will have a broad appeal to staff and students in colleges of education, and in social science departments of polytechnics and universities.

More recently, at its third meeting (Bristol, 1975), the seminar has discussed the kinds of research in language in education. Reports on the second and third meetings are contained in this volume, which is completed by a related report, 'Research on Spoken Language in the Primary School' originally prepared for the Scottish Education Department by the editor of this book, Alan Davies, and Clive Criper.

The research seminar on language and learning was set up with the intention of promoting the exchange of information and the discussion of common problems among researchers. It was also intended to provide a stimulus to new and promising directions of research. The size of the seminar was necessarily restricted, and this record of the debate is published so that the many others who are interested can know something about it.

J. D. NISBET
Chairman
SSRC Educational Research Board

M. L. JAMES
Acting Secretary
Social Science Research Council

1975

Introduction

ALAN DAVIES

The topic *Language and Learning in Early Childhood* was a natural sequel to the more general survey of the relations between language and education undertaken in the first joint SCRE–SSRC Seminar in January 1973, now published under the title: *Problems of Language and Learning* (Davies 1975). The 'early childhood' focus was a deliberate attempt to examine in depth one educational area that has been neglected and which has recently enjoyed attention and merits investigation in view of its developmental interest. The 'early childhood' topic therefore contains interest for linguists interested in theory and for teachers concerned with practice. This volume in Part 1 reports the Seminar concerned with language and learning in early childhood which was held in Leeds in January 1974.

The volume contains two other sections. In Part 2 Gordon Wells, himself a participant at the Leeds Seminar, reports (with colleagues) on the third Seminar in the Language and Learning series, the one held in Bristol in January 1975. In Part 3 Clive Criper and Alan Davies review the research literature on 'spoken language in the Primary school', a report originally written for the Scottish Education Department in September 1974. It is appropriate that the account of the Bristol Seminar and the research review accompany the Leeds Seminar report in this one volume. The Leeds Seminar papers considered ongoing work, both theoretical and practical, in the narrow area of early childhood education. It was to be expected that at the end of the Seminar the question should come up again and again of what kinds of research should be most highly prized in that area. Hence the origin of the Bristol Seminar for which, as Wells explains (p. 89), three papers on putative research projects were contracted as the basis for a discussion of fruitful future research. Similarly, the Leeds Seminar came back again and again to the question of disadvantage in education. It is appropriate therefore that the Criper and Davies paper and bibliography should form

A*

part of this volume since that paper deliberately viewed language in education against the background of current discussions of educational disadvantage. The Criper and Davies bibliography has in fact been expanded to include references from Parts 1 and 2 of this volume.

Any discussion of language and learning in early childhood necessarily ranges over both psycholinguistics and sociolinguistics, concerned as it is with the relation between language and cognition on the one hand and language and society on the other. We were warned in the Leeds Seminar by a number of speakers that in research we see what we want to see, or, as Joan Tough put it: 'the way in which the problem is conceived determines the way in which it will be met', and the present writer is well aware that in summarizing the discussions at the Leeds Seminar and highlighting the main themes he may be seeing what he wants to see. This Introduction does not try to summarize the Leeds papers. What I am attempting to do is to recapture some of the main concerns of the discussions. The papers, after all, will stand for themselves. What appeared to happen was that the major interest in Leeds came to rest more and more during the Seminar on sociolinguistic concerns possibly reflecting a change in academic fashion in the last few years. Roger Wales made a plea for the psycholinguist's interest in psychological reality, and for the importance of investigating children's own awareness of their linguistic competence. But the centre of interest in the Seminar was on interaction rather than on cognition.

From a sociolinguistic point of view there is more to speech events, more to language ability than linguistic competence. Hence the attempts still vague and unsatisfactory, to establish the notion of communicative competence. Investigations of language learning and language interactions as well as the experience of language teachers make it clear that there is more to using, learning and teaching a language than knowledge of the linguistic rules indicates. Knowing the grammar is just not enough as a model of how speakers behave or indeed of how to imitate them when learning a second or foreign language. From this point of view second language teaching is both evidence for, and a vindication of this notion of communicative competence. But of course, it is not being suggested that communicative competence consists of grammar plus intuition since intuition explains nothing, being a way of accepting the unexplainable. Communicative competence is a combination of rules of grammar and rules of language use. There is no doubt among sociolinguists that such rules of language use exist; precisely what they are remains unclear, hence the vagueness and unsatisfactoriness referred to above.

Much second language teaching has assumed that what is necessary is to teach the grammar. Many programmes for the disadvantaged have taken over this belief and have taught disadvantaged children as if they were second language learners. Bereiter and Englemann (1966) are good examples of this approach. But in both situations, second language teaching and teaching the disadvantaged, it is rare to find rules taught *as rules*. The stuff of the teaching corpus, of the curriculum, is texts of various kinds and lengths designed so as to exemplify the rules of the grammar. Now in the Leeds Seminar this kind of approach in language programmes for the disadvantaged was labelled, quite properly, structural. It was contrasted (by Courtney Cazden among others) with an approach seeking to achieve communicative competence and labelled from different points of view as functional or concentrated or language use. It was precisely in these oppositions, precisely in the discussions of non-structural approaches that there was obscurity as to what exactly can embody communicative rules. Joan Tough and others wanted functional materials and Courtney Cazden spoke of concentrated as opposed to the more structural, contrived encounters in her discussion of assessment. And although the label was not used there was the further implied contrast to language use and that was the more structural *language usage*. So we have three pairs of contrasts, on the one side aspects of linguistic competence: structural materials, contrived encounters, language usage, all to be avoided according to the general view of the Leeds Seminar; and on the other, aspects of communicative competence: functional materials, concentrated encounters and language use, all to be embraced. But the nature of the texts conveying these aspects of communicative competence was left vague, understandably so, because it is difficult to set out exhaustively what makes up communicative competence—or functional materials.

At times it seemed to be being suggested that *any* bits of mother–child dialogue of the 'enabling' kind could be used as good examples of language use. But it is clear to us all that no teaching syllabus or language programme, no data that are investigated remain completely 'authentic' in the sense of being unidealized. As soon as it is selected as an example, used again, removed from its unique and original occurrence, then it becomes unauthentic. The very fact of selection, of sampling for a purpose means that language use is as text-bound as language usage is. Like language usage (or like structural drills) it does not at the one extreme set out rules as lists of categorial procedures. Like language usage it does not, at the other extreme, gather bits of any old data to exemplify 'the language'. It selects carefully and exactly in order to exemplify just those rules that it is desired to teach, only they are communicative and not grammar rules.

From this point of view disadvantage becomes easier to under-stand as a linguistic phenomenon. Much of the argument in the language deprivation area has been semi-philosophical, concern-ing itself with the status of such sentences as 'this child is linguis-tically deprived' and querying whether it is proper or meaningful to make such a statement, hence the very different explanations for the 'same' evidence of language performance as either lan-guage deficit or language difference. William Labov has, of course, asserted that 'the notion of verbal deprivation is part of the modern mythology of educational psychology' (Labov 1969) and indeed the names of Labov and Basil Bernstein were appealed to during the Leeds Seminar as apparent protagonists of the two views, of the language difference explanation, which Labov has certainly espoused and the language deficit explanation, which Bernstein is thought to have supported.

Bernstein's own work seems to illustrate a parallel development to that in the Leeds Seminar, moving from a concern with children's perception, and measurement of this by grammatical data of language usage, to a much more direct interest in the socialization of different sub-groups in society. He has always been interested in socialization and in language data as evidence for this but his research shows a change in emphasis on the data that seems to move further and further away from performance evidence. Three stages may be suggested which illustrate his changing use of language data. At the first stage he was anxious to show that lower-working-class and middle-class children exhibit grammatical differences in their writing and speaking and these differences are of an obvious surface kind. There is no doubt that he found such evidence, as indeed have most researchers who have followed him in this attempt to correlate language perfor-mance and social class. What many commentators, many critics and eventually Bernstein himself concluded was that such dif-ferences might be reliable, in the sense of being systematic, but they were not valid. Children did exhibit grammatical differences but as Labov and others have pointed out this said nothing about their perception or about their logic. In any case Bernstein was interested in socializing as illustrated by language and so he moved on to Stage 2 as we see it now.

At Stage 2 it is language use rather than usage that interests him. He compares two short texts, in which two boys, again differentiated by social class, describe a series of pictures telling a story of a broken window. Bernstein has accepted that language is more than forms, e.g. grammar; it is also functions, i.e. what language is used for. Examples often quoted are requests, commands, giving information, persuading and so on. Although he does not talk about language functions in any categorial way (i.e. with a tight-knit set of categories) at this point it is clear that he is differentiating these two boys and, by implication, the social classes in terms of the ways in which they use their common language. It is an appeal to frequency and to habit, not that the working-class child cannot but that he does not do what the middle-class child does, which, for example, is to set down explicitly for a general audience, rather than to imply meanings to his own reference group. It is not clear why Bernstein became dissatisfied with this kind of language-use data unless he realized of course its glaring sampling problem. On what principles does one select data of this kind? The very fact that the same two texts were used again and again suggests that there was a difficulty about selecting other data which would provide supporting evidence.

In his Stage 3 it seems that Bernstein has abandoned a linguistic interest in language for some kind of reflexive interest. He has, for example, in a recently published work with young children (Cook-Gumperz 1974) used language as a way of collecting socialization data rather than as evidence of those data themselves.

Disadvantage as a linguistic phenomenon then has to do with differences in language use. If the investigator chooses to examine differences in language usage then he will find them and be led into some kind of deficit view. If he examines language use he will find that there is differential use, that social classes and families differ both in the functions they use language for and the ways in which those functions are verbalized. This is in no sense a linguistic deficit at the individual level. What it argues for is differential language use, i.e. language difference. Of course this could be regarded as linguistic deficit at some kind of social level. In so far as some groups in a society have prestige, money, authority and power, and in so far as their pattern of child-rearing is mediated through language functions which differ for the social classes, then so far can the working class be said to suffer from a language deficit, because they do not use language the same way as the middle class. Demonstrating this systematically is difficult, as Bernstein has found.

What we can conclude here then is that disadvantage may be related to language deprivation, if that deprivation is seen as being a matter of different (often deliberate) language use, and it must therefore be evaluated in terms of Cazden's concentrated encounters. Of course, as Wales reminded the Seminar, correlations between language scales and social class imply no causation. At the same time different groups do use different languages (e.g. French and English in Quebec). It seems not unreasonable that, within one language, language use differs for social classes in terms of language functions and that as a result socialization does differ.

If we are to do anything about this, whether for the Black American child or the working-class child and if our way is to be through language then it is necessary that we stop at Bernstein's Stage 2. If we can sort out the categories of language functions then we can produce meaningful and valid language programmes. But if we go on to Bernstein's Stage 3 then there is no way in which language can be used any more as a mediator or a catalyst. How could it be, since it is not clear what it is in the language that indicates differences or could bring them about. At Stage 3 language is evidence for something else and it is the latter that would need to be acted upon. So it is firmly in the language function/language use area that language deprivation needs to stay, and it is work of a more theoretical kind that needs to be done in order to help with the desired applications. It is understandable that the Bristol Seminar was still exercising itself on this matter of language functions and the tricky form—function relationship.

This relationship is tricky because it is not consistent. Different forms do not always convey the same functions. In other words there is variety here, one major aspect of language variation. Now sociolinguistics does not catalogue language varieties one after the other like a family snapshot album. In its attempts to be theoretical it concerns itself with language variation as an idealized form of behaviour. It is because of this deliberate avoidance of so-called authentic data that sociolinguistics brings within its scope *language use* as an ideal form, *rules of discourse* and the concept of a *paralinguistic pragmatics* as accounting for a grammar of mother–baby communication, which Bruner suggested at Leeds.

For the opposite reason there was at the Bristol Seminar a good deal of objection to the suggestion that raw language data might be collected in nursery and primary schools. The objection was not, of course, that you cannot use observation to collect authentic data and eventually idealize it but that you cannot do anything else, i.e. that there is no such thing as 'raw data', that all data depends upon some theoretical construct which needs to be determined in advance. As long as sociolinguistics claimed to be studying language and society as discrete variables it remained possible to take linguistic form for granted, i.e. use the categories of linguistics such as nouns, verbs, modality—as given, and relate them to social functions and situations. But such essentially correlational approaches have come increasingly under attack and in their place attention has turned to a more composite approach of language-with-society as one variable. This can be seen as an attempt to extend the scope of linguistics by taking in social situation as a necessary linguistic level. At the Edinburgh Seminar, the first in this series (Davies 1975), Halliday claimed that what sociolinguistics seems to be studying is what linguistics, as he understands it, always has studied. Language functions, the units desperately needed for all applied educational work in language, have thus become the object of the newer sociolinguistic quest. Various taxonomies have been suggested often for different purposes and all so far lacking in that essential quality of descriptive adequacy. Indeed it may be that sociolinguistics has tried too hard for explanatory adequacy in its theories before satisfactorily establishing descriptive adequacy. A discussion of some of the work on language functions is given in Part 3 and Gordon Wells *et al.* in Part 2 point to the danger of producing more and yet more idiosyncratic function taxonomies.

Why is there this need in applied educational work for information about language functions? This question collapses into the broader question about language programmes in general and that into the yet broader one of 'why education?' The fact is that institutions, of which education is one, are normative and as such must involve programmes or curricula. However much choice and time are allowed for, there have to be units and sequences laid down to be learnt. What is needed then is the best information about language units and sequences. Language programmes for early childhood, which have largely concentrated on the disadvantaged, have foundered not because they exist but because their analysis of language and language needs has been inadequate. What is needed is not, on the one hand, emphasis on linguistic forms, nor, on the other hand, random selections of enabling dialogues between enabling mother and child, but that content which somehow combines the two.

As might be expected therefore there was general acceptance at the Leeds Seminar of the need for language programmes even though Joan Tough was critical of the general trend of programmes. What criticism there was was aimed at badly conceived ones and those with unsatisfactory content. The Peabody Language Development Kit for example was found unacceptable by teachers in Scotland because, Joyce Watt suggested, both its content and its orientation towards children were wrong. But dislike of the Peabody should not be generalized into a closed view on language programmes. It is instructive here that Joyce Watt should have quoted the view of Bereiter and Englemann in favour of language programmes, instructive because these two protagonists' names tend to be used synonymously with bad language programmes (see for example Criper and Davies, p. 151). Watt approvingly quotes their criticism of conventional nurseries, that they have 'a broad unfocused educational programme, that recognizes no priorities and tolerates no omissions'. If this flatulent liberalism is true, all power to the preparation of purpose-built language programmes. It is only through good programmes that most nursery children can receive the language preparation they really need. It is no good relying on there being enough good teachers to act as the tutoring adults Joan Tough suggested are required. And even good teachers may not be aware of the small importance that current practice gives to language. 'Most nursery teachers,' said Joyce Watt, 'would claim that language is a priority. I think that in practice it is not.' In other words it does not receive the central place teachers think it does.

What is a good programme? In a way it is pedagogically selected adult–child dialogue, just what Joan Tough advocated but with the right bits of the right dialogues in the right order. Enabling dialogue then, on its own—that is the confrontation of adult and child in the nursery—is not enough though it forms the content of the language programme. Here indeed is a great field for research and development, for sociolinguists and materials writers, to produce innovative language programmes that do what all good textbooks do, intrigue, instruct and reassure.

As always with curriculum innovation it appears that the teacher is being turned into a dummy, expected to hand over his authority and creative talents to a machine-like programme. How machine-like, how much room remains for teacher initiative depends on the programme. But the objection of usurping the teacher's authority is both true and refutable. No teacher can expect to supply the needs of all his pupils however good or recent his training. When there is a sudden leap in knowledge or switch in emphasis of diagnosis, as here, then it is essential to make available to teachers the linguistic knowledge and insights and the pedagogic tools all together in the same programme. To demand that every teacher be a tutoring adult puts the professional threshold too high, as Joyce Watt pointed out. Cazden too had doubts about the value of the adult–child dialogue as a pedagogic instrument. How does dialogue, she wanted to know, transfer into cognition; what value does it have in promoting thinking, one of the major activities of education. Cazden had another doubt related to the transfer possible to the child from dialogue to dialogue. What matters in the long run is not whether the child has learned off, by rote or practice or whatever, all the dialogues he is exposed to but whether he is in a position to generalize from them to all the new dialogues he meets in real life both within and outside the school nursery. This is the generative question turned on its head. It is axiomatic, as Chomsky and others have pointed out, that the child does generalize from the utterances he hears to new ones he has never met before. Can the same be said for dialogues? Surely it must be. Otherwise the child can never proceed beyond the corpus, the curriculum, the programme, provided for him in his nursery. The 'good' language programme selects and idealizes dialogues in such a way that they are generalizable in exactly the same way that grammatical rules are generalizable. Cazden mentioned a third doubt, that the adult–child dialogue might be too restrictive, in that it prevented or at least did not allow for the child bringing into use in the school those language skills and knowledge he so capably and clearly deploys outside. Formalizing these in the educational context, being shown how, might well be the quickest way into the cognitive development that is so necessary.

Cazden herself can properly be asked to face the same demand that she presented to Tough—how to generalize from dialogue to dialogue; but in her case it is encounters that need generalizing. There is no problem here for the child. It is the teacher who has to face the demand of generality. Now, by encounter Cazden means an assessment which is not a test or rather does not have attached to it the features normally associated with tests. The encounter (better the concentrated encounter since an encounter that is contrived rather than concentrated is a test) is open and not closed: its limits depend upon the interaction of the moment; it is non-scripted, not scripted: its discourse dependent on the particular interaction; it provides familiarity to the child both in the expected task and in the known evaluator (usually the teacher). All this puts a heavy burden on the teacher, as heavy perhaps as the generality demand that Cazden insisted upon for dialogue. If the encounter is of the moment without limit or script and involving the routine of a daily or at least frequent task then judgement is not easy for the teacher. Not only is judgement not easy; the representativeness of the encounter used for assessment is also open to question. Of course, if the curriculum, the language programme is right then it may well be that sampling any part of it (which is what Cazden wants the teacher to do) will give evidence of the child's over-all progress. Indeed it may and so we return once more to the urgency of providing the right sort of curriculum. There will of course remain a sampling problem but the teacher can herself overcome this by repeating encounters frequently.

What Cazden is advocating is the good language programme with which the teacher fully cooperates, observing and recording her children's performance daily. The assessment she makes will be of the internal achievement/attainment kind rather than the external proficiency, since she can rely on the programme (much as in programmed instruction practice) to produce learning through its deliberate structure. 'The "evaluation" question collapses,' says Cazden, 'to the more general question of how to analyze child language.' This is another way of saying that good language programmes are based on adequate child language analysis which by definition can be used for the concentrated encounters Cazden advocates. What remains problematic is that we do not have available such child language analyses and in the meantime do require the generality that good tests, Cazden's contrived encounters, provide. As Chazan pointed out, Cazden is somewhat hard on tests.

In the Criper and Davies review (Part 3 of this volume) it is suggested, not for the first time, that too much can be made of language. Bernstein's early work supports this view inasmuch as the restricted codes hypothesis indicates the importance of other forms of communication than the verbal one. While we concentrate on kinds of language deprivation arguing as to whether or not it is innate and whether or not it is better described in terms of function than form, we perhaps neglect those other representational systems in which middle-class children may be deprived. Lovell wanted to bring into the discussion the systems of intellectual skills and the ways in which these interacted with linguistic growth. Joan Tough, while firmly convinced of the existence of language deprivation, does point, if unconsciously, to the danger of basing language programmes on middle-class children's language use. After all to postulate deprivation is to assume that middle-class children have a different language use from non-middle-class children. But can we so easily dismiss the normative dilemma? Can we be sure that one type of language use is necessarily better for schooling than the other? At any rate Joan Tough does raise this issue by noting that, as with encounters and dialogues in our earlier discussion, language programmes do not transfer to other situations and other language uses.

Educational disadvantage is nonetheless a useful myth. Gordon Wells suggested some possible causes of disadvantage and Joan Tough expressed firm convictions about disadvantaged children—that they may well be different from others because of an aptitude for rote learning, they may not be able to project into other children's problems and viewpoints, i.e. they are egocentric and non-reflective, they may have very different experiences of language in use. It is, of course, to this explanation of the causes of observed educational disadvantage that Tough has directed her research work in Leeds. It is such problems as the disadvantaged child or the disabled child (which Lovell noted) that tend to lead into applied research, precisely because they are problems. Wales, however, was loath to generalize from the disabled to the normal child. What happens equally often is that we generalize from the disadvantaged child to the normal child. As Tough said 'the majority of programmes . . . currently in use . . .[are] conceived as curricula for the disadvantaged child.' Criper and Davies in Part 3 make the same point. But it is surely time that more applied interest in language in education was given to normal children and that language programmes for them were designed. What is needed is more theoretical work on child language development, which is what Wales advocated most strongly; what is also needed is concurrent work dealing with serious language materials preparation and development so as to experiment with language programmes. We cannot innovate without innovating and there is no doubt that work in this very applied field of preparing curricula and trying it out can feed back into more theoretical work on the nature of the form–function relationship. There is no need to assume that all research and all discovery must be one way, from theory into practice.

This concludes the introduction to Part 1 of this volume. Parts 2 and 3 have a separate origin and since each contains its own introduction it has not been thought necessary here to do more than refer to them in passing. At the same time there is a direct connection between Parts 2 and 3 and Part 1, apart from the obvious connection of all having language in common. It is this, that Parts 2 and 3, the account of the Bristol Seminar and the review of the research literature on spoken language in the primary school, each separately takes up the question of relevant research, both quite deliberately. The Bristol Seminar, as has been explained, had as its theme appropriate research in language in education, taking up the reiterated claim in the Leeds Seminar that more research was needed. The Criper and Davies review was written explicitly to advise the Scottish Education Department on areas where research into language in education should be concentrated. What is of interest therefore is where these two considerations of appropriate research coincide. The Bristol Seminar concluded that the three general areas where research is needed are those of:

a. initial language acquisition
b. language and social background
c. language and educational practices.

The Criper and Davies review recommended research into:

1. teacher prescriptivism
2. the study of form–function relations particularly at the cross-over from nursery to primary school
3. the use and interpretation of intonation
4. an anthropological study of peer-group language behaviour.

The emphasis is clearly different, the Criper and Davies suggestions being more linguistic and more particular, but there is a good deal in common. Thus we can equate as follows:

Bristol	Criper and Davies
a	2 & 3
b	4
c	1

These are crude matchings but it is significant and reassuring that there should be agreement in general on the research that is needed within the field of language in education.

PART I

I

Language and Learning

R. J. WALES

In this paper I will discuss aspects of child language, particularly that of pre-school children, in an attempt to focus attention on some of the issues which might be relevant should, say, an educator ask 'What can you tell me that would help me understand better the child that is beginning school?' This seems the best way of providing a basis for dialogue between those representing a variety of disciplines as to what avenues of child language research might be most usefully pursued. As we proceed I hope it will become clear that much less information is available than might be, and that some of the educators' more detailed questions might usefully be rephrased. Regarding the child's language, a question like 'What do you make of it?' necessarily involves asking both 'What do we make of the child?' as well as 'What does the child make of it?' Of necessity therefore what we think is interesting moulds what we go looking for and thus, substantially, what we find. Because of this it will always be necessary to work from the theoretical preconceptions of the student of child language in order to correctly evaluate what is known, and what the consequences are for asking for certain kinds of answers. Since time and space are fairly short, we are fortunate in not needing elaborate or exhaustive reviews of recent literature. These have been provided for us from a variety of points of view by Braine (1971), McNeill (1970), Clark (1970) and by Brown's superb synthesis of his own work (1973). Slobin and Ferguson (1973) provide a most useful collection of fundamental research papers. From these and many other sources it will become clear, I think, that the major emphasis in early language studies is on understanding it as a representation of some system. Why this should be the major interest will, I hope, become clearer as we proceed.

1. *Sounds Like Language*

While we are intending to stay mainly with syntactic and semantic issues, some recognition must be given to studies of child
phonology. Many of these have been crucially influenced by
Jakobson's theory of linguistic sound systems. This is based on the
notion that such systems are complexes of oppositions which
taken together define the domain of what we can meaningfully
manipulate in producing a linguistic utterance. Applied to child
language this results in the hypothesis that what the child does in
acquiring its language is to proceed from the optimum (maxi-
mally distinct) oppositions towards more and more complex sets
of distinctions. While a general similarity to Jakobson's hypothesis
has been observed by such as Leopold (1939), Velten (1953), the
detailed support hoped for is absent.

Recently an elegant study by Smith (1973) has suggested that it
is possible to characterize precisely the child's phonology. He
showed by simple tests of minimal pairs in different word positions that his subject did not have perceptual problems, that is
that he knew from the age of two all the adult's phonology. However he consistently mispronounced words and the nature of these
mispronunciations changed as he developed. Smith states a number of rules to describe what happens. He observes that at any one
stage of development the child was consistent in the pronunciation of a particular word, and that the child developed his phonology in discontinuous steps indicating that instead of just the
pronunciation of a single word having changed, a rule or set of
rules had changed. In comparing his own detailed study with less
substantial data from a number of different languages, Smith
proposes some universal constraints on phonological acquisition
which may reveal themselves in different ways in different languages and different speakers of those languages.

What is worthy of note in this study is what is being assumed by
way of its basic structure. Instead of approaching the child's
phonology as standing in a very abstract relation to the adult's
such that we assume it perceives and produces in terms solely
of its own system, Smith assumes that the adult system determines
the child's. His view of the child is thus (roughly): child phonology
is equivalent to adult phonology plus its own realization rules.
On the face of it unexceptional enough—until we note the
apparently astonishing claim that the child understands the
adult phonology from the word go. Some studies by Emias *et al.*

(1972) and Fodor and Garrett (1970) have been interpreted as indicating that young babies make discriminations amongst sounds which are consistent only with innate capacities for recognizing distinctions crucial for understanding speech. So although such studies still require further clarification as to what detailed speech characteristics the children are in fact responding to, Smith's view starts to look much less astonishing. In 1972 Kornfeld presented some very preliminary findings suggesting that a child's phonetic realizations may mark physical distinctions in the sounds which the conventional phonetic descriptions would fail to capture. She concludes 'that $1\frac{1}{2}$–$2\frac{1}{2}$-year-old children do not produce the same distinctions as adults; instead they selectively abstract from the adult set of features.' If this were corroborated, and the perceptual end of the descriptive game also needs to be modified, then we will have to reconsider the impact of Smith's findings. Meanwhile his analysis poses some intriguing and, as yet, unstudied questions regarding the impact of phonology on other parts of the linguistic system. For example, the frequent use in young children's language of such expressions as 'gonna', 'hafta', might be the consequence of phonological constraints, social conventions, syntactic or semantic relationships, or some interaction between some or all of these. If we are interested in precise answers to questions regarding what effects dialects might have, and what we might do to change them if we wanted to, we must rely partially on answers relating to the representational systems the child has at the phonological level as much as any others.

2. What's in a Word

After babbling, the sounds of the child's language are indissolubly linked to words, and as a general rule these come initially one at a time. It has been most natural to study these early one-word acquisitions by way of diary studies. Sometimes a diarist has collated earlier studies but perforce such an exercise had to make sweeping assumptions regarding the compatibility of the methodologies of the sundry diarists. Only recently (to my knowledge) has anyone addressed himself to collecting data on say the first fifty words from a variety of children in the same way—Nelson (1973) presents such results. Among these is a striking commonality in many of the words the children acquired, e.g.

negatives of some sort, *more*, *big*, some deictic terms such as *that*, some 'prepositions' such as *up*, and relatively few object or person names, characterize all the children's early speech. It seems that this commonality ought to provide the basis for interpreting the development which follows it—how, will be illustrated in the next section. As indicated by putting the descriptive category of *up* in italics there are some fundamental issues involved in deciding, from the interpretation of both the child's phonology and the context of utterance, the significance of what the child has said. Without indulging in personalized polemics, we ought to seriously question the criteria by which the adult's syntactic and semantic categories are attributed to the child. It has been established by many workers since the fine context-defining study of Bloom (1970), that the productions of the young child may be interpreted in terms of a larger set of semantic intentions than are superficially evident. Some have been tempted to claim that the categories of adults' major semantic intentions are represented from the word go in the child's speech. Unlike the analogous claims of Smith (1973) the present inexplicitness of these descriptions does not allow any evaluation beyond pointing out that at the moment they seem to reflect the interpreter more than the interpreted. What is at stake here is whether or not it is possible to 'derive' the basic semantic categories from underlying more general cognitive categories. This is a question which many of us are interested in because of an interest in trying to say more about how far, and where, language is distinct from the other parts of cognition. The importance of this question has, I suspect, resulted in some being too rapidly enthusiastic about some possible inter-relations. Take, for example, the description of children's early utterances such that the prominence of their dependence on location is brought out by for example suggesting 'locative' as a primitive term in that description (Wales 1971). It still needs to be demonstrated how and where in the development of language it is that the child's prelinguistic spatial/cognitive conceptions of location make contact with the linguistic ones. Until something substantive can be said about that, the hypothesis of inter-dependence remains open or empty according to one's point of view. Much the same can be said of the proposal made first by de Laguna (1927) that even the first of the child's words are implicit predications. If one wishes to argue (as McNeill 1970 does) that it is theoretically interesting to try and chart all the child's utterances as essentially sentential then such a move may be very attractive—

and it may be worthwhile living with imprecise criteria in the context of elaborating a complete theory—but presumably we are well advised to take careful note of where we have been inclined to skirt problems in the interests of developing a more general framework. Without making such a move as de Laguna's, of course, we are saddled with a serious problem deciding when and how sentences start. For a decade or more the influence of Chomsky (1957) resulted in the search for syntactic relations, which in turn resulted in starting from utterances where syntactic relations were definable, i.e. had at least two words. The problem of the significance of the earlier one word utterances was ignored. With the revival of interest in semantics we can expect increasing study of this area.

3. Between Words

Although Roger Brown and others worked with it, the originator of pivot grammar was Martin Braine. In looking at the distribution of two-word utterances he observed that there was a sub-set of words, which while small in number, occurred frequently, usually in initial position, and rarely on their own. These he dubbed 'pivot' (P) words, which, when concatenated with the larger, constantly growing class of 'open' (O) class words, defined the rule for the child's first sentence structure (S) as S → (P) + O. To find that something systematic could be defined this early in the child's syntax attracted a good deal of attention. Unfortunately as Bloom (1970, 1971), Bowerman (1973) and Brown (1973) have all concluded from further scrutiny of data, the pivot grammar is wrong; though Brown does indicate the data which have a 'pivot look' to them. The approach which these three scholars take (though in differing ways) is to emphasize the semantic content of these utterances and elaborate a set of semantic relations to characterize the children's sentences. Thus among the semantic relations Bloom assigns to noun–noun combinations are: conjunction, attribution, genitive, subject–locative and subject–object. All this is very interesting and, at times at least, persuasive.

There are however a number of problems which in a sense carry over from those discussed briefly in the preceding section. It is not always clear for example how we are to decide when an utterance like *daddy chair* is genitive (i.e. daddy's chair), subject–locative (daddy on chair) or subject–object. Of course, from observing the context the observer can come to some decision between these interpretations. There remains the question of how we can be sure that is what the child intended. It is not enough to indicate (correctly) that there are regularities in what the child says in relation to the possible set of coherent interpretations available in the situation. It is surely desirable and in the long term essential that we elaborate criteria for deciding when children may be using linguistic formulae because they recognize that saying that gets them to some desired communicative end, or when they are in a position to unpack the utterance into its constituent parts and utilize that level of knowledge to achieve more specific or varied ends. That is, how far and in what way, is the young child able to progress beyond relatively thoughtless speech habits which may be elaborated expressions of a kind of phatic communion equivalent to 'look I can talk' to which we as adults can respond 'look I can reward you by putting an interpretation on what you say'. This kind of issue of course points to all manner of fiendishly difficult questions, and it is important that the semantic orientation of such studies as Bloom, Bowerman and latterly Brown should be seen as at least giving us the framework in which to address them. One interesting suggestion on the same theme is from Hakes (1970). He has suggested that the uniformity in some of the two-word utterances that gives them the 'pivot look' is that there is 'a single kind of construction, the existential sentence, that appears sufficiently often both within and across children to warrant its characterization as the archetypal pivot construction.' Thus *see* $+\mathcal{N}$ is interpreted as having a 'noticing' function and is read as I see N. What is particularly valuable about Hakes's discussion is his attempt to give an account as to why there are wide individual differences in the number or exemplars in the children's speech. Given his analysis he suggests this may be due to differences in the activity or passivity of the child—the latter being more likely in his view to produce 'existential' sentences. What is important about this suggestion is not only the address to individual differences and the concomitant sampling problems, but that in raising explicitly the possible interaction of biological/social variables on such differences he may have pointed the way to a method for getting closer to unravelling the problems relating to what the child makes of its own utterances, i.e. what construction we may validly place on them. Methodologically this boils down to being able to trade one kind of interpretation against

another by juxtaposing them in contexts where say one interpretation predicts constancy and the other predicts change.

Another area where such studies seem possible derives from the
discussions by Bever (1970) of the role of perceptual strategies
in the child's language processing. Bever's basic contention is that
the children selectively sample the speech they hear using sundry
short-range strategies for this purpose; notably interpreting
noun–verb as actor–action. Thus, in simple sentences where this
rule is applicable, the children (even at two years) will, according
to Bever, perform appropriately. However when confronted with
passive sentences, where this rule is strictly inapplicable, their
performance drops to chance. This last result is interesting since
if they applied the rule regardless they should always misunder-
stand these sentences. This suggests they do recognize that something is wrong, and this somewhat weakens the strong and simple
version of Bever's case. Garman (in India) has found examples in Tamil which allow the juxtaposition of the noun–verb as
subject–object, versus actor–action interpretations, that they
overlap somewhat in their use but that the former seems to precede the latter. Slobin (1972a) in a wide-ranging review of studies
of around fifteen different languages has argued for a number of
what he has called 'universals' arising out of 'operating principles' many of which take an analogous form to Bever's strategies,
e.g. 'operating principle A: Pay attention to the ends of words'.
So, according to Slobin, English-speaking children have greater
difficulty acquiring prepositions and articles than children
learning highly inflected languages do in acquiring related
inflections. 'Operating principle C: Pay attention to the order of
words and morphemes—Universal C1: The standard order of func-
tor morphemes in the input language is preserved in child speech'
(perhaps the reason for the child blocking the noun–verb and
actor–action rule in Bever's study?). 'Universal C2: word order
in child speech reflects word order in the input language' etc.

The utility of cross-linguistic study is brought out in a very
different context by some studies conducted by Suppes and some
of his colleagues. They collected large sets of utterances and wrote
a number of Phrase Structure grammars to account for these—
rather like solving a problem in different ways. For each set of rules,
probabilities were assigned so that each grammar could be evaluated for goodness of fit with the initial data. They thus indicated a
possible way of evaluating one Phrase Structure grammar against
another. Although there are numerous problems associated with

such ambitious studies, nevertheless the difference of approach has already thrown up some important issues that earlier studies had largely overlooked. One of the things such an approach allows us to do is get a much better idea of those features of children's utterances which by virtue of their frequency suggest their centrality to children's speech. Thus pronominal constructions are among the three most frequent in the English, French and Chinese corpora. Yet little of current, even semantically based study, has been addressed to this topic in child language.

4. More Words

Two classical questions which are asked from the first word of a child onwards are 'How are the meanings of the child's words different from those that the adult gives to those words?' and 'How do the child's meanings change into those of the adult?' One of the standard means for trying to figure out answers to these questions is to study how the child's conceptual structure, as it may be related to words, differs from that of an adult. This approach is notoriously ambiguous in that the child's misunderstandings have often been held to represent an inherent difference in conceptual structure, rather than how that structure has been related as the 'meaning' to particular lexical items.

Take as an elaborate example the case of the child's understanding of spatial adjectives; if one adds to such adjectives as *big, long, high*, etc., such items as *same* and *more* we can develop a whole network of terms which in their inter-relations define a coherent semantic domain, or field. Now it is a matter of common observation that these terms occur crucially in the vocabulary of Piaget's conservation tasks either in setting up the problem for the child or in the child's justification of its responses. Because the lexical items occur in the child's spontaneous speech at this stage it is assumed that the 'misunderstandings' on the part of the pre-operational child are due to a conceptual deficit—namely a lack of a sufficiently coherent operational system. That the problem might be a consequence of how the child related its concepts to the meanings of its lexical items seems never to have been seriously considered within the Piagetian framework (at least until the recent work of Sinclair de Zwart 1967). A number of studies of the linguistic issue have lent support to the notion that there is a fundamental problem in relating the child's concepts to its developing lexical structure. Thus Donaldson and Balfour (1968) and Donaldson and Wales (1970) reported that while pre-school children would probably respond in an adult manner to instructions containing *more*, their responses to similar instructions containing *less* tended to be identical to those containing *more*. This was summarized by the title of the Donaldson and Balfour paper 'Less is more'. The Donaldson and Wales paper reports similar results for the understanding of *same* in relation to *different*, and in general that linguistically simpler adjectives like *big*, *long*, *tall*, etc., are better understood than *small*, *short*, etc. Our general conclusion—that in such pairs of autonomous adjectives the simplest 'positive' adjective is acquired first and its 'negative' opposite is acquired in relation to it—has been taken by Clark (1973) and systematized as part of a theory whereby she argues word meanings in such a semantic field are acquired. Thus in her view the *high–low* pair would be acquired in the following manner: first the child acquires a feature which might be labelled 'having physical extent', and then a feature specifying dimension—'height', this allows *high*; *low* is interpreted in the same way as high on the positive extent of 'height' until the opposition is marked by the acquisition of the 'positive' 'negative' distinction. In her view therefore the process of acquiring word meanings is that of an ordered acquisition of semantic features (labellable distinctions of meaning). This is an elegant and helpful hypothesis, with the virtue that it is clear enough to be challenged as to its relation to the empirical evidence. Unfortunately, it seems to fail here on a number of grounds: (1) apart perhaps from the *more–less* and *same–different* pairs there is no evidence of an intermediate stage of 'synonymy' in the child's uses of the meanings of any pairs of adjectives; (2) as Wales and Campbell (1970) point out, it seems much more likely that the spatial adjectives are differentiated from each other on the basis of the meaning the child has for *big*; (3) Clark's own data on the errors in the childrens' production of opposites support the contention that they have the notion of opposition and can apply it in such a task before they have differentiated the pairs of adjectives on the relevant dimension; (4) in some work on three distinct languages with Garman, Griffiths and Clayre, we have found that the *more–less* distinction is available to the children if the task is made simple enough. Also, by using a different form of analysis for the matching classification task Donaldson and Wales report for studying *same–different*, we have found evidence that the children are making systematic differences in their use of these terms; even when their use, if categorized simply in terms of conventional adult responses, would be categorized as the same.

What these studies seem to suggest is that the child's meanings only represent a sub-part of the adult's, and this sub-part is fundamentally determined by some general, biologically determined concepts, which are differentiated and added to in rather more complex interactions with environments of acquisition and strategies of use than we have yet been prepared to admit. It would surely be rather surprising if, after umpteen centuries, semantics were suddenly to be simple and clear! However, the usefulness of these studies is to try and point to the central determinants of the mapping of the concepts the child already has onto lexical items. Through all the messy data and slippery theorizing we can hope to get some general idea of the central 'innate' concepts—not only in the adjectival domain but also, for example (Wales 1971), on the role of movement in the interpretation of some prepositions (or related syntactic forms in inflected languages) and deictic demonstratives. Yet another area of really encouraging research is that of Eleanor Rosch (1973) attempting to generally define 'natural' semantic categories on the model of Berlin and Kay's (1970) demonstration of the 'universality' of focal (best instance) referents of basic colour terms. There are inevitably a number of methodological and theoretical problems with these studies, but for example our own developmental studies of colour terms suggest sufficient agreement with Berlin and Kay, and Rosch's position to encourage us to believe that more study may well make possible revealing accounts of the interaction of physiological constraints, psychological response strategies and social communicative constraints in determining not only the main 'central' 'natural' categories but also how and why shifts from them occur.

5. *Between Words and Situations*

The questions here revolve around the relations between (a) the children's words and the physical situations of their use, and (b) the speaking child and the persons who define its social context of discourse.

(a) *Words and events.* The context of the 'real world' and its influence on the child's speech can be exemplified in a number of ways. First there is an elegant pair of studies by Eve Clark on the child's understanding of sentences involving temporal order of events—e.g. involving the use of terms like *before* and *after*. In a study of their spontaneous speech and in a subsequent experimental check she found that the children first acquired the linguistic forms which reflected in their order of mention of events the order in which the events had in fact taken place. Thus, the form *X before Y* was acquired before *Y after X*; and *Before X, Y* after *After X, Y*. In another kind of study, Huttenlocker and Strauss (1968) and Huttenlocker, Eisenberg and Strauss (1968) have shown that the child performs much better if the physical object to be performed with (i.e. held in its hand) corresponds to the grammatical subject of the relational term of the instruction. Huttenlocker and Strauss sum up that 'one's understanding of a statement may depend upon the relation between that statement and the extra-linguistic situation it describes'. By presenting children with end state information Bem (1970) has shown that such problems as Huttenlocker's are amenable to training, therefore the relation between the statement and the situation is malleable.

Another study, by Donaldson and Lloyd (1971), seems to suggest such a relation; in fact the study is interpreted as suggesting that the child works from the perception of the situation to the interpretation of the statement. In a situation with four garages, and with either only three cars in them, or five cars, four of which are in them, the children are asked to evaluate as true or false such statements as 'All the cars are in the garages'. None of their sample of pre-school children were errorless in evaluating this statement—typically asserting of the first situation (three cars) that it was false, and of the five cars that it was true.

Using a simpler situation involving sand in beakers, Wales, Garman and Ross (1972) have shown that both in Edinburgh and in Tamilnadu about 25 per cent of the pre-schoolers could answer correctly and consistently, and that many of the others were using when they could a semantic interpretation for *all* which might be crudely glossed as 'full', but, when the sand was not contained by anything, switched to an interpretation akin to *more*. (This pattern of interpretation we suspect to be strongly related to the 'central' semantics of *big, more*, etc., as suggested in the preceding section.) Given this result (and despite the syntactic oddities of Donaldson and Lloyd's task) it is apparent that task difficulty is a crucial variable in determining the child's interpretation. This however is not to dismiss but rather to emphasize the importance of the context in influencing what the child makes of the linguistic content of the statement.

(b) *Words and people*. In our culture (which is in the minority in this respect) it is from their parents that children acquire language. One of the tantalizing myths perpetrated in recent years is that young children hear highly deviant adult speech by way of hesitations, false-starts, etc. A number of studies recently have however confirmed Brown and Bellugi's (1964) claim that the mother's sentences to the child are typically short, simple and grammatical. One of the questions which these studies pose (e.g. Snow 1972; Freidlander *et al*. 1973) is whether this adult simplification is an aid by virtue of the repetition and emphasis that paraphrases, etc., provide, or whether by virtue of simulating the child's speech communicative ends are enhanced (or both). No data I know of clearly relates to this problem. Another issue which does have some preliminary evidence to bear on it is the question 'is the adult's tendency to simplify speech to children a mark of an advantaged background?' Slobin (1969—cited in 1972b) reports a comparison of children from an urban ghetto, who conventionally have to rely on other children's speech for input, with that of Brown's Harvard mother–child data. He found 'on all grammatical measures reported for mother's speech by Brown, Cazden and Bellugi (1968), the relative frequency profiles for the Oakland children were the same as those for the Cambridge mothers'. This result is not only interesting in its own right, but does seem to go a long way toward undermining one leg of Bernstein's (1964) hypothesis regarding differences in language use as a function of social class background. Labov (1970) has already cast considerable doubt on the appropriateness of such hypotheses by his beautifully clear demonstrations of the systematic complex rules which govern the dialects of Black English he has studied. Bernstein's position is exemplified by the notion that children asked to describe a picture for someone who cannot see it will differ radically in how they do so as a function of social environment. Thus the working-class child will use a 'restricted code' and refer to objects and persons by pronouns without the aid of linguistic referents. The middle-class child apparently does not do this, but uses an 'elaborated code'. However the examples given us in the literature also indicate that the working-class child typically uses past tenses whereas the middle-class child uses the present continuous—that is just that tense which is only appropriate if the hearer can view the events simultaneously with the speaker. Thus they are by this criterion the 'restricted' encoders! Apart from the wider issues of attitudes and interest, this example should give pause to anyone who desires to account for differences in language use on the basis of fundamental differences in the availability of linguistic capacities. Since Bernstein's work can be seen as but a particular instance of Piaget's (1928) broad notions of egocentric speech, it may well be that the latter's view ought to be similarly challenged. As more studies are pursued of the social basis of linguistic interaction in early childhood so the picture on this point may become clearer. Is it perhaps the fact that nurseries constrain children (and if so, how?) to see other people as people to communicate with, that makes for the main usefulness of these institutions. Is there a difference in talking while playing, and conversing while doing nothing else since it's intrinsically fun to talk? If so, when and under what conditions does this start? Doubtless these questions have been asked before, but if so we still wait for some answers.

One of the intriguing sources of potential new insights to the social inter-relationship of structure are the successful studies of Gardner and Gardner (1971) on teaching a chimpanzee sign language. Although such studies are as yet in their early days it seems at first glance that Washoe (the chimp in question) has developed a set of signs which may be concatenated but which do not respect word (sign) order in the way that is characteristic of young children. However, McNeill (in press) has suggested that Washoe may have developed a 'new' syntax which is socially based and reflects orders determined by addressee—non-addressee. Whether or not this is a valid case in relation to the facts remains very open. But so does the contention that this is a radically distinct form of syntax from that of human language in that it is socially based. Nevertheless it does directly pose a challenge for any who now wish to claim that human language in its structure cannot be separated from its social function.

6. *What Issues in Learning?*

The days when psychologists were tempted to study man as if there was nothing between the ears are obviously on the wane, and they have been replaced by an era marked by a proper respect for the complexities of language. With the stability which derives from serious successes we can now discuss such questions as 'what do you have to be equipped for to learn language?' and 'what can you do to affect the rate of learning?' without an automatic descent into polemical dogmatics. Thus we can point to the serious possibilities of empirical support for the kind of innateness hypotheses canvassed by Chomsky, Katz and Postal and at the same time regard the questions concerning environmental influences as important (for extended discussion see Campbell and Wales 1970). A number of instances illustrating these issues have already been marked for attention. The suggestions that the child already 'knows' a great deal relevant to its language before uttering a word; that in the semantic domain this may derive from spatial and temporal consequences of the action patterns of the child and of others; the regularity of the linguistic input to the child; and the different extra-linguistic strategies which it may put to use in interpreting that input and the consequences of its own output—these suggest real grounds for supposing that theoretical coherence in describing child language is not a false hope. However we have marked down a number of deep problems (theoretical and empirical) which can only be overlooked at the cost of trivializing the conclusions we may wish to draw. The most serious of these concern the grounds for relating one set of phenomena, described within a particular conceptual framework, to another set described within another framework, the danger is great of drawing conclusions simply on the basis of the commonality of the descriptive names used, and, in practice it is not easily recognized, let alone circumvented. Take as a general example the set of ways in which actions, sight and hearing may be related to 'language'. Nearly everyone would agree that these representational domains interface with each other, but how are we to state these relations? Is there a 'language' of neural 'information' which allows this 'inter-communication' to occur? That these are perplexing questions is presumably clear enough—some of their ramifications have been discussed by Fodor, Bever and Garrett (1974) and Marshall and Wales (1974). With these complexities, and others stemming from them, it should presumably be evident why so little has been done to try and establish any consensus as to what children learn first. Or to provide general statements concerning the order in which they acquire the several parts of adult language. The problem is not whether such claims can be made, but what meaning they would have. Even assertions that comprehension precedes production need to have a specified empirical context to be made intelligible.

Much of this interest in the representations appropriate for describing the child's language revolves around what the young child can make of what it is doing. Crucially this involves what used to be called the 'psychological reality of the linguistic description'. Some of the discussion of this recently has been based on a misunderstanding of where Chomsky has placed the restriction on subjectivity—moving it from the data base of behaviourist conceptions to the need for formal systematic description which does not require or allow of intuitive interpretation once the description is constructed. In fact, it was because of this move to make intuition an acceptable basis for initial data analysis that some of the earlier studies of child syntax (e.g. the first grammar approach) were charged with being 'performance grammars'. As the emphasis has moved progressively towards what the child is able to make of its own language, so the issue of eliciting judgements of acceptability from the child have been interpreted as related to the child's intuitions—see, for example, studies by Gleitman, Gleitman and Shipley (1973), and de Villiers and de Villiers (1972). However, as Hakes (1973) has suggested, intuitions such as those involved in judgements of synonymy, anomaly and ambiguity may emerge later than and independently of the child's ability to understand and produce the sentences involved. What we have here is a three-term problem: (1) necessary and sufficient knowledge for given performance; (2) subjects' awareness of that knowledge; (3) description of that knowledge. Both (1) and (3) might be described as intuition. It is, of course to (1) that (3) must correspond. However if we are concerned with 'psychological reality' we will also be concerned with (2); and only with respect to (2) will we be able to claim that those features which exhibit psychological reality are in fact features of the individual rather than merely features of the descriptive model, i.e. rules (cf Wales 1968).

It is presumably clear from this that the answers sought are in no way trivial or simple, and that the search for descriptive adequacy is faced with serious obstacles because such descriptions cannot easily be abstracted from considerations of process and situation. For example coming to grips with such questions as 'how soon and at what stage can children liberate themselves from their immediate environment?' involves considering representations of space and time in their interaction with processes of perception and memory. Similarly 'when and how do children use complex (embedded) sentences in conversation as distinct from conjunction, e.g. "S and S and S", etc.?' Traill (1967) found, in a task where one child was asked to 'tell X ——' with the blank filled by an embedded sentence, that they frequently produced the sentences with the appropriate constituent sentences in a conjoined rather than embedded form. Again, note the influence of perception and memory in distinguishing the structures accessible to comprehension from those of production. In a different though related context Chomsky (1965) has said 'we must be careful not to overlook the fact that surface similarities may hide underlying distinctions of a fundamental nature, and that it may be necessary to guide and draw out speakers' intuition in perhaps fairly subtle ways before we can determine what is the actual character of his knowledge of his language or of anything else'.

It is the strength of recent psycho-linguistics to emphasize the point that questions concerning the 'how' of learning are contingent on questions regarding 'what it is that is being learned'. The juxtaposition of these related sets of questions has directed attention toward some fundamental issues. In selectively expounding these I hope that enough has been said to provide the basis for serious further discussion and research.

Finally, that there are fundamental issues for theories of learning, and not just for conceptions of language can be best indicated by looking at the kinds of errors children make. Virtually every theory of learning from S–R to Piaget assumes that as the child progresses, whether linearly or by stages, this progress leads to the kind of improvement that results in the elimination of errors. However, in a variety of domains in linguistic and cognitive development there are indications that this is sometimes not so. Thus having apparently mastered a particular verbal skill—say the use of the past tense forms of irregular strong verbs, or the use of *big*—the child starts to give inappropriate uses just in those contexts where previously it had given appropriate ones. To suggest that the strategies of use have changed—the past tense forms of the regular weak verbs being overgeneralized, or the use of *big* restricted as the result of differentiating dimensions—tells us little about the learning mechanism which underlies the change. It isn't even clear how the data of such developmental sequences are to be formally analysed (Wales and Campbell 1970). Nevertheless the generality of these kinds of phenomena do point up rather vividly the inherent inadequacies of presently available theories, and the necessity when looking for mechanisms to be aware of the representations those mechanisms articulate.

Discussant: *Kenneth Lovell*

I intend to keep rather more closely to language and learning in the home, and in the nursery and infant school, although I shall return to points made in the paper by Wales from time to time. My thesis is divided into two broad parts: first, language and learning from the perspective of language capacities; second, language and learning from the perspective of the uses to which language is put.

In the first part I am asking for more research into interrelations between language and intelligence since both affect learning, and for more knowledge of the semantic analysis of vocabulary change and the understanding of quantifiers which express logical relations. I begin by suggesting that in infancy language acquisition depends upon prior non-linguistic referents. Whatever else Piaget has or has not done, his work suggests that language is one of a number of representational systems emerging around twenty-one months of age with the onset of the semiotic function. Macnamara (1972) has suggested that infants learn their language by first determining, independent of language, the meaning a speaker intends to convey to them. They then work out the relation between the meaning and the language. Such a viewpoint rests on the assumption that their thinking has been developing for some time prior to the beginnings of language acquisition. Vygotsky (1962) and Piaget (1963), for example, bring evidence which generally supports this assumption. Indeed, by the time the infant begins to understand language at around twelve months of age he has already built some relationships between his own activities and the movement of objects. Again the work with deaf children suggests that those severely behind in language development still reveal the essentials of human thinking processes. Francis (1969) too, indicates the importance of developing intelligence when she brought evidence that the structure of speech of a two-and-a-half-year-old is more related to the kind of activity in which he is engaged, and to his limited intellectual growth, than to the hierarchical structure of sentences as such.

The general view expressed here in no way necessarily contradicts the view that once the young child has made progress in acquiring language, the latter may well enrich the thinking. Language possibly focuses thinking; it certainly acts as an analyser and synthesizer, plays a role in the storage and retrieval of information, gives a flexible representational system enabling the child to deal with the world in its absence, and having been socially elaborated it has a notation for a whole range of intellectual tools like classification, seriation, which are used in the service of thought.

My first suggestion then is that we need research beginning at around twelve months of age into the developing relationships between intelligence and language. But I believe the parallels persist between linguistic capacities and intellectual performance in both early and late childhood, and these parallels need to be explored further. There are similarities about the way children detect linguistic rules and gather information about other aspects of their environment. When we look at young children's syntactic and semantic categories we see that, judged against those of the adult, they are often arbitrary, context-bound and over-generalized. So too are their categorizations of objects; compare Piaget's notion of graphic collections. While I believe the bulk of evidence suggests that there are parallels and interrelations between the linguistic and intellectual domains I admit that the interrelations established to date are not high. The work of Scholnich and Adams (1973) involved relationships between certain language and intellectual skills. These were passive voice comprehension and backward repetition on the one hand, and matrix permutation on the other. Correlation coefficients between the variables of around ·45 were obtained in kindergarten children. While this figure is statistically significant it certainly is not large, and must be looked upon as a first step in estab-lishing an overlap between these particular aspects of language com-petence and intellectual skills.

Sinclair de Zwart (1971) points out that since the five-year-old has acquired most of the adult's linguistic structures it is legitimate to ask what is the difference between the linguistic competence of the four/five-year-old and that of a six/seven-year-old. She suggests that the changes in thinking around six to seven lead to new verbal behaviour. First, there is a certain reflection on language itself for sentences can be dissociated from their content. Thus when asked to make a sentence with the words 'coffee' and 'salt', the six-year-old no longer says 'You can't, nobody puts salt in coffee'. Or when the six/seven-year-old is asked, 'How many words do I say when I say "Susan has six dolls" ', he will count on his fingers and get the answer, and not reply 'six' as the four-year-old will. Second, this capacity for detachment makes it possible for the six-year-old to find different verbal formulations des-cribing the same event. The child can now conserve the semantic con-tent while changing the form of the utterance. Unfortunately she does not give hard data supporting her view. In the Piagetian view then, the new changes in thought, the moves from semi-logic to more systematized thought, permit a restructuration of the linguistic acqui-sitions of the pre-operational period. Such restructurations are bound to affect comprehension and learning.

At the end of last term one of my Ph.D. students finished collecting data on certain linguistic tasks involving surface and deep structures, and tasks involving conservation of quantity, seriation and decentra-tion in the three-mountains experiment devised by Piaget, at each age level from four to eleven. It is clear that there are substantial corre-lation coefficients between the tasks in the four- to seven-year age-group, also a substantial first principal component, suggesting a clear link between intellectual and linguistic structures in this age range.

I must also draw your attention to the work of Lunzer *et al.* (1973) who obtained data on seventy very varied measures for each of two hundred children aged five-and-a-half to six years. It was the tasks involving intellectual development as in classification and seriation tasks that best predicted performance in reading and mathematics after one year at school—taking the group as a whole. But when the children were divided into three socio-economic groupings—the less advantaged, average advantaged and more advantaged—language scores correlated more highly with classification/seriation scores in the less advantaged group than they did in the other two groups. This was particularly so when the less advantaged group was compared with the more advantaged group. From this study then, language measures seem to be more closely related to intellectual behaviour in less advantaged groups.

We know that young children's ability to recall sentences is less than linguists would expect (Weener 1971), as is children's judgements of sentence meaning. This over-expectancy on the part of linguists could be because they assume a rule is learned before it is constructed by the child, rather than the converse. On the other hand, Piagetians may underestimate children's capacities, because tasks given to assess a child's logical thought may be less relevant to him than the language tasks he is given. So it could be that we need more research using intellectual tasks as familiar and relevant as linguistic ones, and linguistic tasks which ask the child to make equivalence judgements and transform word strings. In this way we are likely to find out more of the precise relations between the domains of language and intellect, and because of this, get a clearer view on the way both influence learning.

I want now to turn to some other studies more concerned with comprehension than with language production. In recent years there have been investigations into the development of the semantic and conceptual frameworks of quantity words such as 'more', 'less', 'big', 'tall'. Donaldson and Wales (1970) suggest that it can reasonably be maintained that most language is composed of relational terms and then proceed to give details of a study of children's acquisition of the understanding of the terms 'more'/'less', 'same'/'different' in three-and-a-half-year-old children. The data obtained indicated that in the case of the two pairs of antonyms, the children failed to differentiate between the two opposing members of each pair. However, as Wales pointed out in his present paper, there are major problems in relating a child's concepts to his developing lexical structure. He then outlined in his paper Clark's views on the acquisition of word meanings in such a semantic field and suggested that her hypothesis was not confirmed for a number of reasons. He further suggests that children's meanings are a sub-set of adult meanings, the sub-set fundamentally being determined by some general, biologically determined concepts – an idea I would like further explained – and then differentiated and added to in more complex interactions with particular environments in which the terms were acquired. Here I would add a few details of the work of Maratos (1973) who showed that around three years of age the word 'big' is defined in terms of overall size. But by four to five years of age children define 'big' almost exclusively by referring to a greater extension along the vertical dimension. Yet four-and-a-half to five-and-a-half-year-olds were clearly able to judge overall size in terms other than height. Thus the problem seems to be a semantic one—the meaning of 'big' is that taken to be appropriate for 'tall'. Here the semantic analysis in terms of one dimension seems to be overextended giving an incorrect definition. Later on the child will have to restrict severely the situations or contexts in which 'big' is defined by 'tallness'. Maratos suggests a number of reasons for the child introducing the vertical dimension into his definition of 'big'. Adults emphasize children's relative size by 'tallness'; the ground is a baseline for vertical measurement whereas there is no corresponding baseline for horizontal measurement; and around five years of age there is a tendency to 'centre' on one dimension when dealing with concepts of quantity.

A study by Donaldson (1972) involved the comprehension of quantifiers. She studied three- to five-year-olds' comprehension of the terms *all, each, only, some, none, not any*—all quantifiers which have as their function the expression of logical relations. Some comprehension of the basic meaning of *all, each* and *some* seemed to be acquired by four years of age since in some contexts the majority of children made no errors. However, in the case of *all* and *each* there were other contexts in which errors were widespread. For example, the statement 'all the cars are in the garages' tended to be judged true, if and only if, all the garages were full. But as Wales points out in his paper, if there were three cars and four garages the statement was held to be false, but with five cars and four garages it was held to be true. As Wales indicated, after considering this and his own unpublished evidence, context remains very important in influencing what the child makes of the linguistic content of a statement.

Donaldson's data in respect of the comprehension of negative statements is also interesting. The consensus of opinion is that adults have more trouble with true negative statements than with false ones. Yet she found among her three- to five-year-olds that this was not true. Moreover, she found that they handled true and false negative judgements with much greater competence than Slobin had earlier with six-year-olds. This difference in competence, in Donaldson's view, may have been due to the experimental procedures used, to the sentences involved or that children go through a sequence pass–fail–pass. She also judged that young children tend to convert a negative to an affirmative before it is judged, so that we find 'None of the doors are open', judged to be false, 'Because you said they were all shut and they aren't'. Clearly there is an area here for research; we need to know in more detail how nursery and infant school children judge negative statements.

To this point I have suggested further research into the interrelations between linguistic and intellectual growth in the early childhood period, for both domains will affect learning. One has only to observe in Junior Educationally Sub-Normal Special School children the limited linguistic competence, the limited intellectual growth and the limited learning. While I believe we have some evidence that intellectual growth at this age affects linguistic competence, we know little about the effect of language on intellectual growth in these years. True we have the evidence from the deaf, some evidence from Joan Tough's longitudinal study, and some very fragmentary evidence from the study by Lovell *et al.* (1968) of speech-delayed children aged three, four and five years. But the field remains wide open for further research.

I have also pointed out some studies which involve the semantic analysis of vocabulary change, and the comprehension of quantifiers whose job it is to express logical relations. Here we find that experience, social practices and the contexts are important. Without precise definitions and without the correct use of logical quantifiers in early childhood learning will be adversely affected. Here too we need much more knowledge.

Now to the second part of my thesis—to language and learning from the perspective of the functions or uses of languages, which are also seemingly constrained by children's thinking capacities. Here I must consider children from linguistically advantaged and disadvantaged homes. And I am not forgetting Labov—I shall return to him later. At the outset I want to support what Wales stated in his section on *Words and People*— namely that we should be careful of those who desire to account for differences in language use by fundamental differences in the availability of linguistic capacities.

I know of no data showing that children from linguistically disadvantaged homes as such, cannot elaborate the basic linguistic forms so evident in children from linguistically advantaged homes. They are able at times to elaborate complex linguistic constructions, they can at times be as explicit and precise as children from more advantaged homes. The point is that they do not so frequently make complex constructions, and they are not as explicit as frequently, perhaps because their early upbringing does not demand it. The potential for complexity of linguistic utterance is more limited by intellectual growth as I suggested earlier, although in saying this I am in no sense belittling the importance of the language those children hear around them, and of the uses to which language is put in the home and nursery.

It seems that children from linguistically disadvantaged homes learn to use language somewhat differently from those from more favoured homes. As a result of her work with pre-school children of average and above average measured IQ, Tough (1973c) concluded that all children seem to learn to use language to protect their own rights, interests, comfort and pleasure; to initiate and maintain relationships with others; to report the present; and to direct the actions of themselves and others. But children from less favoured homes, compared with children from more favoured homes, used language less often and less extensively to report on the past and anticipate and predict the future; to elaborate possible alternatives; to see causal and dependent relationships; to give explanations as to why things happen; to create imaginative situations; and to reflect on their own feelings and on those of others. Reflection on the feelings of others leads the child no longer to speak for himself, but to shape the message according to his reading of the other person—to understand the other's role rather than merely to play it. These differences in the uses to which language is put may affect intellectual growth—a research topic of importance—and are likely to be of considerable importance in respect of learning.

It is my belief that much could be done to help the less advantaged child if we had the will. Such help would be comprehensive—it would embrace the home, the nursery and the school. Slowly, over the years and over the generations much could be done to help all children to use language in ways in which the more advantaged children use it, and so render educational opportunities more equal. All societies of the future will need the strategies in using language indicated by Tough, for all mankind will have problems of agriculture, engineering, medicine, psychology, etc., to face, discuss and solve.

A recent study by Robinson (1973) further suggests to me that the differences between working-class and middle-class mother/child interactions need not be as great as they sometimes are and this again encourages me in the belief that change is possible. True, Robinson was comparing upper-working-class—not lower-working-class young children—with children from middle-class homes. Pupils were matched by groups using scores on Raven's Progressive Matrices Test for this purpose. Topics were nominated, children were encouraged to say what they knew about them, to play with related objects, and to direct any questions they had to their mothers.

There were no social class differences in the number of questions asked by children, but the questions of the middle-class children were more complex, more varied and longer. For the majority of topics the middle-class mothers provided more meaning, gave more information likely to be related to the child's previous experience, and gave more encouraging and correcting feedback, and feedback seems to be very important in all learning. Middle-class mothers were more likely to maintain a theme for more than four utterances, and less likely to repeat what children had just said. But in respect of two topics, the Bingo Card and the Family Allowance Book, the upper-working-class mothers provided their children with more meaning through informative statements than did the middle-class mothers. Thus while some social class differences in mother/child interaction may be topic independent, others are not. When knowledge is available to the mother and its transmission is deemed important, it seems that it will be passed. Robinson points out that the weakness of a similar Hess and Shipman study was that they relied only on two simple tasks which had a middle-class flavour, while the weakness in Robinson's own study was that the mother's knowledge of, and attitudes to, the topics were not assessed at the beginning of the study prior to their passing information to their children.

However, he points out other interesting ideas. He does not accept that the working-class children asked the same number of questions as the middle-class children because the former were upper working-class, for there *were* social class differences in maternal behaviour that were thought to be relevant to the growth and continuation of curiosity in children. For Robinson, the maternal behaviours which seemed relevant to the children's knowledge and questions were those that allowed the children, or helped them, to decide what to do with such knowledge. On the other hand, knowledge made available by the mother must, of course, be assimilable by the child; and productions made by the child must be confirmed, extended or corrected. But it was the maternal 'pulling' rather than 'pushing' that for Robinson is so important in the development of children's learning. Tough's research is directed to this kind of problem.

In concluding this section I would refer to the work of Labov (1973). It's fashionable to do so these days. His general thesis is that speakers of non-standard English do have the necessary linguistic and cognitive experience to learn in school. The language of urban-ghetto Afro-American children—and perhaps by implication that of lower-working-class English children—is capable of argument, logic, conceptualization. Such problems as working-class children have in handling logical operations are not to be found in the structure of their language. Such non-standard English should be looked upon as a dialect and not differentiated from the forms of speech necessary to handle abstractions. Personally I would like to see more hard evidence backing his initial claims. His suggestions again raise the question of the interrelations of language and intelligence, and the need for research. Even if there is some substance in Labov's views, his followers often fail to realize that he himself twice points out in his Georgetown Monograph that the children he has in mind do need practice in paying attention to the surface components of language although they understand its meaning all right. And twice in that Monograph he points out the need for them to learn to be explicit. Let me quote one sentence, 'We have conceded that NNE children need help in analysing language into its surface components and in being more explicit.' And again, 'As we have seen, being explicit is one of the main advantages of standard English at its best.' So even for Labov, children who use non-standard English could take, with profit, a few leaves from the language book of what we regard as the more linguistically advantaged child.

Finally, I would like to say a brief word about an important topic that Wales raises towards the end of his paper. He asks how representational domains interface with one another. Now I cannot agree with his text when he includes sight and hearing as representational domains – for me these are figurative instruments, which are not a sub-set of the instruments of the semiotic function—nevertheless the interfacing of, say, imagery, symbolic play, gestural language and oral language is an important issue. We want to know how they aid, abet or hinder one another in young children, and how the necessary intercommunication occurs. Of course, symbolic play and imagery may form a framework, but not a system, whereas language is structured into a system. Moreover, language not only represents what is known, but is itself an object to be known. The child has to infer rules and regularities of language and derive an interiorized grammar so that he can construct and understand an unlimited number of sentences. Thus we cannot study language acquisition as we study other modes of representation.

The Genevan work suggests that in the pre-operational thought period imagery in the child deals almost exclusively with static events. A child at this stage has great difficulty in reproducing in imagery, movements or transformations he has observed, or anticipating in imagery, movements and transformations. This does not help us much to understand the problem of the interface of the behaviours of the semiotic function.

In our study of speech-delayed children (Lovell *et al.* 1968) we found no difference between delayed and normal speakers at three years of age in respect of quality of play organization or in degree of play cooperation, but differences did appear at four and five years of age. Our data were very limited and here is a research area bearing on the interface, which is wide open. Again we need to know how fantasy – creative imaginations involving emotions clothed with images—which seems so important in the years up to six and seven, affects language, and intellectual growth, and learning. In general terms it seems that fantasy is important in our age range, for it can be both a facilitator and distractor, but we need more research here and hard facts.

The interface of which we have been speaking is important at all age levels. We know from such workers as Paivio, also Bower, that imagery in adults has relevance to language and learning. Paivio argues that in adults imagery is centrally important in facilitating retention; among children the role of imagery in retention is less well understood. Again, when we pose problems to older school pupils we sometimes see them making movements with hands, arms, face, in searching for strategies and solutions and then they formulate their strategies and solutions in language. They also tell us at times that they use visual imagery before they formulate their solution in words. But we need knowledge—not snippets of information—as to the ways in which the different representational domains interact with one another.

We are concerned in this book with language and learning in early childhood. In my concluding sentences I must say that however important language is in respect of learning, the changes in intellectual processes and learning in the years five to seven are connected with many other changes in this period and seem part of a broader developmental movement. The vast related literature dealing with this topic has been surveyed by Sheldon White (1969).

Concentrated versus Contrived Encounters: Suggestions for Language Assessment in Early Childhood Education[1]

COURTNEY B. CAZDEN

The most usual way to evaluate the effect of an educational programme on child language has been to compare the language of children who were in the programme with the language of those same children at an earlier time and with children who had different experiences during the same interval. Thus the 'evaluation' question collapses to the more general question of how to analyse child language, with the exception that aspects of language are selected for assessment from judgements about what help children particularly need and what help a deliberate educational environment is most apt to provide. In its general form, the question is this: given any two sets of utterances by child A at two points in time (whether the intervening period is filled with natural development or deliberate education), or by child A versus child B (who may differ in home background or by their presence or absence in a particular educational environment), beyond saying that one child said X and the other said Y, how can we more economically and informatively describe how their language differs?

I have addressed this question on several previous occasions and will review them briefly here by way of raising the central question of whether it is possible to measure as a product, independent of the contexts in which they have been learned and practised, the functional aspects of child language which I believe are both

---

[1] While preparing this paper, I benefited from discussions at the Rand Corporation panel meeting on the evaluation of Headstart (and the position papers prepared by Butler, 1973 and Featherstone, 1973); and from discussions with staff members of the Follow Through project at the Bank Street College of Education.

most vulnerable to environmental differences and most amenable to environmental assistance. I will try to characterize what seem to me to be essential features of any assessment procedures which attempt to do just that, under the heading of 'concentrated encounters' versus 'contrived encounters', and then turn briefly at the end to the differences between 'formative' and 'summative' evaluation.

First Thoughts About Assessing Child Language as Product

In a chapter for a handbook on formative and summative evaluation, Cazden (1971) tried to bring together suggestions from many sources for ways that teachers could listen more sensitively, and interpret more informatively, many aspects of their children's language, both in natural observations (or 'listenings') and in the more contrived and structured situations we call 'tests'. Chart 1 shows the scope and framework for these suggestions. An 'X' on the chart indicates a possible educational objective for which I tried to suggest assessment procedures.

Joan Tough's guide, The Schools Council Language Project: Listening to Children Talking (1972), is a more useful solution for at least part of the same purpose, more useful both because it is more selective and because Tough has tried out her suggestions with teachers and I have not. Another difference between the two sets of suggestions is that Tough limited her suggestions to observations of speech in ongoing educational contexts because she found that teachers simply did not have time to carry out any separate 'tests'.

Quite separately from questions of how to assess a child's repertoire of language structure and functions, I became increasingly aware of situational effects on everyone's language, adult as well as child. Cazden (1970) reviews all the studies I could find in which the research focus was on how the same child responded differentially in different speech situations. Chart 2 shows the framework for this analysis. Note that whereas the framework in Chart 1 attempted to be exhaustive (admittedly in a simplified way), Chart 2 simply categorized the research that existed to date and is as limited as the variables being investigated at that time.

If children's speech is influenced by the situation in which it is spoken, then important aspects of any assessment situation must be

CHART 1

TABLE OF SPECIFICATIONS FOR PRE-SCHOOL
EDUCATION: OBJECTIVES IN EARLY LANGUAGE DEVELOPMENT
(Taken from Chart 14-1, Cazden 1971, p. 348).

BEHAVIOURS

| | Cognitive | | | | | | | | | Affective |
CONTENT	Understand and produce simple language forms	Understand and produce elaborated language: describe	Understand and produce elaborated language: narrate	Understand and produce elaborated language: generalize, explain, and predict	Use language effectively for specific purposes to others: communication	Use language effectively for specific purposes to oneself: cognition	Operate on language: analyse	Operate on language: transform and translate	Operate on language: evaluate	Demonstrate the use of language frequently and with enjoyment
	A	B	C	D	E	F	G	H	I	J
1. Sounds	×							×	×	×
2. Words	×						×	×	×	×
3. Grammar	×						×	×	×	×
4. Objects		×		×						×
5. Events			×	×						×
6. Ideas				×						×
7. Reality: discussion					×					×
8. Fantasy: dramatic play					×					×
9. Thought						×				×

CHART 2

EFFECTS OF THE SITUATION ON CHILD LANGUAGE
(CLASSIFICATION OF RELEVANT STUDIES)
(Taken from Table I, Cazden 1970a, p. 44.)

Language Characteristics	Characteristics of the situation				
	Topic	*Task*	*Listener(s)*	*Interaction*	*Mixed*
Fluency/Spontaneity	Strandberg Strandberg & Griffith Williams & Naremore (a, b) Berlyne & Frommer	Heider *et al.* Brent & Katz	Labov *et al.*	Cooperman (personal communication)	Cowan *et al.* Cazden (1965) Labov *et al.* Pasamanick & Knobloch Resnick, Weld, & Lally Kagan (1969) Jensen
Length/Complexity	Standberg & Griffith Cowan *et al.* Moffett Williams & Naremore (a, b) Labov *et al.* Mackay & Thompson	Brent & Katz Cazden (1976) Lawton Robinson (1965) Williams & Naremore (a, b)	Cazden (1967) Smith	Plumer	Cowan *et al.*
Content or Style	Labov *et al.*	Lawton			
Approximation of Standard English	Labov *et al.*	Labov *et al.*			

Note—See original (Cazden 1970a) for references.

considered. These methodological issues are discussed in the Appendix on 'Methods of analysing child language' in Cazden (1972a). One section of that appendix deals with tests, which I would now define broadly as any situation in which Person A asks person B a question to which Person A knows the answer. To make this an interaction acceptable to both persons, Person B must realize that Person A has certain characteristics (such as age, greater knowledge, higher status) and accept such characteristics as legitimizing this non-symmetrical, non-reciprocal relationship. Note that this definition combines, as I think it should, what we normally think of as 'tests' and many (most?) of the questions which many (most?) teachers ask children in school recitations and even 'discussions'.

The Appendix in Cazden (1972a) discussed the complex intellectual and interpersonal demands which tests place on the child in five categories: (1) the intellectual processes or knowledge the test is designed to evaluate (e.g. auditory discrimination); (2) the content to which (1) is applied (e.g. words or sounds which may be more or less familiar to the child); (3) additional abilities presupposed by the particular task in which (1) is evaluated (e.g. knowledge of the meaning of 'same' and 'different'); (4) attending behaviours and motivation which are particularly important in any group-testing situation where a child has to be listening and/or watching at the right time and place and respond on demand; and (5) interpersonal relationships which at their most universal are usually called 'rapport', and which at their most culture-specific will affect what particular children consider appropriate (and 'safe') behaviour towards a person of 'Person A''s characteristics. In a review of the *Test of Basic Experience* (TOBE), Cazden (1972c) applies these evaluative categories to one specific published test.

If these contextual influences on speech are as significant as I believe they are, especially on young children, they will limit the inferences that can be made from any test response, and thereby limit the validity and reliability of the information the teacher or researcher seeks.

Language in Context

Still separately from the foregoing, I have argued for assessing process as well as product in early childhood education. By 'process' I mean the actual behaviour of teachers and children during the educational experience; by 'product' I mean measures of what the child has learned in that experience, what the outcomes of that experience have been. Under what conditions one can expect a valid demonstration of that learning is the central question of this paper.

Cazden (1972d) presents three arguments for assessing process, using the framework shown in Chart 3. In the order in which

CHART 3

VARIABLES IN EDUCATIONAL RESEARCH

(Taken from Chart 1, Cazden 1972d, p. 188.)

Curriculum model (A): objectives and strategies for achieving them	Process variables (B): behaviours of teachers and children in the educational setting	Product variables (C): scores on tests either immediately after educational process or later
degree of implementation of model	relationship between process and product	

they were discussed: (1) process measures can yield a measure of the degree of implementation of some curriculum theory or model; (2) process variables may be the primary focus; that is, the experiences that children have in classrooms are important in themselves; and (3) information on process variables is critical for understanding the relationship between what children do and what they learn.

Arguments (1) on implementation and (3) on process–product relationships remain critical for teacher training and research. Here I want to stress the second argument, that the experience provided by an educational environment must itself be assessed, especially in the language domain.

In general, if we as parents were selecting a school for our own children, we would go as observers to see how children and teachers spend their time and probably give less weight to evidence from test scores of previous pupils. This is true unless we were concerned about the school's track record of preparing students for college entrance examinations, and the mere mention of that unnaturally pressured situation at an older age highlights further the more natural basis on which judgements are otherwise made.

Parents in general seem alike in this respect. At least Butler (1973) reports that 'interviews cited [as part of planning at Stanford Research Institute for Follow-Through programme Consumer guides] demonstrate that parents were more concerned about classroom processes than about what transformations took place in their children over the Headstart year'. (p. 10.)

When we consider language experiences more specifically, the argument about process versus product is different in important ways for language structure and language function.

Assessing Language Structure

In the case of language structure, the argument is simpler. All children learn the basic system of their native language, or dialect, despite considerable variation in the nature of the input to that language acquisition process (for instance whether they spend more time with other children or adults). On some of the more complex details of their language system, individual variation does exist, for example in the structures investigated by C. Chomsky (1972), and here exposure to written language seems to provide a qualitatively unique kind of data for the child. But the general point remains: there is sufficient research, both on language acquisition and on the assistance children get from the environment, to say with assurance that if a child participates in inter-actions which include examples of language somewhat, but not too much, more mature than his own, in situations where the meaning of the new, growing edge of language structure can be gleaned from the more familar verbal and non-verbal context, he will take what he needs to build his own language system. This sequence is so inevitable, unless there is some unusual defect in the child's basic information processing system, that we can assess the environment for the necessary ingredients and be confident that if they are present, they are sufficient. We do not need to test the children to make sure that learning is indeed taking place.

I say this while acknowledging that aspects of language structure can be assessed by tests (see example of tests in Cazden 1970a and b, and Slobin 1967) all of which have been used by many researchers. In the case of the learning of language structure, assessment via tests is possible but unnecessary. In evaluating educational programmes, assessment of the environment, I believe, is enough.

One excellent example of this kind of environmental assessment was done in residential nurseries by Tizard *et al.* (1972). Their study is almost unique in showing a relationship between aspects of an educational environment and growth in the child's receptive language system.

A quite different example comes from suggestions (Palmer *et al.* 1971) for obtaining 'formative' evaluation—that is, information which can be used by teachers and programme directors to help improve what they are doing. The example happens to be focused not on oral language but on children's interest in books.

Goal: *To interest children in books and encourage mothers to borrow books to read to their children at home.*

Evidence: During free choice periods, how many children go to the library corner and look at books by themselves? How many requests do adults get to 'read to me' during a day? How many children sit without being disciplined during story time? How many books have been borrowed by mothers during the week? Which books have become special favourites, as shown by signs of extra wear? If observations are made to answer these questions in October, December and February, are there any trends during the school year?

Replanning: Is the library corner placed so that children starting to look at a book are protected from visual and auditory distractions? If adults are too busy to read to individual children, can the staff be increased by getting high-school volunteers? If one adult is particularly good at keeping children's attention during story time, can he or she be freed to read or tell stories on a regular basis? Are procedures for book-borrowing as simple as possible, including help in filling out cards for adults who need it?

Assessing Language Functions

The argument for the importance of assessing opportunities in the language environment for the acquisition of a repertoire of language functions is somewhat different. Since another paper in this book will discuss curriculum, I will not attempt a full discussion of language goals here. Briefly, one can derive goals from many sources, for example, our knowledge about development itself (e.g. Kohlberg and Mayer 1972); theories about language use (e.g. Bernstein 1971); research on the different results of formal versus informal education (most recently Scribner and Cole 1973); or accounts of what sensitive teachers intuitively do (e.g. Rosen and Rosen 1973). To focus the discussion, let me suggest one general language function which would emerge as an important educational goal within any of the above frameworks: the ability to communicate meanings in a verbal form of appropriate explicitness, for a particular audience, without undue reliance on a shared physical or interpersonal context. Starting from Bernstein's theory, Cazden and Bartlett (1973) tried to spell out programme specifications for achieving this language goal. Although we used these specifications for reviewing a book (Gahagan and Gahagan 1970), the same specifications could be used to evaluate programmes:

The first three specifications characterize experiences with language that children should have in school.

(1) Restricted codes and elaborated codes draw on the same language system, the same repertoire of syntactic structures and words (lexis) in Bernstein's terminology. The difference between them lies in the functions and contexts in which those resources are used, in particular in the degree to which meaning is made explicit and context-independent. Emphasis in an educational programme, therefore, will be on changing patterns of frequencies of use of certain forms, not on teaching new forms themselves. Curriculum design thus becomes largely a matter of creating tasks which will elicit these forms—tasks which require the child to define and express ideas he otherwise would not talk about. In coding these ideas in particular contexts, the child will be changing his habitual syntactic patterns and learning new vocabulary.

(2) A full programme to stimulate the use of elaborate codes requires language experiences for four separate language functions: regulative, instructional, interpersonal and expressive. In the *regulative* function the child should help to formulate rules and negotiate about their enforcement and teachers should use personal rather than positional control. In the *instructional* function children should reconstruct knowledge for themselves, rather than receive it from some authority, and they should then discuss, even argue, with their peers. In the *interpersonal* function, there will be more emphasis on individual identity and differentiation than on

group solidarity. In the *expressive* function, feelings encountered in that differentiated individuality must seek expression in words as well as dance or painting.

(3) While the influence of the momentary context on speech is acknowledged, Bernstein distinguishes 'code' from 'speech variant'. Code refers to a more pervasive or underlying regulation of speech, while 'speech variants' are more superficial variations in that underlying code in response to particular situations. It is a child's code that we wish to extend in order that every child can use an elaborated code whenever it is necessary to accomplish some personal goal. ('Use' entails knowing, albeit tacitly, both what such a code is and in what kind of situation it would help.) Changes in code, in contrast to changes in speech variants, follow changes in a child's conception of his roles vis-à-vis others, and his conception of what language can accomplish in these new (and newly perceived) situations. For example, when a child explains to others something he can do, the need for explicit communication follows from his new role as 'expert'. Somehow, the impact of these new language experiences taken together will be greater than the sum of the style-shifting that each would evoke alone.

The last three specifications characterize more detailed aspects of a school environment which could provide such language experiences.

(4) Meeting the first three specifications in a classroom group poses an important problem: the feeling of community created must be based on organic rather than mechanical solidarity, according to Bernstein's adoption of Durkheim's terms. That is, there must be a division of labour so that children carry on different activities but also need to discuss their ideas and plans with each other—individualized learning, but not just everyone doing his own thing. Outsiders to the classroom community, transients like visitors, or more permanent like children or adults from the rest of the school—can play an important role in sustaining the need to communicate more explicitly than classmates might require.

(5) Language use in the total school environment, not just in a particular period of the day, should be the object of concern. And in addition to the situations that can be created in school, dramatizations and games can simulate additional contexts and provide more concentrated encounters. Such simulations can be particularly important, as intensive practice in new roles and their communicative demands, to help some children overcome previous habits of coping with their world in non-verbal ways or through restricted codes alone. Simulation situations are better than pattern drills for two reasons. First because the focus is

always on communication, not imitation, on meaning, not form. Second, because they can provide a variety of communicative contexts while pattern drills, by definition, offer the child a more limited range of contexts and options.

(6) In terms of content, the specific topics that communication is 'about', education should start where the child is. One can be explicit about anything. And as Bernstein makes very clear, the particular non-standard forms referred to as a 'dialect' are no hindrance either. . . . Problems may arise in using indigenous content in classrooms with older children if they feel strongly about a boundary between their in-school and out-of-school worlds. . . . But with younger children, it should be easier. In either case, familiar content must not stimulate only routinized clichés; fresh individualized use of familiar material must be encouraged. . . .

While Harold Rosen has been critical of Bernstein's theory (as in Rosen 1972), the above specifications seem completely compatible with the detailed account of language usage in good primary school classrooms in *The Language of Primary School Children* (Rosen and Rosen 1973).

Turning back to the problem of assessment, I believe that assessing an environment for its opportunities for learning to use language must be different from assessing that same environment for its opportunities for learning language structure, because different learning processes seem to be involved in the two cases.

Briefly, unlike the learning of language structure, the learning of specific language functions seems to depend on the child's actually practising those functions. While with structure, the child may well learn what he hears, in using language he seems to learn what he himself says. (See Cazden 1973 and 1974 for more detailed arguments on this distinction.) Thus the child's language-using environment must be assessed not only for the opportunities it provides, but for the extent to which individual children take up those opportunities. It is not enough to know that productive talk of desired kinds is 'in the air'. Even if one wants only a comprehensive valuation of an environment, not outcome data on individual children, one still must monitor individual child participation.

One aspect of any group setting is that teachers must distribute their attention and their conversational time among a group of children. In addition to the simple matter of a division of talking time, there is the more complex matter of an unequal division.

A group environment can be twenty-four different environments for twenty-four children. Because teachers themselves respond to reinforcement, they may talk more to the children who talk most to them. In other words, how individual children talk (or don't talk) affects the teacher's behaviour and that in turn reacts back to them.

A student at Harvard, Anne Monaghan, did some research on this problem in a Cambridge nursery school which has a child group mixed in age, race and social class. Ignoring these differences, Monaghan kept track of who initiated conversations and then compared the list of children ranked according to number of verbal contacts they initiated with any teacher with the list of the same children ranked according to the number of verbal contacts any teacher initiated with them. The two lists were very similar, and more so in the spring than in the fall. In Monaghan's words, over the course of the year,

The teaching staff appears to be reinforcing and amplifying what already exists when children enter—those children who initiate a great deal get teacher initiations in return, while those who initiate infrequently are not frequently sought out by teachers. By omission or commission, the general configuration of social abilities or deficits which a child brings with him to school will be strengthened as classroom policy now stands. (1971, p. 16.)

With this consideration, assessing any environment for language use by naturalistic observations assumes large and perhaps unfeasible dimensions. If child performance is important for child learning, then observations in completely natural settings have their limitations. The density of evidence on whether, for example, individual children ask questions as well as answer them, or construct coherent narratives or explanations, is likely to be thin, even over the course of extended observations. So one seeks supplementation, in situations which represent or simulate the larger whole but which can yield more information in less time. Just as the programme specifications above suggested more 'concentrated encounters' in simulated situations like dramatizations and games for instructional purposes, so such 'concentrated encounters' may be useful for assessment as well.

Concentrated Encounters

In contrast to the more contrived situations we call 'tests', the most important characteristic of concentrated encounters is that they are condensed forms of familiar interaction experiences. They represent our best examples of teaching encounters and are as close as possible to them in setting, participants and topic. But they are more focused by teacher direction for assessment purposes, and involve a smaller than usual group of children so that the participation of each child is maximized.

Familiarity is the key precisely because the situational influences on speech are so powerful that it is difficult if not impossible to get a young child to transfer language skills he has demonstrated in a natural situation to some more contrived situation in which we wish to elicit them on demand. Shapiro (1973) has documented the failures she encountered in trying to assess behaviours of young children, previously observed in a primary grade classroom following a Bank Street model of education, in an artificial context where those same behaviours had no functional value for the child and were now requested only in response to a test-like question of some unfamiliar adult.

Concentrated encounters in which observations would be focused should include both teacher–child interactions (as in a discussion of a story, or science experience, or field trip) and child–child interactions (as in role-playing, or some kind of two-person communication game where one child has to give directions or ask questions of another).

Formative and Summative Evaluation

One remaining question needs to be addressed: can results of such concentrated encounters be used as evaluation of both teacher and programme on the one hand, and of individual children's growth on the other? Or, in other words, can the same data contribute both to formative evaluation of programme process (and used in teacher education and programme improvement) and for summative evaluation of a programme's 'success'?

The report of a task force at the Educational Testing Service (ETS) posed the problem as follows:

The decision to use either natural or contrived settings often appears to be a matter of the investigator's taste, when it should depend on the proposed use of the 'scores' in subsequent analyses. If the observational measures are to serve as dependent variables, they should be derived from standardized situations. If they are to serve as independent variables describing the program or treatment, they may be derived from naturalistic settings, although valuable predictive (independent variable) information can also stem from standardized situations. Confusion on this point may result in such anomalies as treating the number of questions a child asks in class as a descriptor both of the kind of educational process he is experiencing *and* the outcomes of the particular educational treatment.

It is important to add that in a systems view of the organism interacting with his environment, the labelling of variables as 'dependent' or 'independent' may not be as important as recognizing their interdependence. However, this view does not eliminate consideration for each variable of the logic of measurement and experimental control. For instance, in the example of question-asking given above, there would be little hope of predicting individual consistencies in question asking behavior from observations obtained in a naturalistic setting where children had widely varying opportunities and occasions to ask questions. (Anderson *et al.* 1972, p. 8.)

How would the concentrated encounters suggested above be analysed in these terms?

The important issue is not whether the teacher or some separate 'experimenter' conducts the encounter. The teacher *can* do it, whether one seeks measures of the programme or the child. For example, a new set of tests for pre-school children being developed at ETS, called CIRCUS (ETS, 1973), are all designed for teacher administration. Whether the teacher *should* conduct the encounter depends on judgements of feasibility and advisability. Feasibility depends on the availability of other adults to attend to the rest of the children. I think the teacher is the most advisable adult both for getting the best from the child (unless we wish particularly to assess his ability to relate to strangers), and because the teacher will herself obtain first-hand information on the child's behaviour which should be useful in planning future language experiences.

The more important issue is the degree of freedom or standardization of the teacher's behaviour. If the teacher's behaviour has been 'scripted', as it is in traditional tests, then no information on her 'typical' behaviour is available; the information on child behaviour is more comparable across teachers, but full interpretation of that behaviour would depend on some notion of the representativeness of the task in the ongoing life of the school. Does the script fit the norms of interaction in the classroom setting? How often are opportunities for practice of the requested behaviour available and taken up by each individual child? These are both type 3 questions of process–product relationships.

If the teacher's behaviour is not scripted, then the encounter can be well used to describe typical teacher behaviour, but information on individual children will be less clear. The teacher may bring out the best in a child or not. The child's responses would at least have to be weighted in terms of the opportunities provided in the encounter for particular kinds of response. Joan Tough describes both the value of non-scripted encounters and their limitations:

As conversation progresses, decisions will have to be made about the direction in which the child's interest seems to lie, and what aspects of the experience are likely to have the kind of meaning which he will be ready and perhaps eager to express. . . . We must remember however, that in our examples the teacher asked different questions and we cannot know whether it was the questions which restricted the answers . . . or whether this would have been the character of the children's responses if the questions had been more open. (The Schools Council Pre-School Language Project 1972, pp. 42, 50.)

Perhaps if the same child participates in several such encounters, then the context-dependent evidence from each can be accumulated across encounters to yield corroborative evidence for a more complete picture of each child.

Discussant: *Maurice Chazan*

The task which has been assigned to me of responding to Professor Cazden's thought-provoking paper, is a particularly difficult one, for two main reasons. Firstly, I have tended to agree wholeheartedly with almost all I have read of Courtney Cazden's work. She has contributed in no small measure to the arousal of interest in the language development of young children—until not so long ago, a surprisingly neglected field of study. Her writings have been valuable and influential in the formulation of a meaningful theoretical framework for understanding early language growth and in encouraging a more sophisticated approach to issues of practical concern relating to educational intervention in early childhood, notably to questions concerning the assessment of the effectiveness of language programmes for young children.

Secondly, it is impossible, in a brief response, to do justice to the many important questions which the paper raises about the evaluation of product and process in language programmes. These questions are always highly complex, but especially so in the case of pre-school programmes, in which case, apart from the factors discussed in Cazden's paper, it seems particularly necessary to separate out the effects of stimulation at home from that provided by the school. Having designated groups of children as 'disadvantaged', 'lower working-class', 'middle-class' and so on, on rather loose criteria, we tend to assume too easily that the kind and amount of language stimulation these children receive at home is fairly constant within the group. However, as Brandis and Henderson (1970) found in their studies, and the Schools Council Project in Compensatory Education based in Swansea (Chazan et al. in press) found in comparing relatively advantaged and disadvantaged children within 'deprived' areas, there are variations in the linguistic environment within the broad social groupings often used in research that have an important effect on children's language growth. As we develop ways of helping parents to provide appropriate stimulation for their children during the pre-school years—and I believe strongly that programmes focusing on parents will pay off as much as school-based intervention—the interaction between home and school will need to be increasingly taken into account in evaluation studies. This is a question open to discussion, but I must turn now to my expansion—or perhaps extension is the more appropriate word in this case—of Cazden's paper.

I will begin by commending the general emphases of the paper, in particular the stress on situational effects on language, on the need to know more about the actual behaviour of teachers and children in the school setting, and on the importance of functional aspects of language. Any attempt to improve and to add to the armoury of techniques and approaches likely to be of value in language assessment is to be welcomed, and, although more thought needs to be given to the purposes to which Cazden's 'concentrated' and 'contrived' encounters may be put, as well as to the practical issues involved, these approaches clearly deserve to be tried out on a wide basis. However, without in any way wishing to detract from the merits of approaches emphasizing encounters in a more or less natural situation, I think that the paper is somewhat hard on tests. Perhaps as an educational psychologist I am over-fond of testing, but I should like to say something about the use of tests in the assessment of early language development, and then to make a few comments about the role of the teacher in evaluation, which seems a crucial matter in the consideration of situational approaches to language assessment.

Use of Tests

Cazden tends to underline the limitations of tests in assessing language and, if I interpret her observations correctly, would be quite happy to develop evaluation procedures that do not include tests of the more conventional kind. Language tests indeed have many weaknesses, and as Mittler (1970) has stated, psychologists have been severely handicapped by the shortage of tests of language skills, particularly tests of language comprehension. Recently a number of new tests, some quite imaginative, have been devised, but most are poorly standardized and lack reliability and validity. With young children it is often difficult to get verbal responses even when the child is friendly to the tester and at ease. Researchers, because of a lack of time or resources, tend to use a very limited range of tests or even a single test, which may not be appropriate, or which may give very little information about the child's language development, but is chosen as being quick to administer. Further, as Cazden herself has stated elsewhere (Cazden 1972b), test results may be deceptive. For example, what the child has learned to express on a test may not have been assimilated into his total linguistic and cognitive system. Nevertheless, in spite of all their deficiencies, tests—both norm-referenced and criterion-referenced—are still needed for the purposes of evaluation. Difficult as the concept of 'normal development' is, we should be able to evaluate specific programmes rather better if we know more about the norms of language development, including norms relating to language structure. (In this connection, it does seem rather sweeping to state, as Professor Cazden does, that 'assessment via tests is possible but unnecessary'.) Criterion-referenced tests can be very helpful in the early identification of individual language deficits.

The pre-test/post-test, control/experimental group design, too, has its weaknesses and has only a limited function in evaluation, but it does have a place, and, although this approach needs to be supplemented by the kind of techniques outlined in Cazden's paper, I cannot see that we can afford to jettison it. So I think that it is still well worthwhile developing new and better language tests for young children to contribute towards evaluative procedures, and also to attempt to relate different strategies of assessment more precisely to specific objectives in evaluation. This question is touched upon at several points in the paper, but clearly much more needs to be said about it. Different considerations arise if evaluation is being carried out in a spirit of pure research, or if it is intended to influence general policy or to provide feedback for the teacher. At the present stage, it seems especially relevant to consider the role of the teacher in language assessment.

The Role of the Teacher in Evaluation

Questions relating to the evaluation of educational programmes at the pre-school stage have assumed an important status in this country following the 1972 White Paper published by the Secretary of State for Education and Science. In spite of financial restraints, there will be a substantial increase in facilities for the under-fives within the next decade, and, as a result of the pioneering work in the USA and to a lesser extent in Britain, it is likely that the emphasis in pre-school education will be on language development. Further, the Department of Education and Science is actively planning a research programme to monitor the development of the new provision, which will include 'studies of the results and effectiveness of nursery education in reaching its several goals', which studies 'will take a wider view of results than the children's educational attainment, though this will naturally form an important part'. In this evaluation programme, the teacher is bound to play a considerable role, partly because teacher-variables are extremely important and partly because external evaluation is a very expensive business.

At first sight, Cazden's concentrated and contrived encounters seem to be ideally suited to giving the teacher her proper place in assessment, but I am somewhat bothered by the idea of giving the teacher a central role in evaluation. I cannot agree that 'whether the teacher or some separate experimenter conducts the encounter' is not an important issue. Admittedly, a strange outsider is not the best person to obtain uninhibited responses from young children, but a stranger with the right approach can soon become fully accepted. Admittedly, too, it is important that the teacher should be getting feedback about her own effectiveness as a person and about the methods which she uses; but can a teacher, even with help, really sustain the role both of the teacher and of a systematic evaluator? And will not the encounter situation itself be influenced by the individual strength and weaknesses of the teacher in the teaching situation? Certainly the teacher can obtain a good deal of useful first-hand information from unscripted encounters, but I cannot see that she will be able to make much more than a crude evaluation of what is going on in the classroom or to obtain a great deal of detailed information relating to individual children, without stressing the role of the evaluator at the expense of the teaching role. Perhaps, whenever evaluation is being taken seriously, the programme needs a 'programme assistant' such as was used, for example, in the Tucson, Arizona, compensatory programme for six- to eight-year-olds described by Lavatelli (1971). As part of the programme, children engaged in varied activities such as excursions, cooking, or observing animals. A child's remarks about these experiences are recorded by the teacher, an assistant or the child himself with all errors and deficiencies included. A programme assistant, who 'serves as a resource person or agent of charge', helps the teacher to analyse the sample and plan subsequent steps.

The teacher's own behaviour is a crucial variable in any educational programme. How is this behaviour to be judged, and how is the teacher to be faced with the judgement? The findings of Anne Monaghan about teacher–child contacts are very important, being particularly relevant for the education of disadvantaged children, and are consonant with those reported in a recent article by Garner and Bing (1973) on a study involving somewhat older children. This inquiry was concerned with the ways in which teacher–pupil contacts were distributed among 179 pupils in five first-year junior-school classes in England. The main data used were the verbal contacts between teachers and individual pupils. Some children had little contact of any kind with their teachers, and contacts generally were unequally distributed. The children receiving high levels of contact were either active, bright, personable children or else active, duller miscreants. The writers comment that contacts between teacher and pupil are of very short duration, and that it is difficult to see how teachers can become deeply involved in children's problems of understanding when only a minute or so is available for them to make their diagnosis and give their help. It would seem, therefore, that an important function of evaluation is to help to increase the awareness of the teacher of her own behaviour towards her pupils.

In this connection, the use of teachers' ratings merit consideration. In our own work in infant schools, we made use of teachers' ratings of a wide range of behaviour, and in the case of language skills found a reasonably close correlation between teachers' ratings and test results. The teachers themselves found the rating schedules useful for their own purposes, in recording the children's progress. The schedules also directed the teachers' attention towards particular skills or specific aspects of development. Should use be made of self-rating schedules too, or would this be undesirable?

Future Needs

To sum up, I have been arguing for attacking the problems of evaluation on a broad front, and for the development of new and more imaginative tests of the outcome of language programmes for individual children as well as the development of such approaches as have been outlined by Cazden. We must not expect too much from a single evaluation technique, but rather attempt to fit specific approaches to specific goals in assessment. In particular, the teacher's attitudes, personal qualities and idiosyncratic methods need to be assessed as part of the evaluation of the educational environment, and we need to think about ways of providing the teacher with feedback without unduly upsetting her self-image. In assessing an educational environment, we must be careful not to regard it, even when carefully planned, as necessarily the same for all children. A particular kind of linguistic environment in class may be stimulating for most of the pupils, but be inappropriate for those children who most need help in their language development. In fact, as previously mentioned, some children may hardly be in real contact with their environment.

We need also to remind ourselves how little we have to offer to teachers in the way of ideas about language stimulation, in spite of the good work which is currently going on in several centres. Moore (1971) was able to say, about the American scene, that 'with respect to the effectiveness of language intervention programmes, no more than a handful of carefully controlled language training experiments have ever been conducted in this country' (p. 43), and this is no less true of the situation in Britain. Yet such evidence as we have suggests that it is from carefully structured programmes that the best results are likely to be obtained, particularly in the case of children from unstimulating home backgrounds. As Moore states, the analysis of the cognitive and social demands of the environment which places an informal emphasis on language shows that it is very unlikely that this situation facilitates the development of verbal skills needed by disadvantaged children. The extension situation and others in which the teacher's response is contingent upon the pupil's seem, in Moore's view, to have some potential value, but it is the structured tutoring situation, in which the teacher plays a more active shaping role and where a warm relationship exists between child and teacher, which 'seems the most effective one for teaching the grammatically elaborated and referentially precise language use that seems to be the major subcultural language deficit having adverse effects on the educability of pre-school children' (Moore 1971, p. 42). This means that, in addition to helping teachers to 'listen more sensitively, and interpret more informatively many aspects of their children's language', as Cazden puts it, there is a need for a great deal more in the way of innovative and imaginative material to help teachers to provide meaningful and relevant 'structured tutoring situations'.

3

Children and Programmes:
How Shall We Educate the Young Child?

JOAN TOUGH

Perhaps all those of us who are concerned with the education of young children would endorse certain general objectives for the curriculum: that the child should gain physical skills, acquire a wide vocabulary, achieve control of the language system, learn to classify, be aware of temporal and spatial relationships, develop the concepts of number, acquire a range of general knowledge about the physical, biological and social world, become familiar with some stories, rhymes and music, be able to solve problems, express ideas in words, in pictures and through a variety of other materials, and develop an understanding of other people's needs and views. Most current programmes, including our own nursery school practice, include some or all of these goals, but the methods of achieving them are very different.

There might be some disagreement amongst us about the relative value of the facts and skills to be taught, and differences in the order of priority in which we would set them. Whether or not we should include the teaching of reading might be hotly debated, although probably all would agree that attention should be given to those basic skills upon which reading is founded. There might also be argument about the kind of experiences to be offered in terms of relevance to the child's own background of experience. Some of the current discussion of the problems of teaching disadvantaged children is to do with the *selection* of materials through which the content of the curriculum is presented.

In spite of such disagreements, however, it would seem that in considering a curriculum for young children the matter of the content is likely to cause less dispute than the matter of *how* the child should learn, that is, the context in which his learning should proceed. The methods of teaching, the relationships between teachers and pupils, the expectations set up concerning children's behaviour, all these induce other kinds of learning; attitudes and values are transmitted which in the end, particularly in the education of the young child, may be more important for his continuing education than the content of what has been learned.

In this paper I shall argue that in planning curricula for the education of young children it is the context of the situations which we devise and the relationships that we promote that will be crucial in determining the effective learning that will take place.

My own approach to the curriculum stems from a general view of the aims of education, which has been expressed by Bruner as:

to produce the kind of generalist in skill, the 'skill intensive' worker who is capable of acting as a controlling factor in regulating, running or curbing of a technology such as we are developing in the West, or one who is capable of understanding it well enough to serve to criticise, to be the controller rather than the victim. (Bruner 1971, p. 158.)

In this view the outcome of education, to put it at its lowest, is the ability to think critically, and to communicate that thinking to others. In this view it is perhaps skills of thinking and communicating that the educated should hold in common, skills of thinking that make knowledge accessible, skills of thinking that can be brought to bear on personal problems of living, as well as upon the problems of runaway technology, and skills of communication that ensure participation in the making of crucial decisions.

In the climate of growing awareness of the importance of early learning for later achievement this general objective can be seen to be one which is relevant for early education no less than for later education. It is also true that there has developed a general recognition of the part played by language in the child's learning. If we are not yet sure how language functions to promote learning, there are few who would argue that its role is not an important one and that it is central to, and should permeate, the whole of the curriculum for young children.

Language Programmes as Curricula for the Disadvantaged

The problems of those children whose experience of the use of language diverges greatly from that of the majority have already been recognized and considerable effort has been spent, particularly in America, in devising programmes which aim to redress such disadvantage.

The majority of programmes that are currently in use, therefore, have been conceived as curricula for the disadvantaged child. The language components of most of them have similar content, for example, vocabulary building, the practice of syntactic structures and the use of locational prepositions, but they adopt different methods to achieve similar goals. Some rely on syntactic patterning and repeating drills, as in the Distar programme (Engelmann *et al.* 1969) and the Peabody programme (Dunn, Horton and Smith 1968). At the other end of the range are those which expect the same kind of learning to emerge from efforts to communicate which are stimulated through social interaction in structured situations, as for example *Talk Reform* (Gahagan and Gahagan 1970). (In contrast our traditional nursery school practice would perhaps include similar goals, not necessarily explicitly stated, but would seek to exploit opportunities arising spontaneously from children's play and activities to help children accomplish such learning.)

Underlying the design of most of these programmes is the assumption that the disadvantaged child is a special case and needs special treatment. The rationale of Bereiter and Engelmann's programme, for example, is that disadvantaged children have a different style or mode of learning which should be used to his advantage. The children it is claimed have an aptitude for rote learning, which therefore should be exploited as the most effective mode of learning for them (Bereiter and Engelmann 1966).

The way in which the problem is conceived determines the way in which it will be met. Should we accept that disadvantaged children are essentially different from other children? Should they be given a different *kind* of education? In looking for answers to these questions we are faced with an ethical as well as an educational problem.

The danger is that if we see the disadvantaged child's problem as one of just being unprepared for school, one of not knowing how to play the role of pupil, then we may neglect more fundamental causes, of which unfamiliarity with the ways of schools and teachers is just one symptom, amongst others, that needs to be taken into account when trying to arrive at a diagnosis of the causes of the child's failure.

Underlying some of the programmes for the young disadvantaged child are a number of assumptions. The child is seen as being deficient in some basic knowledge and skills, for example, in knowledge of the structures of language, and skill in producing them. It is assumed that the disadvantaged child has a predisposition to a different mode of learning from other children, and can learn best in group sessions in rote-learning contexts. Hence we find language being taught by the drill and sequencing familiar in second language teaching.

There must also be an assumption that rote learning of this kind will transfer into other contexts and become a generalized skill, for if every possible answer has to be learned by rote there never will be time for the child to catch up on all he should, and could, learn.

Finally it must be assumed that motivation which stems from praise by the teacher will persist when the teacher is no longer present, and when learning becomes difficult and tedious.

In this paper I shall challenge both the conceptualization of the problem, and the assumptions which underlie such language programmes. Can curricula planned on such assumptions ever lead to the development of skills of thinking and of communication? Will the automatic observance of rules and overt practice ever lead to the application of critical thinking to problems of living and learning outside the school, or even to success in later schooling?

An Alternative Conception of the Problem

First of all the conceptualization of the problem must be challenged because it is from this that inferences are made about the goals which ought to be pursued through the curriculum.

In the first place it seems likely that we shall learn more from examining what an 'educated' child can do, and the process by which he reached this state than by examining only what the disadvantaged child is unable to do. Margaret Clark in a paper at the last seminar made a similar proposal and suggested that we should learn more about reading failure by studying children who have learned to read easily before coming to school (Clark 1975).

The learning that most five-year-olds have accomplished is the outcome of their experiences in the home environment during the pre-school years. By that time it is clear that some are much better equipped for starting school than others. It is difficult to discover exactly how they have come by their advantaged position. We can, however, examine what it is they have learned during the pre-school period, and by examining also what the disadvantaged child has learned we may perhaps see the nature, if not the causes, of their advantage or disadvantage.

To do this I refer to some of the findings from a longitudinal study undertaken in Leeds. Some aspects of this work have already been reported (Tough 1970, 1973a) and a full report is given in 'The Development of Meaning' (Tough 1976).

The children in this study were selected at the age of three and their parents either had received the minimum period of education and followed unskilled or semi-skilled occupations, or had received higher education and were in professional occupations. There were twenty-four children in each group and there were equal numbers of girls and boys. All scored above 110 on a Stanford Binet Test of Intelligence at the age of three, and the mean scores for the groups were about the same. All the children were talkative and generally friendly and large samples of their language were collected at the ages of three, five-and-half and seven-and-a-half years. The mothers of all the children were interviewed twice, first when the children were three and again when the children were seven-and-a-half.

I refer first to the differences between the groups in the amount of complexity in their language.

On any aspect of complexity of the language of these children that we measured there were differences, generally at a high level of significance. At each age the mean length of their utterances, complexity within the noun and verb phrases, complexity in the structure of the utterances, the frequency of the use of pronouns, all showed that the advantaged group used greater complexity more frequently than the disadvantaged group.

But we agree with Labov (1970) and others that unless the differences in the complexity of structure can be shown to be a reflection of differences in the kind of meaning expressed then we would not assume that complexity is of itself important. However, when the uses of language were analysed the differences between the groups were also highly significant.

All the children in both groups used language to maintain their own status, rights and property and for threats and criticism of others. But, and this appears to be the important issue, the children in the advantaged groups used language more frequently for recall, to make associations, to analyse details, to make a synthesis, to anticipate and predict, to collaborate and plan, to give explanations and to project through the imagination, to hypothesize and approach logical reasoning.

What is the cause of these differences in learning to use language? What experiences have the advantaged children met which have fostered these uses of language? Before going on to examine what these experiences seem likely to be there are some important features which call into question some of the assumptions upon which some language programmes are based.

First it appears that some of the differences found reflect a lag in development, that is, the disadvantaged group are learning some uses at a later age than the advantaged group. For example, at the age of three some of the uses listed above were appearing in the talk of the advantaged group, but they were absent in the talk of the disadvantaged group. By the age of five-and-a-half they were appearing in the talk of the disadvantaged group but not so frequently as in the talk of the advantaged group. By seven all the advantaged group were using synthesis as well as analysis, whilst analysis now begins to be used more frequently by the disadvantaged groups.

How can such a lag be explained? Can we infer that it is the change in their experiences of language in use when they come to school at five which promotes the development of uses which home experience has not initiated? This explanation would fit the 'lag' phenomenon quite well.

Again by seven-and-a-half the advantaged group are regularly using synthesis and hypothesis, logical reasoning and imaginative projection, whilst the disadvantaged group rarely use them spontaneously. Yet it is important to note that it is not the case that the disadvantaged group never use complex language or display these particular uses. The difference between the group lies generally in the frequency and extent of complexity and incidence of particular uses.

A further interesting feature appeared in the responses of the disadvantaged group at the ages of five-and-a-half and seven-and-a-half years in interviews in which they responded to certain materials, pictures and models, and carried out particular tasks, for example drawing, demonstrating an experiment and constructing a model: the advantaged children tended to make an immediate, appropriate response in which meaning was well organized but the disadvantaged group gave only partial answers, and the meaning possibilities were not fully realized. How can this be explained? Is it that the disadvantaged group have an inadequate inner framework of meaning against which to organize such experiences?

But there is a further point to make here. By using a number of probes, which encouraged the children to think again and helped to focus their attention, they were often able to reach a similar construction to the one made immediately by the advantaged children. Without the probes certainly the observer would not have known of their ability to organize the experience; it seemed as though they needed the probe to help them discover what they knew. With the adult's help the capacity they had for organizing meaning was demonstrated.

It might be argued that these children just did not see the task as a relevant one, although they were clearly enjoying the activity and there were no closed questions requiring a correct answer, and all answers were acceptable. In looking at the data it seems that many of these disadvantaged children had an inner knowledge of which they were unaware. It would appear that the adult's probing served to uncover this neglected knowledge and focused the child's attention on it so that it became available for use. This again would seem to be an explanation which fits the facts of the data.

There are also points to note about the disadvantaged child's ability to use complex structures. Whilst it is the case that at all three ages there are significant differences between the groups in the use of complex structures it is not that the disadvantaged child never uses complex language. For example, when he repeats a story that has just been told to him by his friend, the length and complexity of the utterances he uses equal that of the advantaged child. Indeed, he may surpass the advantaged child since the latter now tends to make a synthesis of some parts of the story, saying for example, 'Spot defended the butcher' instead of 'Spot barked and took hold of the robber's ankle so that the butcher could run away.'

However, the disadvantaged child generally tends not to be explicit, although it is clear that on some occasions he can be provoked into explicitness. For example, he is asked to direct his friend, who is hidden behind a screen, to make pictures from tiles. In this situation the disadvantaged child uses nouns, modifying them liberally with adjectives, gives locational description and is driven to giving redundant information. We see in this situation that the disadvantaged child's problem lies not mainly in a lack of command of syntactic structures but more in the difficulty which he seems to have in projecting into the other child's problem and viewpoint. He has difficulty in selecting information of the kind which will give most help to the other child. It is not, however, that the disadvantaged child cannot attempt the task. He is driven to use the same strategies employed by the advantaged child, but he apparently finds taking the other's view of the situation difficult.

So we see that the disadvantaged child can be explicit when the situation presses him, but he does not anticipate correctly what the other child needs to know. This seems to be an indication of the difficulty he has in projecting into the other's perspective.

However, these are some situations in which explicitness and complexity of structure are used more readily. For example when he is left talking with his friend to make a picture or model together we see that he sometimes draws on complexity of structure as he seeks to maintain his status, or what he feels to be his rights, and for threatening and criticizing his friend. These conversations contain some of the most complex utterances of the whole interview although there are also many one word utterances. The child who says –

'If you've gotten all those little wheels then I'm not going to have any to put on to this motor I'm doing that's going to zoom across yonder after that nit there.'

can hardly be said to need instructions in how to use complex structures, but nevertheless in some parts of his interview he seems unable to organize meaning at any but the simplest level.

To summarize, there is plenty of evidence from our study to show that although there are significant differences between the groups in the complexity of the structures used, the disadvantaged child shows that he has access to complex structures and he produces complex utterances in some contexts with some facility. Although he does not seem to have the ready command of complex structures that the advantaged children show, the disadvantaged child may have more resources of language than is made evident by his answers to questions.

But there are great differences between the groups in the purposes for which they use language. This might lead us to infer that the disadvantaged child is organizing his experiences on a different basis. Nevertheless it also seems to be the case that with help he can be led to impose a structure on his experiences which resembles that imposed by the advantaged group.

From the evidence of this study it would seem that the disadvantaged child has two major problems.

First he does not seem to project readily into the needs of his listener; he seems to assume that the listener shares his own viewpoint. This seems to suggest that he is still egocentric in the view that he takes of the world outside himself.

This conclusion is supported when we look at what happens when the child is left to talk with his friend. Even in this situation the advantaged child and the disadvantaged child seem to take up different viewpoints. The relationship which is reflected in the way in which the advantaged child initiates and responds to talk tends to facilitate the exchange of information whereas the disadvantaged child seems to close down the possibilities for exchange. This does not mean that there is necessarily less goodwill amongst the disadvantaged but that the child's own viewpoint, particularly his need to protect his status and rights, is dominant, so that there is rarely a basis for the reciprocation of views.

The second problem seems to be that the disadvantaged child does not reflect upon his own experiences, anticipating how things will turn out, looking for clues from past experiences to predict what developments might be. Nor does he seem to project so that he can take account of more than the immediately observable. His problem seems to be an inability to take up a standpoint other than that supplied by his immediate perception.

At seven-and-a-half one of the tasks he was given was to respond to the pictures in which a stick figure appeared in an ambiguous but partially structured setting, for example, apparently running round a corner. The children were asked to give possible explanations, to project and suggest any appropriate context. In this task the disadvantaged children tended to give their attention only to the figure—for example 'He's running.' When asked why they tended to give replies like 'I can see he is' or 'Cos I can see his legs are far apart' or 'He's going like this'.

Those disadvantaged children who did project made only a general projection 'He's running away from someone' or 'He must have done something bad'.

On the other hand the other children tried as it were to project round the corner or look forward, and find explanations, and were able to offer a range of possibilities 'There might be a big boy chasing him' or 'He might have stolen something and the policeman's after him', or 'Perhaps he's running to catch a bus or perhaps he's late for school'.

The explanation of the disadvantaged children's response might be that they were just unfamiliar with the task, but this was as plainly true for all the children. It was not that the disadvantaged child did not offer an explanation, it was the strategy he used to find an explanation that was different. Again, it seems that he finds great difficulty in projecting beyond the immediately perceptible. In this last task solutions are to be found by making a survey of possible situations in which 'running away from' or 'running to' might be a result. This means drawing on the imagination in order to perceive what might be hidden from view.

This brief summary will I hope be enough to support the challenge to the underlying assumptions of some language programmes.

The problem of the disadvantaged child is not usually that the child is deficient in knowledge of language. It is not that he has not a knowledge of syntactic structures. The child is able to use complex structures in some situations although he may not use them in all situations. A programme based on drilling structures may be doing no more than practising overtly structures which are already known but rarely used in the classroom. A similar point has been made by Courtney Cazden in a report of the findings of a research student (Cazden 1972a). During the period in which children were being drilled in the use of negative statements this student noted down negative statements that were being used in the children's spontaneous talk in any situation but the language lesson itself. All the children in the groups were heard using negative statements, and examples of four categories of negative structures were collected from all of them. Cazden comments that although these children might have benefited by being helped to sort out the meaning of a negative statement, for example, 'Draw something that is not a circle', drill of this kind may be ignoring the language competence which children already have, and be doing nothing to help them use it for their own purpose.

But it is also clear that the assumption that what is learned is likely to transfer into other situations is not justified. The disadvantaged children in our study demonstrated that this just does not happen. They use complex syntactic structures to convey complex meaning in some situations but in other situations there is little evidence of such knowledge. The use of complexity does not appear to have become generalized from one kind of situation to another. There seems to be little to support the view that structures learned in a rote-learning situation will transfer into other contexts.

Nevertheless it is clear that the disadvantaged children are using language differently. Does this mean that they learn by different means? We will briefly consider some of the differences in the children's early experiences.

The Learning Environment

The home can be considered as providing a curriculum for the young child's learning. What are the differences between the curricula that have been offered to the disadvantaged children and those which the advantaged children have experienced? It is not the case that the mothers of the children in our two groups provide environments for the child's learning which fall neatly into contrasting models, but there is a tendency towards such a dichotomy and on most of those factors, which can be seen as contributing to the kind of opportunities for learning offered to the child, there are differences between the groups, which reach a level of some significance. To illustrate the differences that seem likely to influence the kinds of stimulation offered to the child a number of aspects are referred to here. The evidence is drawn from interviews taken with mothers when the children were three years of age. Further interviews were undertaken by my associate Elizabeth Sestini when the children were seven-and-a-half.

In both interviews we were interested in the factors in the child's home environment which seemed likely to relate to the differences which emerged in the children's use of language. These might be expected to be the nature of the activities allowed and encouraged, the interests and activities of the parents, the activities they engaged in with their children and in which the child engaged with other children, the parents' view of their children, the value they set on education, their view of school and teachers, and the parents' methods of controlling their children. All these seem likely to contribute to and be a reflection of the kind of environment in which the child is growing up.

In addition, and inextricably bound up with these activities, is the experience in using language that the parents provide through their own talk with others, and particularly from the way in which they engage the child in talk.

In an interview, however open the questions are, and whatever care is taken to avoid inferring value from particular kinds of behaviour, answers must be viewed with caution. Reported behaviour and actual behaviour may not match. Particularly in the case of mothers of the advantaged group there may be a tendency to report what might be seen to be desirable ways of behaving. However, even if one should be wary about the reliance placed on the information given in interviews, the ways in which answers are given, the organization of ideas, the bases on which arguments are built, are a reflection of habitual modes and are not likely to reflect ways of thinking which are rarely expressed. All the mothers saw the interview as a means of helping us towards understanding their children and none sought to curtail the interview.

The points to be made here are general ones that emerged from both sets of interviews.

First, it is clear that talk went on in all their homes and that the children were engaged in it at some time. All the mothers talked freely to us and it is unlikely that they were silent in their own homes.

Both at three and at seven it seemed that all children asked questions and most mothers tried to answer them. But the mothers of the disadvantaged group indicated that they either had not the resources or the patience to give satisfactory answers.

In both interviews it became clear that the mothers tended to have different views of their children and what was appropriate for them to do. From what mothers said the disadvantaged three-year-old may have learned an independence denied to the advantaged three-year-old. Many of the children in the disadvantaged group were reported as spending much of the day playing outside in the company of other pre-school children. The advantaged three-year-olds on the other hand were reported as rarely out of sight and sound of some adult and it seems likely that they were therefore more frequently in talk with the adult.

At three the advantaged child it seems experienced more stories and rhymes, and games. Where there were older children they were reported as frequently attempting to join in the word games and problem-solving activities of the older children. When they were seven it was clear that the advantaged children were being encouraged to read, to be constructive and creative and to follow individual interests. They were frequently placed in problem-solving situations and were supported in their efforts to find solutions. The disadvantaged children on the other hand spent a great deal of time outside the home and in the company of friends about their own age.

A question was designed to reflect the methods of control by which mothers managed their children at the age of three. If the answers of mothers can be taken as a true picture of what actually happened it would seem that the advantaged children received more explanations about why their behaviour was unacceptable or why mother was annoyed with them. Such explanations were not so likely to be offered to the disadvantaged group. There was nothing to suggest that the mothers of the advantaged group were more permissive or that the mothers of the disadvantaged group were more punitive.

But what of the experiences that the children have in using language? We were not able to record all the mothers talking with their children, but we recorded a number of them. The examples we have show the differences that there are between mothers, although we have not enough data to show that these differences are characteristic of the two groups in the study. But we shall be reporting on the differences we have found in the way in which mothers organized their own meanings in the interviews. This supports the view that children are likely to have very different experiences of language in use and perhaps indicates something of the nature of the difference.

In the examples we have we see how some mothers enter into conversation with their young children almost as though they were adult, though the subject is likely to be something on which the child's attention is focused. The characteristic of the conversation is one of projecting into the child's position or viewpoint and giving explanations and information. The child's response is taken as new evidence of his problems of understanding and the mother projects again, helping him to move towards her own understanding. In conversations of this kind we can see how the dialogue between the adult and the child becomes a major means of learning for the child. As he is helped towards his mother's understanding he is also helped to see her viewpoint and in time he comes to project in the same way both into the needs of his listeners and into the ways of the world outside himself. The listening adult both necessitates and rewards efforts to express thinking.

Clearly the mother sets up a relationship in which this can happen, but the relationship is the result of her view of the child either as a developing person or as playing the role of learner. This results in the mother making efforts to project into the child's needs for information in order to facilitate the transmission of meaning.

Other conversations display the mothers' different views of their children and illustrate what happens when the mother fails to project into the child's developing meaning. Questions are ignored, or answered summarily, and the child and the adult's interest and meaning fail to come together, almost as though the conversation is two monologues which have one or two common items. Generally this kind of conversation develops where the adult is intent on the child's behaviour whilst the child has some other point of interest which he is pursuing. Such experiences, however, do little to help the child to project into the mother's feelings, or meanings, and do little to help the child take account of the needs of the interested listener.

There is already a considerable body of evidence about what are likely to be the important influences on the experiences the child will meet in his home. The works of Hess and Shipman, and of Bernstein and his associates, are well known. The study of different 'teaching styles' of mothers (Hess and Shipman 1965), the way in which mothers view the use of toys (Bernstein and Young 1967), the mother's view of the purposes language serves (Bernstein and Henderson 1970), and the way in which mothers seek to control their children (Bernstein and Brandis 1970) all provide glimpses of the nature of the differences in experience which are likely to account for differences between children in what they have learned already before they come to school. The work we have done at Leeds endorses and extends this view.

From the interviews with mothers we gain a view of the attitudes and activities which are predominant in the home. But the central experience, with which all other experiences will be associated, clearly emerges as the adult–child dialogue. Through this dialogue, values, information, structure for experiences are mediated. It becomes the source of the child's outlook on the world, on what he will see as meaningful, and the kind of meaning he will seek to impose on each new experience he meets.

It may be that the differences we find between children in their disposition to use language is mainly a consequence of differences in their experiences of participating in dialogue with adults.

The Nature of the Adult–Child Dialogue

What emerges as likely to be the most crucial factor in the education of the young child, the adult–child dialogue, is one which has so far been little explored. It is not that the importance of this dialogue has not been recognized. Bruner has drawn attention to it many times, for example:

There are doubtless many ways in which a human being can serve as a vicar of the culture, helping a child to understand its point of view and the nature of its knowledge. But I dare say that few are so potentially powerful as participating in dialogue. (Bruner 1971, p. 107.)

In communicating with the child we are essentially concerned with the transmission of meaning. But meaning is essentially individual, personal and residing within. There can be no direct communication between minds, as Vygotsky has pointed out, and since communication can be achieved only in a roundabout way, language has to be pressed into use for the mediation of ideas (Vygotsky 1962, p. 150).

The problem when communicating with the child is not only that his knowledge and skill in using language are immature but that his meanings are also underdeveloped and immature. He is dependent on the adult not only for the model from which to extend his use of language but also for the development of meaning.

What is it that the child must learn to do if he is to be able to take part in the exchange of meanings through the use of language in dialogue? In discussing the development of semantic theory Cicourel puts forward one of the conditions for the successful exchange of information as follows:

The member's ability to monitor his own output and the output of others involves a reflexive embedding of thoughts, perceptions, and spontaneous acts into subsequent outputs! Simultaneously the speaker-hearer projects this reflexive activity prospectively and retrospectively so as to create 'traces' and 'glimpses' of what was intended by participants including the speaker-hearer himself. (Cicourel 1973.)

So the participants in dialogue, if meaning is to be exchanged, must not only look inwards to their own meanings but must look outwards and try to read the clues to the meanings intended by the other participants.

Each individual carries within him his own 'subjective texture of meanings', to use Kellner's phrase (Kellner 1970), built up from past experiences, and it is these meanings which are projected into his actions and behaviour in any concrete situation. For meanings to be transmitted in dialogue Kellner proposes that there must be a 'reciprocity of perspectives' in terms of an intersubjective intentionality. Mead refers to this as 'taking the role of the other' (Mead 1934). Language cannot perform its mediating function unless there is projection from the communicator's meaning into the meanings of each other. For dialogue to be effective for the exchange of meanings, each participant must enter with a stock of information and a reflexive awareness with which to select information relevant to the dialogue, but in addition, each must be able to project into the other's position to examine what is needed to complement the relevant information which the other holds. Thus dialogue necessitates on the part of the participants projection into the perspective of the other, alternating with an inward reflexive inspection of relevant knowledge in order to select what might be made available to the other.

But the child is not able to take part in a dialogue in this way, and there is much evidence in young children's talk of their inability to consider the other's viewpoint: they are essentially egocentric even when they talk for an audience. The child's first success in communication comes when there is a mutuality of experiences and interpretations so that what is symbolized through language meets similar meaning in the other. Such communication may take place, for example, between children in the same family because of common experiences and similarly transmitted subjective textures of meanings.

But where such mutuality of experience does not exist there is likely to be difficulty in communication. When the child is in dialogue with an adult there is likely to be a gulf between their meanings. This communication gap can only be overcome by efforts 'to get inside' the other person in order to see what meanings he will need to have made clear to him. This is always the position the tutoring adult will need to take in order to project into the meanings of the child.

But for the child to begin to project and take the other's viewpoint, to 'take the role of the other', is major learning, to be accomplished by the patient efforts of the tutoring adult to bring to the child insight into the other's perspective. In doing this the adult necessarily must turn the child back to reflect upon what he knows, to make a selection from his own stock of knowledge in an attempt to match the communication need of the other. It is the gradual building up through dialogue of the alternating projection–reflection activity on the part of the child which seems to be vital to the process of his education.

The adult as he engages the child in dialogue must always be projecting into the child's problems of meanings, trying to assess the question or comment which will help the child to reflect on his own store of knowledge, and draw out that which is needed by the listener. The adult must display his own need for information, the kind of problem he has in gaining the child's meaning. In this way the child is invited to look at the recipient's predicament in making sense of the information offered by the child. Skill in taking part in dialogue cannot be taught to the young child by instruction, but he can be led gradually to see what activity is entailed in the exchange of meanings.

In helping the child in this way the adult does more than facilitate communication. Bruner has made the point that:

one of the most crucial ways in which a culture provides aids in intellectual growth is through a dialogue between the more experienced and the less experienced providing a means for the internalization of dialogue in thought. (Bruner 1971, p. 107.)

The characteristic of reflection is that of internalized dialogue. This means the inner self must play two roles, that of the self as participator in a dialogue, with access to a range of meanings, and also that of the 'other' who is questioner and challenger, one to whom explanations and justifications must be given. The model from which this role can be learned is that of dialogue with the tutoring adult: internalized it may become a model for thinking.

The dialogue with the adult may be important, then, for two reasons. First it perhaps provides a model on which the child can base his inner activity of thinking, and second it may give the child the help he needs to learn the alternating inwards–outwards switching from reflection to projection which enables him to meet the requirements of dialogue.

The Communication Problems of the Disadvantaged Child

To return now to the problems of our group of disadvantaged children. They showed a knowledge of language, but frequently showed an inability to communicate effectively: they used complex structures, but generally only in situations where mutuality of experience was the basis of the relationship. In response to experiences where an initiating open question was used, they responded with partial insight only; yet frequently, with probes from the adult, they were able to organize meaning more effectively. The adult's probes in this case offered a view of the listener's communication-need to which the child responded awkwardly but with relevance.

Moreover, the disadvantaged child appears to have great difficulty in making any projections either into the views of others or into the possibilities of situations. We might infer from this that these children have not met enough dialogue either in the home, or with a tutoring adult in school, from which to learn the alternating projection–reflection strategy without which the communication of ideas and the extension of meaning can hardly proceed. Might we infer also that they are unlikely to have internalized a dialogue model to form a basis for their thinking?

But if these differences exist should the disadvantaged child be regarded as different, and so be taught differently? There is nothing in our data to suggest that disadvantaged young children learn by a different means. The disadvantaged child learns by exactly the same means as the advantaged child: he learns from the talk around him and with him, as well as from the concrete experiences he is having; he absorbs the values, he learns the language structures. What he learns is different, because what is made available to him is different. He is the victim of his own experiences and is not able to detach himself and reflect upon them.

The child does not internalise the world of his significant others as one of many possible worlds. He internalises it as *the* world, the only existant and conceivable world . . .

(Berger and Luckmann 1966, p. 154.)

If the disadvantaged child is to be helped he needs to be given access to the skills of thinking, and the skills of communication through the use of language. It seems unlikely he will learn these except through exchange with an adult skilled in the use of dialogue.

The Enabling Curriculum

The advantaged child has learned in his home what the enabling mother considers as everyday knowledge that the child should become acquainted with. Her talk centres around the routine business of organizing a home, around the play in which the child engages in a concentrated focus of attention. She takes whatever is happening in the immediate environment as a source of interest, the people, the activities in shops and streets, in living things—that is the immediate biological and social world. She stimulates the child's curiosity, directing his attention to interesting everyday phenomena around him. She introduces him to books and stories and rhymes. She invites him into communication through written language, not by the formal instruction of reading, but by directing his attention to the things which display reading and the use of writing.

Above all, this enabling mother helps the child to look back on his experiences and reflect on them, to anticipate and predict, to hypothesize about possible explanations of phenomena and to look for problems to be solved. She does it all because she sees the child as a learner, a developing person having all the potential that being human implies. The crucial experience for the child, perhaps, is the relationship which promotes interest, inquiry, and motivation for learning; the relationship which draws the child into a continuing dialogue in which ideas are transmitted and extended.

It is true that this mother may provide an education for her child intuitively, but it is also true that she is applying skills of thinking that are the product of her own education.

Is this the model that we should follow? To those who cry that this is a middle-class model we would retort that if the skills of thinking are to remain a middle-class monopoly, education will remain accessible only to the middle classes. We should distinguish very clearly between the product of education, that is particular kinds of skill in thinking, and the goals to which such skills are directed. It is not necessarily inevitable that these skills should be used for middle-class goals.

The Question of Structure in the Curriculum

The enabling curriculum described above is clearly set to produce advantage for those who experience it. Yet in writing about curricula for young children Courtney Cazden refers to the paradox of the 'good home' curriculum. Although this curriculum, provided intuitively by parents, produces advantage for their children, those curricula which most nearly resemble that of the enabling home have been shown, in the United States, to be less effective than 'structured' programmes (Cazden 1972a, p. 25).

The methods by which such comparisons have been made, however, might be questioned. It would not be surprising for children's scores to rise on tests if the items tested were those for which the answers had been learned in programmes. Nor would it be surprising if children in the 'open education' type of school failed to give answers if questions and ways of questioning were quite unfamiliar. But we must question whether the 'open' education of our nursery and infant schools is set on the model of the enabling home, and, if it is, whether the model is ever achieved.

The strength of most cognitive or language programmes is their structure. Content and skills have been analysed and placed in a stepwise sequence so that the child's daily progress might be guaranteed. Lessons are planned in detail for the teacher to use, and teaching materials may be provided as a basis. In the didactic programmes where the relationship between teacher and child is conceived as authoritarian, however, the child's role is likely to be a recipient one rather than participant. Even where participation is required the child may be responding always to the programme's presentation of meaning. The result may be that the potential he has for reflection on those experiences which are most relevant to him will be neglected.

Such programmes may serve to reinforce the disadvantaged child's view of the role of the adult and his own non-questioning egocentric position. Such programmes appear to neglect the need to extend the child's ability to reflect on and use his own inner knowledge, to project into the meanings of others, and to develop a wide range of strategies in using language for the communication of his own thinking. Though the child may build up a stock of answers, he may do this without gaining insight into meaning. He must always rely on the teacher to supply the sources of learning and so may not be helped to initiate his own learning. But within a narrow framework he may gain confidence in playing the role of pupil, and perhaps feel secure in the instruction-centred regime.

If structure as seen in the didactic programmes appears too narrow and to make the curriculum inflexible, that does not mean that structure is viewed as unimportant, only that structure may not be most usefully conceived as a linear sequence in the acquisition of concepts and skills. In looking for a structure for the curriculum it may be more useful to recognize three dimensions upon which it should be based.

i. Knowledge of the potential that the child has for learning,
that is the kind of learning that is possible for him, particularly
his capicity for language development. It includes also
recognition of the possibilities that exist for developing
self-motivated learning, including the capacity the child has
for curiosity, for play and exploration.
ii. Recognition of the potential of the environment, for providing a basis for learning both the natural immediate
environment and the devised environment of the classroom,
including a range of experiences structured deliberately to
promote particular learning.
iii. Knowledge of communication strategies, both the skills to be
promoted and the strategies which will provoke them in
dialogue with the child.

It is not the structure of the content which should be the main
focus, but the total structure of the enabling environment, at the
centre of which is the tutoring adult, the teacher who manipulates
and exploits the potential of this structure to achieve the objectives
of the curriculum.

In this kind of structure, the everyday knowledge and concepts,
the curriculum goals with which all programmes are concerned,
are the necessary by-product of the strategies of interaction
through dialogue between child and teacher. It is not just that
they take care of themselves, but that they should become the
outcome of an active exploration of the child's own meanings. This
is essentially what Moffett (1968, p. 213) proposes in discussing a
curriculum for older children. In his view there is only one subject
to be learned and that is dialogue or discourse itself: the traditional
subjects are seen either as bodies of content to be symbolized, that
is providing the content for discourse, or as ways of processing
information, that is ways of symbolizing, or acts of discourse. The
tutoring adult in the enabling environment will be alert to the
possibilities for centring dialogue, on (for example) opportunities
for classifying, the development of concepts of number and spatial
relationships, for developing all manner of representation.

The structure of this curriculum can hardly be accommodated
in a programme which has a sequence of specified topics or
activities to be presented day by day. The structure becomes
evident in the nature of the dialogue in which the teacher engages
the child, which might draw on any of the sources for learning
that can be made available to the child within this enabling

environment, according to the direction in which his thinking moves. The structure lies in the knowledge the teacher has of the kind of skill she is seeking to promote in the child, skills of thinking made evident through skill in using language, skill in communication made evident in the skill he develops in taking part in dialogue.

But it is not that the teacher's role is one of waiting for chance opportunities. The child's interest and thinking may be readily led into planned experiences which the teacher anticipates will provide a basis for promoting particular kinds of thinking. There is a need for designing experiences, as well as a need for being alert to the possibilities of spontaneously developing opportunities.

We have already the evidence of the work of Marian Blank to indicate that the exploitation of planned exchanges between child and the tutoring adult is likely to be effective (Blank and Solomon 1968). In Blank's view the central limitation of disadvantaged children is that they lack an internal symbolic system with which to organize and codify the world. It is reported that the child made considerable progress as the result of daily sessions with his tutor but it is not clear from what Blank says how he spent the rest of the day.

The enabling environment should be set to be provocative of thinking, conducive to the expression of ideas, inducing problem-solving attitudes, developing awareness of other people's needs and views. The regular engagement of the child in a dialogue by his teacher on a one-to-one basis should arise from and be embedded in the ongoing interest and activity of the environment. This is the characteristic of the enabling environment that we should seek to provide in schools for the education of all young children. But in the long run the enabling environment should be guaranteed to all young children as the outcome of a total, effective education for all.

Discussant: *Joyce Watt*

My comments are made, not from the viewpoint of an expert in the field of language, as that I cannot claim to be, but from the perspective of a teacher of young children who has also been concerned with the education of teachers and with research in the field of educational deprivation. I trust that my perspective is the appropriate one, for, as I see it, Tough's paper is primarily the paper of an educationist who sees educational contexts and relationships as central, and who, while concerned to establish her research findings within a valid theoretical system, is, at the same time, determined to translate those findings into practical curricular terms and establish them within a framework of beliefs and value systems.

I take as my first point of reference a comment made by Joan Tough in the first pages of her paper and which, I think, is central to her theme —'the way in which a problem is conceived determines the way in which it will be met'. This is obviously eminently true of the field of educational disadvantage in general, where definitions are formulated and solutions are sought in both global and specific terms against a background of political and social bias as well as educational, psychological, sociological and linguistic interpretation. In the linguistic field alone, we have already had ample evidence, even within this seminar, of personal perspectives and interpretations which presumably would lead to very different programmes of support or remediation. In the wider linguistic field, we have had in recent years many elaborate theories of the nature of linguistic deprivation, ranging from those which have seen the disadvantaged child as a deficit system, to those which have seen linguistic deprivation as part of the 'deprivation mythology'. *The Myth of the Deprived Child* (Ginsburg 1972) and *Tinker Tailor: The Myth of Cultural Deprivation* (Keddie 1973) add illustration to Labov's well-known assertion that 'the notion of "verbal deprivation" is part of the modern mythology of educational psychology' (Labov 1969).

Personal and professional perspectives are important, but, in the realms of disadvantage, they must be reserved for the theorist–specialist. Policies conceived in narrow terms, without reference to other perspectives, may well be doomed in their practical application to disappointment and rejection.

I use Tough's comment at this point and before a discussion of programmes because, unlike those which have preceded it, this paper *is* essentially about policy—'how shall we educate the young child?'—and any discussion of programmes must be prefaced by a recognition that they represent personal and professional perspectives in action, and their strengths or weaknesses may well be in the extent to which they relate to the perspectives of others who 'conceive' and try to 'meet' the problem in different terms.

Joan Tough of course introduces the statement 'The way in which a problem is conceived determines the way in which it will be met' in the context of her discussion of programmes *per se* with the implication that the programme represents the way in which one particular perspective meets the deprivation problem.

I would like to digress slightly to underline a conspicuous lack within this seminar as a whole, which is pertinent at this juncture to Tough's paper—the lack of a precise definition of terms. Few words within educational terminology are used as loosely as 'programme'. According to the context, it may be taken to mean any group of learning activities ranging in turn from those organized within a strictly Skinnerian framework to those assembled in a very loose and ill-defined way.

Within the context of educational programmes for pre-school disadvantaged children, Weikart (1967) distinguished three forms of 'programme', the 'traditional', the 'structured' and the 'task-oriented'. The 'traditional' programme, through progressive, child-centred methods, seeks to promote all aspects of a child's development—social, emotional, physical, as well as cognitive and language, through an emphasis on play, creativity and individual self-initiated activity. 'Structured' programmes emphasize cognitive and language development promoted through deliberately pre-planned sequenced activities. They rely heavily on teacher control but aim to encompass a number of intellectual skills. Lastly 'task-oriented' programmes, often using their own specially designed equipment and materials, emphasize a particular skill and prescribe in detail not only the nature of the problem which children should meet, but the exact nature of their expected response.

In a more recent classification, Weikart (1972) distinguishes four interpretations of the pre-school curriculum. The 'programmed' model is geared to strictly defined curricular goals, behavioural objectives are clearly specified, and learning is said to be achieved if the correct response is elicited from the child. The 'programmed' model maximizes the initiative of the programme producer and minimizes that of the child. It is teacher-proof. The 'open-framework' model is likewise tied to a theoretical framework and is normally geared to cognitive and language goals, but differs from the 'programmed' model in being more broadly based and in relying much more on the initiative of each teacher to meet the individual needs of children in her group. The 'child-centred' model has much in common with the 'traditional programme' as previously defined. Emphasis is on social and emotional growth but the 'whole child' philosophy is central. The 'custodial' model is scarcely definable in curricular terms, its function being largely supervisory.

It is regrettable that in her discussion Joan Tough does not attempt some such analysis of the rationale behind different types of programme but leaves us rather to infer a definition on the assumption that the programme is the 'way' in which verbal deprivation can best be 'met' if it is conceived in the following terms:

1. that the deprived child is a deficit system whether by virtue of his heredity or his experience
2. that the deprived child needs a 'special' kind of learning method which minimizes his conceptual weaknesses and capitalizes on other cognitive strengths. His strengths are likely to be in the field of

associative learning, and therefore his curriculum should be based on regularity, rote, and repetition and should be essentially adult-initiated.

It is apparent that programmes defined in the above terms have much in common with the task-oriented and programmed models defined by Weikart and it is this specific conceptualization of the problem and the assumptions of language programmes built on it, which Tough is challenging. While I share her reasons for rejecting the above conceptualization of the problem and its associated assumptions, I accept that those reasons are based not entirely on rational grounds alone, but also on a value system which rejects the apparently facile categorization of children at a time when our knowledge of their patterns of learning is incomplete.

It is of some significance that in fact no programme as defined above, and as exemplified by the Bereiter and Engelmann programme to which Tough refers, has been used experimentally in this country. The only programme which has been used—and it would fall towards Weikart's 'structured' category—is the Peabody Language Development Kit. In two studies, NFER 1968 (reported in Quigley 1971) and Halsey (1972), that programme generated a considerable degree of opposition from teachers. Having been involved with one group of teachers in the second of the above studies, I can summarize the reasons for that group's opposition.

Firstly, teachers asked to use the programme within the traditional pre-school framework saw it as disruptive. At a superficial pragmatic level this was because it demanded an approach and pattern which was confined artificially to one specified part of the day and which therefore could not be a genuinely integral part of the total curriculum. At a higher level, there was a fundamental clash of beliefs for, while the programme had its own rationale based on its own theory of learning, that rationale was not in accord with a policy geared to a child-centred curriculum. While the child-centred philosophy may well be open to criticism in some of its practical application, it takes as fundamental a theme which has been reiterated many times during this seminar, that every child has his 'own idiosyncratic way' of learning, and that educational policy must allow for that. Teachers saw little possibility within the programme for personal idiosyncrasy.

Secondly, they were unhappy with their own role as teachers. In one sense the programme inferred teacher domination but, because materials and procedures were preconceived and therefore imposed, teachers saw their creative role as very much reduced. Highly professional people could not accept such minimal responsibility.

As a final comment in this section, I would emphasize that while I agree with Tough's rejection of programmes on theoretical grounds and sympathize with the practical and theoretical objections of teachers,

I would not exclude programmes within specific clinical situations where, if a child's pattern and level of difficulty have been carefully assessed, the programme may have an important contribution to make. Tough's alternative to the programme is thoroughly described in her paper. The rationale of the adult/child dialogue I accept completely, and it is worth noting in passing that it meets fully the objections to programmes outlined above. Not only does it allow and encourage the child's own idiosyncratic way of learning but it also, at the same time, restores the teacher to a full and demanding professional role. There are, however, several assumptions made by Tough which I feel we ought at least to query.

First, it is obvious that Tough sees the skill of the tutoring adult as crucial to the success of the adult/child dialogue, particularly in relation to disadvantaged children. As the controller of the dialogue, the teacher must have a general knowledge of child development, a very particular knowledge of the factors which lead to the acquisition of language skills, and an ability to empathize with disadvantaged young children in order to establish with them, through a language relationship, a complex pattern of learning.

Within her paper, Tough describes a number of response-provoking situations where the disadvantaged group when compared to the advantaged group seemed to lack an adequate framework of meaning within which to organize and give verbal expression to new experience. This, however, proved to be the superficial explanation. The responsible and sensitive adult, who knew how to act as a catalyst to provoke and probe the child's past experience in order to make it relevant to the present problem, could elicit from him a pattern of meaning which, left to himself, he was unable to express. 'Without the probes, certainly, the observer would not have known of their ability to organize the experience; it seemed as though they needed the probe to help them discover what they knew. With the adult's help the capacity they had for organizing meaning was demonstrated.' Within the 'educating' context the disadvantaged child was dependent on the adult being able to translate with him the relevance of his past personal experience to his present individual problem.

To what extent can the teacher of disadvantaged children do this? Tough seems to assume that the inability to make the dialogue meaningful lies with the disadvantaged child alone. She argues for 'a reciprocity of perspectives in terms of an intersubjective intentionality' and claims that 'dialogue necessitates on the part of the participants projections into the perspective of the other—the child is not able to take part in a dialogue in this way'. I would argue just as strongly that, for different reasons, the average teacher of disadvantaged children does not have these abilities either and needs constructive help in acquiring a 'reciprocity of perspective'. This is true in terms of understanding the level of cognitive development at which the child is functioning, but it is most relevant in terms of appreciating the social context within which the child expresses his meanings. Bernstein (1970) makes a plea for a 'reciprocity of perspective' on a wider front when he argues that 'if the culture of the teacher is to be part of the consciousness of the child, then the culture of the child must first be in the consciousness of the teacher'. The literature of 'deprivation mythology' emphasizes the richness of language interchange with disadvantaged children which is possible within the supporting social context: '. . . the social situation is the most powerful determinant of verbal behaviour and . . . an adult must enter into the right social relation with a child if he wants to find out what a child can do: this is just what many teachers cannot do' (Labov 1969). Why is it that many teachers cannot do this? Is it lack of empathy, a culture gap, an intellectual inability, or a combination of all these factors? Can the skill be taught? We are far from understanding the full complexities of this problem, but I believe the skill can be acquired through carefully conceived learning experiences for teachers as individuals at both the pre-service and in-service stage. Certainly the skill cannot be taken for granted. If it is as crucial as Tough would have us believe, the promotion of this skill in teachers warrants a much greater place in our thinking and concern.

Secondly, Tough assumes by inference a virtue in the dialogue which she denies to the programme. Of the programme she says, 'There must also be an assumption that rote learning of this kind will transfer into other contexts and become a generalized skill, for, if every possible answer has to be learned by rote, there never will be time for the child to catch up on all he could or should learn.' She queries whether programmes do in fact have inherent transfer potential, and, at a superficial level, I would share her doubts, but I would query in turn whether she has any evidence as yet of the potential of the dialogue to lead to cognitive flexibility to any greater degree.

A related assumption is that the dialogue, unlike the programme, provides a conceptual mode for thinking. While this may be a legitimate assumption from the evidence of the disadvantaged children who found their own meanings through the probes of sensitive adults, it must be queried whether we have the evidence for presuming that the newfound framework was any more than a temporary construct whose supports would be removed with the immediate context. We are far from being able to accept unquestioningly that 'internalized, it (the dialogue) may become a model for thinking'.

Having queried some of Tough's assumptions, I would now like to pinpoint one area related to dialogue which I would have liked to see discussed further within this paper, that is the relationship between oral expression and physical action. In the videotape of nursery school activities shown earlier in this Seminar, we saw several examples of constructive adult/child dialogue. One in particular was carried through to the accompaniment of the child painting incessantly at an easel. One is tempted to suggest that, but for the opportunity to express himself in parallel through the medium of paint, the dialogue for that particular child at that particular point would have been impossible. Perhaps we are too prone to dismiss such physical communication as a parallel activity geared to the resolving of emotional or social tension and underestimate its possible complementary contribution in the cognitive field. For many disadvantaged children, the adult/child dialogue divorced from physical action must be highly artificial. While many of the dialogues described in this paper did take place in the context of action, e.g. drawing, building, etc., the relationship between the two is vague, and it may be that a further study of the adult/child dialogue 'in action' may be an important development from the present study.

In the final section of her paper, Tough makes a plea for a structure to be given to the learning environment in order that the tutoring adult can operate effectively. Her rationale of the structured environment (which has little in common with the structured programme) I accept completely, and find little to dispute. However, I would like to make explicit one feature of the structured environment which I understand Tough to infer, that the structured environment is an enabling environment to the extent that it recognizes that priorities must exist and that one of the fundamental priorities in the pre-school curriculum is language. Bereiter and Engelmann in their criticism of the traditional child-centred approach for the needs of the disadvantaged maintain that 'the mistake that seems to be inherent in the "whole child" point of view as it exists among educators is contained in the assumption that this concern requires a broad unfocused educational programme that recognizes no priorities and tolerates no omission' (Bereiter and Engelmann 1966). I accept this as a legitimate criticism of the most extreme uncritical approaches to child-centredness, and regret its likely effects especially on those children who may yet today be asked to transfer abruptly from the broad, unfocused nursery curriculum to the even more reprehensible narrowly focused curriculum in a primary school. Many nursery schools would in fact claim that language is a high priority within their curriculum, but the organization and pressures of the school may well be such that that priority remains theory rather than practice.

In an earlier paper Tough (1973c) refers to language as the uniting force which gives an identity to the members of the 'enabling' family: 'Language is provoked in response to the expectations and encouragement of the parents, and because employing language brings its own intrinsic reward of becoming a major means of sharing in the life of the family.' It is perhaps legitimate to extend the analogy and suggest that language could be similarly the uniting force in the nursery school, a power which, within that context, could be for the disadvantaged as well as the advantaged a 'major means' of sharing in the life of another important educating community. But for this to be achieved, language must be more than incidental, it must be acknowledged as central, and opportunities for its use deliberately structured in individual ways by sensitive adults within a planned environment. It is an argument, not for a compromise between 'programmes' and traditional child-centredness, but for a combining of the strengths of the two, for the planning of carefully conceived and sequenced activities within the context of acknowledged priorities, and for a child-centredness which allows for individual response to individual experience and the expression of individual idiosyncrasy. It is an argument, too, for the combination of the child-centredness of child-initiated learning and enlightened teacher direction which Cane and Smithers (1971) see as vital to the successful acquisition of reading skills in infant departments and which I would suggest is equally important for the acquisition of language skills by 'disadvantaged' children in the pre-school years. It is an argument for the adult-child dialogue at its best.

Lastly, to return to a discussion of global and specific concepts of 'disadvantage' and the overall context of this paper, I conclude with reference to a quotation in the first section which is taken from Bruner, that our purpose as teachers is to encourage children from the start to be 'controllers rather than victims'. Joan Tough sees the potential power of dialogue in that light. In the immediate context that is a specific analysis and intended outcome of one curriculum area, but with all its overtones of individuality realized through participation, it is for many the global interpretation of what it is to be 'advantaged'. Such thinking has timely relevance and places the specific objectives of dialogue alongside at least one important interpretation of the global aims of policies geared to the dilemma of contemporary disadvantage.

PART II

4

Research on Language and Learning: Some Suggestions for the Future Report of the Bristol Seminar, January 1975

GORDON WELLS, ALLAYNE BRIDGES,
LINDA FERRIER AND CHRIS SINHA

This seminar concluded a series of three that was sponsored by the Scottish Council for Research in Education and the Social Science Research Council with the aims of strengthening the links between workers in the fields of language development and education, and of promoting research on language and learning. The first two seminars (Edinburgh, January 1973, and Leeds, January 1974) considered broad theoretical issues and reviewed recent and ongoing research in this field; the purpose of the third seminar was to consider future research. In order to give the meeting a specific focus, three people, already experienced in the prosecution of research, were invited to submit proposals for detailed discussion by colleagues with similar research interests. Two results were anticipated: firstly, that the three proposers would receive helpful comments and suggestions that they could incorporate into their intended research, and secondly, that all participants would benefit from the opportunity to discuss theoretical and methodological issues in the context of specific research proposals. A third outcome from the meeting was also hoped for: that it would be possible, in the light of the foregoing discussion, to highlight specific areas in which further research was urgently needed.

With these aims in view, the seminar was organized in three parts:

(a) Three plenary sessions in which the proposals were presented and discussion initiated by invited discussants.

(b) Three series of concurrent small-group meetings, in which the individual proposals, and issues arising from them, were discussed in detail. Reports from these groups were then presented to a plenary session.

(c) A plenary session in which a consideration of future research was introduced by a prepared paper based on suggestions from participants.

An informal addition to the programme was a talk by Dr Marion Blank, from Rutger's University, New Jersey, on her work with teachers of cognitively poorly functioning children.

INTRODUCTION

The field of language and learning provides a meeting-ground for people from a wide variety of professional backgrounds—linguists, psychologists, sociologists, educators and administrators—all of whom share a common concern, in one way or another, with the development and education of children; so a forum, such as that provided by this series of seminars, offers a valuable opportunity for inter-disciplinary discussion, in which problems can be seen from many perspectives, and ideas developed in one discipline can be taken over and used to enrich the thinking in another.

There are attendant dangers, however, not least of which is the obscuring of important theoretical differences by apparent agreement in the use of certain key terms. 'Disadvantage' has been such a term in the recent past, used freely by workers in many disciplines without the underlying assumptions that give theoretical substance to its use within particular disciplines being made explicit. The confusion that this can cause became apparent at the second seminar in this series, where a large part of the final session had to be devoted to a clarification of what people meant by the term 'disadvantage'.

One of the purposes of the organizers of the third seminar was to give ample opportunity for such examination and questioning of theoretical assumptions, in the small-group meetings which occupied almost half the programme. In the event, each group spent some time discussing issues specific to the proposal that it was considering, but inevitably, and desirably, these led on to more general issues, some of which were discussed in more than one group. Unanimity rarely resulted, nor was it expected to, but positions were clarified, and in some cases modified, and an understanding gained of the reasons for the differences that remained.

Such a seminar is not easy to report, however, if only because of the sheer quantity of talk that took place. To select particular contributions for verbatim report would have been invidious, and in spite of the excellent work of the reporters, some key contributions would have been found to be inaccurate or unattributable. The solution adopted, therefore, has been to gather together the many contributions made under topics, and to present the main points made in relation to each topic, irrespective of the session in which they occurred. Inevitably, many points of detail have been sacrificed, but we hope we have succeeded in accurately representing the major trends.

The comments of the invited discussants, and the discussions of issues specific to each of the three proposals, have been included with the summary of the proposals to which they relate. Since the discussants' comments were quite brief, they have been included verbatim. It is hoped that the resulting change in style will not prove too disconcerting. The discussion concerned with future research also follows the introductory paper on that topic.

The report falls into three main parts, therefore:

1. Summaries of the three proposals and ensuing discussion of issues raised by them.
2. Summary of the more general discussion, organized under a number of topic headings.
3. The paper which presented suggestions for future research and a summary of the ensuing discussion.

Acknowledgements. We should like to thank Maureen Shields, Hazel Francis and Alan Davies for courageously submitting research proposals for detailed discussion, and for allowing me to summarize the proposals for inclusion in this report. Inevitably, much of importance has had to be omitted, and the senior author takes responsibility for any misrepresentation of their intentions and supporting arguments that this has led to. Our thanks also to Barbara Tizard for taking on the difficult task of making a coherent presentation out of participants' suggestions for future research.

I. CONSIDERATION OF SPECIFIC RESEARCH PROPOSALS

(a) *The Investigation of Social and Communicative Skills in Children at Nursery School*

MAUREEN SHIELDS

Introduction

This research proposal starts from the assumption that the claim made for traditional nursery schools, that they educate the child in social and communicative skills, should be taken seriously, and is therefore concerned to elucidate the process of development in children's social and communicative skills in the pre-school years, and to discover what types of social and communicative experiences are, in fact, provided for the child in such institutions. It is hoped that the outcome of this research would contribute to an improvement in educational practice.

The research is based on the following theoretical assumptions:

(a) that social and communicative skills have cognitive/affective structures which are built up in the course of social interaction,

(b) that these cognitive/affective structures have a selective effect upon the child's perception of the behaviour of others and this will affect both the way he reacts to them and the effort he makes to communicate with them,

(c) that the attempt to modify the surface structure of social and communicative behaviour may remain ineffective without some attempt at understanding the underlying schemes that organize these behaviours.

Support for these assumptions comes from recent work in three areas: firstly, studies based on cognitive theories such as that of cognitive egocentricity, which has recently been closely investigated by several workers such as Fishbein (1971, 1972), Masangky (1974) and Flavell (1974). It appears from this research that, while the ability to take into account the perceptual viewpoint and emotional state of others does develop and differentiate as the child gains more experience, there is evidence that this group of skills is beginning to form at a much earlier age than previously considered possible. Secondly, studies based on the observation of young babies in interaction with their caretakers and other persons by Bowlby (1969), Schaffer (1971), Carpenter (1974) and others, which appear to show that the child's perception of other persons develops early, and that rudimentary interactional patterns are established within the first six months of life.

Taken together, these two lines of research show the so-called egocentrism of the very young child to be, in fact, a remarkable cognitive achievement. The idea of human identity, that is that he is like others and others are like him, and the idea of the possibility of two perceptions sharing an inter-subjective field must logically precede the development of the idea that the field is shared but with a different perspective. It is this presupposition of a shared field that is one of the twin foundation stones of communication, for it mediates the possibility of a common frame of reference. The other fundamental concept is the idea that others are self-moving and are capable of intentional behaviour and that they may modify that behaviour in response to signals. Together, these presuppositions allow the possibility of speech acts within a common field of interpersonal and contextual meaning.

The third area is that of early communication and language

development. Studies here seem to show that the establishment of an interpersonal field and its partitioning and organization are very early features of language. Many studies of early language, by Bowerman (1973), Bloom (1973), Brown (1973), Clark (1974), Schaerlaekens (1974) and others demonstrate similar, if not identical, forms which appear linked to the mechanics of interpersonal communication. Work by Shields (1972, 1974) also shows that the language of slightly older children contains a developing use of auxiliary constructions to modulate speech acts in order to take account of the status and intention of others, and to express social rules and obligations.

Focus of the Study

The present proposal is distinguished from those already referred to by the intention to focus on the development of *skill* by a qualitative examination of social processes in the nursery school.

The development of skill in initiating, sustaining, modulating and terminating social contacts would, according to the hypotheses used here, imply cognitive organization which would fit the choice of means to what is known about the interpersonal situation, including what is known about how other people see things and how other people act and react. These cognitive schemes would include the child's perception of role, including age role, sex role and status role, and any modification of these gross categories due to individual differences. They would also include schemes of possible relationships between persons, and schemes governing behavioural planning including cue identification in various situations such as approaching or responding to strangers, to acquaintances, to friends, to persons of different sex, to adults known and unknown, in a variety of situations. Among the questions which might be asked are:

(a) What behavioural and linguistic evidence is there for saying that children distinguish sex role?
(b) Does the concept of sex role operate differentially in different kinds of interpersonal contexts?
(c) What behavioural or linguistic evidence is there that children have graded ideas of age, rank and status, and behave differently to persons of different ages?
(d) What behavioural or linguistic evidence is there that children adapt to the perceptions of others?

(e) What behavioural or linguistic evidence is there that children react to the feelings of others?

(f) What techniques do children use in initiating social contacts with friends, acquaintances and strangers?

(g) What behavioural or linguistic means do they use to maintain or check on the maintenance of social contacts?

(h) What behavioural or linguistic means do they use to maintain groups in operation and how do they control the entry of newcomers into the group?

(i) What means, behavioural or linguistic, do children have for claiming or sustaining particular roles in groups?

(j) Do children have standards of behaviour which would categorize what is kind, what is unkind, what is tactful or what is rude? Are these standards reflected in their behaviour?

The questions to be asked could be multiplied ad lib, but the techniques for deriving answers would of course place serious constraints on what might reasonably be asked.

Research Design

It is proposed to base the research on an intensive study of about thirty children, from their first initiation into nursery school until the time they leave, after an initial observation of behaviour at the upper and lower end of the age-range to permit the construction of a preliminary inventory of behavioural differences. Data will predominantly be collected directly from the individuals to be studied, though a minimum of indirect data will be needed, including information about the number and ages of members of the family, the opportunities for social encounters outside the home, the mother's opinion about the child's intra-family sociability and friendliness to adults or peers outside the family, and her estimate of the child's language skills.

Three methods of direct data collection are proposed.

(a) Observation in a free field, where the children would be observed with the least possible observer interference. This would be expected to show the incidence and length of social encounters, and with whom the child interacted, together with some information about social styles. Various observational techniques will be considered, including episode sampling, time sampling and ethological schedules. The latter would have to be revised to include recording of verbal behaviour, in particular certain features of language which are important in interpersonal communication. However there are great technical difficulties in making observations in a free field in the kind of detail proposed, and it may be necessary to stick with observational schedules for the background information and have machine recording of language in a structured field.

(b) Observation in a structured field, in which the child would be introduced to different interaction situations with friends, same sex companions, opposite sex companions, younger children, older children and adults. The interaction, which would be recorded on audio- or video-tape, might yield systematic differences in the child's social and linguistic behaviour.

(c) Experimental situations in which the child would be asked to demonstrate some of the schemes which organize his perception of others by sorting tasks of a repertory grid type, role play with dolls, and other tasks which might throw light on his social perceptions.

It is proposed that both observational and linguistic data from these three sources should be combined to yield a profile of the child's skill in interaction, a major component being his use of language to mediate interpersonal interaction.

Linguistic Analysis

The careful analysis of what is said in social encounters is the most essential feature of the data collection. Human social life is maintained by verbal communication, and interesting though the analysis of proxemic behaviour, gesture and facial expression may be, and essential though it is at an age when verbal communication may not yet be fully developed, observation of this kind can only form a background to the study of talk.

Despite much theoretical development in the study of language, a frame for the analysis of language as human communication is still lacking. Such a frame would have to take account of the field of presuppositions shared by the two speakers and would note the match and mismatch in it. It would note the linguistic devices used to partition the field and highlight the theme of discourse. It would note the nature of the speech act and whether it was appropriately fitted into the shared concept of role relations and the possibilities and probabilities which would structure two intersecting fields of expectation. It would note the devices used by the speakers to fit their locutions one to the other. At the moment the only working frame of this kind known to the proposer is being used by Gordon Wells to analyse his sample of children's language (Wells 1972, 1973).

The frame used by Wells is, however, very complex and deals with many other aspects of syntax as well as those closely related to interpersonal communication. What is proposed here is a simplified frame arranged around the main communication functions into which more detailed categories could be fitted. It is based on the analogy of a field with two or more sources of activity. The following seem suitable divisions:

(a) interpersonal field induction (by eye fixation, gesture and later by such verbal signals as the vocative use of names and words such as *look*),
(b) interpersonal role specification and modulation (initial systems within this function consist of names and personal pronouns which describe primary discourse roles, and which later double up for agency roles),
(c) speech act specification and modulation (including devices, phonological, syntactic and lexical, for indicating the nature of the speech act intended),
(d) field organization (including referential material about objects and persons in the shared field and their states or activities),
(e) field extension (devices used to push the boundary of the shared field back from the here and now (i) by tense and aspectual marking, (ii) by words like *want*, *like*, *remember*, *suppose* that cross interpersonal boundaries into the expression of intrapersonal experience of the speakers).
(f) interpersonal discourse organizing devices (used to relate discourse to the field exophorically and discourse to discourse anaphorically).

Since many of the techniques of both data collection and analysis need considerable further development, a year's pilot study would be needed before the main study could begin.

Discussant: *Ruth Clark*

Children's linguistic development is increasingly coming to be viewed in the context of cognitive development as a whole, rather than as an isolated function. More recently particular emphasis has been put on the social functions of language in early childhood. A study of the role of speech in the growth of social competence would be a valuable contribution to this development.

The breadth of the theoretical source material on which this research proposal draws is most impressive.[1] Understandably, Maureen Shields's focus of interest narrows considerably when she comes to discuss her actual research design. Everyone will have his own views as to whether the right things have been retained and the right things omitted from the narrower proposal.

My own view is that the absence of a ready-made framework for describing social development and the extreme intricacy of the processes to be studied justify a decrease in the breadth, but not in the depth of the treatment.

I feel that the scope of the study could profitably be narrowed still further by decreasing the size of the sample and concentrating the linguistic analysis, if language is to be the focus, on those aspects of linguistic structure which are indisputably relevant to the perception and management of social relationships, such as features of discourse, the specification of rules and deictic functions.

On the other hand, I feel that linguistic structure should not be relied on as the sole index of developing social competence. The relationship between linguistic structures and gestural and behavioural indices of social competence cannot be sacrificed if the study is to achieve the desired increase in our understanding of social development. There is no reason to assume that linguistic skills will perfectly reflect the growth of social concepts. So far as cognitive development is concerned, we know that concepts can be available before the child has the means of expressing them, and also that the child may acquire and use linguistic forms long before he has grasped their full potential significance and the full range of their use. The order in which various exponents of social awareness are acquired will reflect not merely the order of acquisition of the social concepts themselves but the complexity of the syntactic structures that convey them, as this interacts with the child's mechanisms for learning syntax.

Since the study aspires to be 'a tentative step towards developing techniques of observation and experiment which could serve to elucidate the elaboration of social skills. . . .', there is no need for an exhaustive consideration of the whole range of social behaviours and their linguistic exponents with a large number of children.

However, there is a need for the insights provided in the background mentioned to be allowed full play without too much prior restriction on the actual classification structures to be used.

---

[1] Unfortunately, most of the background material had to be omitted from the summary, for reasons of space. [Editor.]

Discussion

One of the first questions to be raised in the discussion period was concerned to clarify whether the primary aim of the proposed study was to investigate features of the language used by children in situations of social interaction or, alternatively, to describe how social relations between nursery school children are established and developed. That is, within the research topic proposed, the emphasis could be placed either on the language used or on the social skills themselves. However, it was maintained by the proposer that the majority of social skills are largely exercised through the use of language and that social acts tend to be marked by the use of particular formal linguistic exponents such as modals; thus, the use of 'will' in the request 'will you do this for me?', or 'will you come and play with me?' was considered to be an habitual indicator of 'concession'. (The more general issue of the relationship between form and function in language which was then raised will be discussed in another section of this report.) It was agreed that the use of social contracts by young children demonstrated more of a linguistic component than other cognitive operations, but nevertheless some discussants voiced concern that instances of social behaviour might come to be judged on the basis of the degree of linguistic sophistication shown by the child. Later questions about the assessment of the social maturity of any particular interchange led to a discussion of the problems of interpretation (see later), although some ways were suggested whereby a child's knowledge and awareness of social rules might be investigated directly, through, for example, the use of telephone commentary or talking doll techniques.

In order to trace any developmental changes in the relative importance of verbal and non-verbal means of communication in establishing and maintaining social relations, it would obviously be necessary to obtain as complete a record as possible of the child's total behaviour, and then to combine an analysis of the language used with a similar analysis of the child's non-verbal behaviour.

During the course of the conference there was considerable discussion concerning the relative merits of different research strategies, in particular with regard to two issues: the aims and objectives of naturalistic 'free-field' studies, and the predictive versus confirmatory roles of controlled experimental studies. In the second area, the debate centred on whether the findings of 'contrived' experiments (in which some aspect of the communication setting is manipulated) should act as the basis for categorizing later observations in a naturalistic setting, or be developed to study children's performance in different, less frequently occurring situations. The related topic of the role of taxonomies in observational research was discussed at some length during the small-group meetings (see later).

In a similar way, 'free-field' observations were seen by some discussants as an opportunity to determine the relative incidence of the full range of behaviours naturally exhibited by groups of interacting individuals, whilst others saw the naturalistic setting as an opportunity for the detailed study of a few, specified types of face-to-face encounters. That is, this latter group differed from the former group in that they were not so concerned to discover the generality or frequency of different types of behaviour, but considered it more valuable to attempt to investigate the processes and rule structure underlying social interaction by concentrating research attention on a restricted set of interchanges involving the repeated observation of one dyad, group or social situation.

As to the practical problems involved in data collection, the entire group agreed that the presence of non-participating adults would be less disturbing to young children within the context of a nursery school than it would be within the context of the child's own home. Since nursery schools generally make claims to provide an opportunity for social development, it seemed particularly pertinent as well as advantageous to concentrate the research efforts on tracing social skill development within the nursery school setting. However it became clear that attempts to produce a satisfactory audio-video recording are bedevilled by considerable technical problems. Several discussants, on the basis of their own experiences in trying to resolve some of these difficulties, called for an opportunity to pool existing expertise and to obtain specialist help in devising recording equipment capable of giving acceptable reproduction of the speech and non-verbal behaviour to be observed in the normal nursery or infant school.

With regard to the nursery school setting, it was also suggested that the development of social skills could be investigated in the light of different staff practices and teaching philosophies apparent within the organization of the nursery school.

Similarly another suggestion was that the importance attached to particular types of social behaviour by parents or teachers in the transmission of social and cultural values could be examined using an interview schedule.

(b) *Language, Social Background and Learning in Primary Schools*

HAZEL FRANCIS

Introduction

There is now a body of research devoted to exploration of social class differences in children's language abilities as they are inferred from their speech in various tests. Since the earlier broad approach, which generally showed rather more developed vocabulary and structure in the speech of socially advantaged compared with that of the relatively disadvantaged, attention has more recently been focused on the use of language in different contexts. Hawkins (1969) found social class differences in the use of nouns and pronouns by children describing a series of cartoon pictures, but such differences were not found by Francis (1974a) in a story reproduction task, although the usual broad delay in development for the relatively disadvantaged was confirmed (Francis 1974b). It seems possible, then, that not only do the relatively disadvantaged choose to use 'elaborated' socio-linguistic codes less than the advantaged, but that all children use different speech patterns in different task situations. These findings suggest that, if educational disadvantage is somehow a consequence of different ability to realize elaborated codes in school, then it might be useful to identify those tasks which give rise to restricted selection, and thereby to help teachers to direct their attention to clearer goals in helping the disadvantaged.

But publicly adequate descriptive speech is not the only objective or context of learning in school. Teachers also hope to foster the understanding of logical and causal relationships. Explanation of these as demonstrated to children is an important part of science-orientated teaching. Hitherto, research into children's understanding has tended to focus on the inferred nature of their judgements rather than on the forms of expression used, but it is evident that in making inferences investigators have made assumptions about the children's use of speech, for example that children use and understand expressions of *more* and *less* as the experimenters do, but Donaldson and Balfour (1968) reported that children, albeit at a slightly younger age, do not necessarily do so. In order to investigate use of language in science orientated tasks one might use a simple physical phenomenon, comparing verbal with non-verbal responses as measures of understanding, and verbal expressions as forms of explanation.

Explanation of observed events is, however, not the only important kind of explanation required of pupils in school. An account of the meaning of a word or sentence is often asked for, and is, indeed, a feature of some vocabulary tests. Children's definitions of 'nonsense' words embedded meaningfully in sentence contexts in such a way as to function as abstract terms, requiring more than ostensive or class membership illustration, might reveal tendencies to use different forms of language in attempted definitions.

For both these tasks of explanation decisions must be made as to the categories of verbal forms to be compared. Accurate referential speech is likely to be as important as in descriptive tasks, and noun/pronoun usage should therefore be examined. But in addition, the use of terms such as *because* and *if* . . . *then* should be explored in the science-type task, and the use of sentence forms that make the definition clear should be sought in the vocabulary task.

A further task required of children in school is learning to read and write. Some idea of the relationship between social class, language forms in speech, and literacy might be obtained by testing children's reading and obtaining measures of structure in story writing similar to those of structure in story telling. Research hitherto has tended to show that little or no correlation exists up to seven or eight years of age between reading scores and measures of structural complexity in speech (Strickland 1962, Loban 1963). No study, however, has correlated reading ability with speech elaboration in different contexts of use.

The research proposed in this paper can now be seen to be in part a replication of the Hawkins/Francis work and in part an extension into the study of children's speech in yet other tasks. It is also a first probe into the major question of the relationship between sociolinguistic aspects of speech and educational disadvantage. Should differences in children's speech in relation to the various learning tasks be confirmed, then it would still remain to be shown whether, and how, these are translated into educational disadvantage.

A further possibility would be to compare teachers' evaluations of the children's speech performance as they have encountered it in class, as they hear it from the 'taped' records of performance in the set tasks, and as they read it from the unidentified transcripts. Whether this could be combined with the present proposal in a larger investigation would depend on the availability of research resources and of teacher cooperation in terms of time, effort and consent.

General Research Design

The major hypotheses are:

(i) There will be differences in the forms of speech used by children in different learning tasks.
(ii) These differences will be related to social background.
(iii) Reading ability will correlate differently with spoken language as used in the various tasks both within and between social groups.

The tasks to be used are:

A Spoken story reproduction
B Cartoon story description
C Explanation of demonstrated phenomenon
D Account of meaning of novel abstract lexical item.

The first two hypotheses will be tested with an analysis of variance design, and the third by means of correlation techniques. The principal variables of interest are social background, age, task, reading ability and speech forms. Extraneous variation in general intellectual ability and sex differences might be controlled by randomly allocating equal numbers of each sex to each task within categories of age and social background. The problem of correlation between social background and general ability will be dealt with by ascertaining mean scores on a test of non-verbal ability and accepting differences as contributing to the overall picture of social class variation, and, if indicated, by analysis of co-variance.

Social background will be categorized primarily, or possibly entirely, on the basis of father's occupation, since this appears to be the most commonly used and useful index in related research. Mother's background might also be an important item of information, however, in that maternal speech styles are likely to be most influential for the young child, and discrepancies between paternal and maternal background deserve attention. It is proposed to group classes as defined by the Registrar-General's categories into an upper social class group from classes 1–3a (occupations in which literacy is valued), a middle group from 3b (occupations of skilled working class) and a lower group from classes 4 and 5 (unskilled and unstable employment). The sampling of children within social class, however, must take into account the interaction between social class and school. It is therefore proposed to select schools according to neighbourhood characteristics in such a way that varying proportions of each social class in school intake are taken into consideration. Thus social background categories will be defined as encountered in different kinds of school. It is intended to test children aged from five to seven years, and possibly up to nine years with four hundred children at each age.

Discussant: *Geoffrey Turner*

Francis's work is in some respects comparable to the kind of work we have been doing at the Sociological Research Unit, directed by Basil Bernstein, particularly our earlier work. I should like to comment on the proposal in the light of our own experiences and to make some possible suggestions based on our recent thinking and research.

The basic view is that the proposal is an interesting one, that it is neat and manageable, but that it suffers from a number of rather severe restrictions, which, if unmodified, would severely limit the kinds of generalizations Francis would be able to make at the end of the research. There are five main restrictions and limitations.

1. The study is restricted to experimental data only. What inferences can be made from the child's behaviour in this unusual context to his behaviour elsewhere in everyday settings? Our view at the SRU is that experimental data is very important and necessary but that it needs supplementing by naturalistic data in the home and school. Bernstein has argued that children who perform differently in experimental settings are following different 'ground rules', ground rules acquired in the home. An important research question relevant to this proposal is: 'How do you get children to switch ground rules in an experimental setting?' If you are making recommendations to teachers, this kind of information seems vital.

2. The social background information is limited to Registrar-General classification of the father's occupation and possibly the mother's. The mother's occupation is important and also her education, but, in view of Francis's research problem, more background information is needed. Similarly with the relationship between language use and reading ability. There are no compelling reasons for thinking that there will be much relationship at five and seven years, though there might be stronger relationship with older children. But if one *is* investigating this relationship, one needs to know about patterns of reading in the home—attitudes to reading, number of books, library membership etc.

One also needs to take into account the type of pedagogy in the school.

3. The concept of verbal ability is restricted. Two of the old measures—total number of words and amount and kind of subordination—are given a prominent role in the proposed study, despite their limitations, whereas the recent work on language, relating form to function (Halliday 1970, 1973; Britton 1973; Tough 1973 and others) is not really reflected. What is needed is a characterization of the semantic properties of the children's texts in such a way as to capture the critical differences in their orientation to meaning, as in the recent work in the SRU using Bernstein's notions of universalistic and particularistic meanings and of contextual specificity.

4. There is no attempt to relate what the child does in one context to what he does in others. It is very important to use the same children in each of the four contexts and to look for patterns of consistency in their behaviour across contexts. Bernstein has defined code as an underlying regulative principle governing a speaker's behaviour in different contexts. It is only by observing the speaker's behaviour in a selection of contexts that one can infer the code. In some recent work at the SRU we identified some patterns of consistency across three contexts—descriptive, instructional and regulative.

5. The final limitation concerns the treatment of IQ. The study is to contain no measure of verbal ability, just a measure of non-verbal ability. The trouble with just taking a non-verbal ability test is the observed discrepancy between non-verbal scores and verbal scores in the case of working-class children. If one does not attempt to control for this variation in verbal ability, one is, in a sense, stacking the odds against the working-class children. And one is also leaving oneself open to the charge that any class differences found are just a function of IQ. I know that there are different schools of thought about the role of intelligence tests in social research and this is a matter that needs to be discussed further.

Discussion

Several participants in the discussion were of the opinion that the proposed research addressed itself to issues of great theoretical and practical significance, but that it required some modification if it was to prove capable of answering the questions it had set itself. In particular, it was felt that further attention needed to be given to clarifying the theoretical bases of the relationships between the four proposed tasks, and the relationships between performance on these tasks and the measures of social background and reading ability which had been proposed. Several suggestions were made concerning the observed discrepancies in the amount of use of exophoric reference by subjects in the Hawkins and Francis tasks. In particular, it was pointed out that an adequate theory of the *appropriateness* of different types of pronominal reference did not yet exist. In the Hawkins tasks, it would appear that the use of exophoric reference is perfectly appropriate to the particular experimental context, in which there is a shared field of visual reference. The same children, who do not appear, purely on the basis of this task, to control anaphoric/cataphoric reference, may be quite capable of using it effectively in the Francis task. It was suggested that a more explicit investigation of the effects of context might be to present identical reference material in differing experimental contexts. Thus, rather than contrasting a story-retelling task with a Hawkins-type picture description task, it might be possible to elicit descriptions of cartoon story sequences under three conditions. Firstly, free recall from memory in the absence of the pictures, secondly, free recall with the pictures present (as in Hawkins' task) and thirdly, a description when the cartoon pictures are in the visual field for the encoder (the child), but are concealed from the experimenter, as in the well-known experiments by Kraus and Glucksberg (1969). This might further narrow down the particular set of contextual variables, and the sets of competences related to them, with which the proposal is concerned. A discussion followed which emphasized that the theory of reference itself had changed substantially since the early Hawkins experiments. These were based upon a theory of reference elaborated by Hasan (1967), who examined primarily discourse structure. It was now held that deictic reference was primary, and that specification of referent within the linguistic system is secondary. Exophoric reference is appropriate and normal when speakers share the same or similar physical or ideological frames of reference. Not only can over-specification be redundant, but it can in fact be inappropriate, in that it is socially distancing. Children might perceive it as implicitly insulting to an authority figure who, under the particular social rules governing the discourse, is assumed to 'already know' the specification of the referent. An implication of this is that in the analysis of *text*, an appropriate analysis must include elements of the discourse which are in fact non-verbal, though strictly speaking they are not non-textual.

This led to a discussion of the relationship between the tasks chosen and the actual practices of teachers in the classroom. It appeared that for many teachers, the skills involved in Task D (the definition of the meaning of a novel abstract lexical item) were accorded a high educational value. It was suggested that rather than examining relationships between performance on tasks and teacher judgements of children's intellectual capacities, an analysis should be made of the relationship between the specific demands of the tasks and the demands made by teachers in their actual educational practice. However, such a study appeared to fall rather outside the scope of the present proposal.

It emerged in the course of discussion that the selection of the four experimental tasks was made partially on the basis of the priorities set by teachers, as reported by them. Thus the rationale behind the selection of tasks was implicitly one of their relevance to the actual context of education, and its assumed goals and orientations. Clearly, then, there cannot be any reason for assuming that the tasks operate in such a way as to *maximize* performance on the particular competences involved, rather they replicate the differences in performance encountered in the educational context.

The problems of selecting and developing experimental tasks can then be seen in rather different terms from those in which they are usually posed—that is, of the artificiality of the experimental context as against the naturalistic setting. Rather, formal identifications must be made of the similarities between the demands of the experiment and of the classroom. However, this leads to further problems. In particular, it becomes necessary to articulate explicitly the stance of the research with respect to the 'difference/deficit/delay' controversy. This is necessary because the tasks chosen are precisely those which can be assumed effectively to *distinguish* between different groups of children in terms of their contextually determined performance; such tasks cannot yield information about any supposed, or inferred, differences in basic competence, or structural resources. Here again, the resolution of the cloudy issue of form/function relations is crucial, since it is proposed to take *formal* criteria for the isolation of functional differences, or of differences *with respect to* a particular function, or functions.

With respect to Task C (explanation of a demonstrated physical phenomenon) it was unclear to some discussants precisely what the purpose of the task was. It was suggested that it was likely that it would be precisely the 'brighter' children who would be most likely to 'fail' these tasks as a result of systematic miscuing based on perceptual strategies. However, it was pointed out that the purpose of the task was not to establish cognitive level or intellectual ability, but to elicit comparable speech data, in particular, expressions of comparison and causality.

Many reservations were expressed about the use of IQ tests, from both points of view. It was felt, on the one hand, that the use of only non-verbal IQ scores restricted the amount of data available about children's verbal ability. Since it is known that verbal IQ test scores are correlated with social class, with working-class children generally scoring lower than middle-class children on verbal IQ, the use of only non-verbal scores, which are less highly correlated with social class, could be seen as discriminative against working-class children, in that actual differences could be argued to be both exaggerated and merely a function of verbal IQ.

In the second place, the use of IQ as a control measure in this type of experiment was questioned from the other point of view, that IQ is not a theoretically explicit measure, and that research should now be oriented towards the isolation of specific competences and the contextual variables determining their situational application.

Finally, a discussion took place on the possible ways in which results of research of this nature could be effectively transmitted to teachers, both through formal means such as more effective in-service teacher training, and by means of a greater involvement of teachers in ongoing 'action research'. The object of research such as that proposed by Francis is the production of a new cognitive frame for teachers which they can apply in practice within the educational situation. The issue of 'what type of practice should our research be aimed at generating?' is inextricably connected with the type of theoretical premises adopted by the research. For example, theories of 'language deprivation' result fairly logically in 'remedial' programmes which supposedly inject previously absent responses into the 'non-verbal' child. However, if the problem of differences between social classes in language use in the classroom is conceived in terms of educational inequality, the outcome of research is likely to be the demand to change the school rather than the child. It was emphasized, however, that while conceptual differences might be wide, in practice the two options of changing the institutional context of learning and of attempting to alleviate the problems of individuals who, within that context, are disadvantaged, are not mutually exclusive. Nevertheless, in either case, it is essential that the practice be founded on a sound theoretical base—a lesson which can be gained from the failure of the 'language programmes' approach.

Another point raised was that much recent research—e.g. that of Marion Blank—challenged existing orthodox pedagogic traditions. If the emphasis on dialogue and the matching of cognitive load to cognitive attainment is to be taken seriously, then this has radical implications for teacher training. In particular, it means that teachers must be given far more understanding of the theoretical basis and empirical findings from which the conclusions of educational research are derived, in order that they may be able to assess their implications for classroom teaching.

The discussion of intervention strategies raised further questions about what was meant by 'special provision'—is it more of the same, or something different? The central principle must be that of making teachers aware of the specific aims of any particular set of practices. To do this effectively, it would appear necessary to 'short-circuit' the usual processes of communication between teachers and researchers; one suggestion was that the traditional concept of 'in-service training' should be superseded by attempts to set up study research groups of teachers within the schools, while encouraging researchers to disseminate their results more widely, through such active measures as promoting and sustaining such groups. It was recognized that part of the problem lay in the common reluctance of researchers to fulfil their obligations to transmit their research more widely—an elitist attitude was still prevalent among researchers, mirrored by an anti-theoretical stance by many teachers. It is essential that this particular barrier be broken down.

(c) *Language Demands at the Transition from Nursery to Primary School*

ALAN DAVIES

Introduction

The research outlined in this paper has a theoretical and a practical rationale. The theoretical rationale is sociolinguistic and is concerned with the form–function relationship which is basic to the relating of linguistic codes to social contexts. The practical rationale is educational and is concerned with the goals of the nursery school. There is a third rationale, in the shape of a pedagogic bridging of the gap between theory and goal, since it will be suggested that at least one measure or realization of success is to be seen in a syllabus for teachers however loosely drawn up. Such a syllabus could, it is maintained, incorporate research findings as to form–function relationships and in doing so go some way towards meeting the anxiety of the nursery school teacher as to what she is supposed to be doing, and how, in doing it, she is supposed to establish whether she has succeeded or not. Furthermore it would be valuable in teacher training.

A deliberately low-key approach towards research is taken, emphasizing a non-programmatic presentation. What is necessary, it is argued, is an essentially anthropological approach in which a 'cultural' observer (in this case a linguist) attempts to inform theory and delimit practice. At the same time the existing participant observers, i.e. the teachers and other adults in the pre-school, should be enlisted for exactly the same theory–practice conjoining.

Success in the Nursery School

Success in the nursery school is a 'problem' in a way that is just not true of, say, the primary school. It is a problem both for the practising teachers and administrators and for the researchers. By what criterion is a nursery school to be judged? Given the inconclusiveness of the evidence about nursery school success it remains curious that (a) they should exist at all, and (b) they should be expanding just now.

Four reasons are put forward by Plowden (1967) for possible expansion (paras. 298–301) but none is conclusive and so reliance is placed on the impressions of involved activists. But these reasons indicate the kind of explanation that has been sought, and their setting aside is suggestive of institutional power. Social institutions may be advocated, as here, on whim, and then wield authority as socializing forces—Bernstein's instruments of power and control. Furthermore, and this is the key point here, their boundaries are arbitrary in origin but become control mechanisms in practice.

The Nursery School–Primary School Cross-over

The fact of the imposed institutional boundary at the age of five between the nursery school and primary school is, it is suggested, more than a curiosity to the researcher. It provides a convenient experimental situation for investigation in that, whatever 'view' may be taken among nursery school teachers of their role, they are inevitably constrained by the existence of the primary school entry at the age of five. Further, this boundary provides a convenient criterion by which to assess the 'success' of the nursery school.

The purpose of this research then is to examine the language demands of first year primary school (Primary One) and relate them to the possibly less overt and certainly more implicit demands of the nursery school. What demands are made on the primary school child and how are they realized—both by teacher and child in production and reception? How far do these match with the nursery school situation? A particular area is delineated below (that of commands) since it is clear that the investigation must be tentative and small scale. It is not even clear that this particular area is the one best suited to investigation, and it will be left until later—after the anthropological period of cultural absorption—before settling on the most fruitful part of the field.

Primary School Demands

Let us consider some primary school demands. First the *pedagogic purpose* of the primary school, as against the nurture purpose of the nursery school. Second, the *school membership* of the primary school, with the tacit assumption all the time of the larger world of the primary school outside Primary One. Third, the *teacher role* in the primary school.

The pedagogic nature of the primary school reveals itself in its deliberateness. The primary school is 'about' teaching and the major goal that is accepted by everyone is literacy. The child is surrounded from the first by the *written* language. Although the modern infant teacher may rarely 'teach' to the whole class, her business is instruction in groups rather than attention to individuals, and this leads to an increase in the use of the referential and metalinguistic functions. The business of the primary school is language whereas the business of the nursery school is activity.

The *school membership* of Primary One has to do with the general move from home into a world of other adults and, more important, the peer group. But it does become important to the primary school entrant that he should understand (and make himself understood by) the other school adults, who exist *outside* his classroom. The emphasis is likely to be very much on the directive language function since their main contact with the child will be with him as a stereotype—new infant—and not with him as a person. Their purpose is to get him to do (or not to do) things. Added to this is the wholly separate language use of *writing* which is so frequently used in the *school* context for carrying messages from class to class. There is just not the opportunity in any of these adult contexts for the kind of use of the expressive function so noticeable in the nursery school.

This appears again when we examine the *teacher role* in the primary school. We have touched on this under both previous headings. The primary school teacher is on her own in the classroom, unlike the nursery school, where there is a choice of adults prepared to let the child practise the expressive function. Everything in the primary school classroom—even when the room is arranged in groups—takes on a public role; and even when the primary school teacher addresses one child, that child is somehow more a member of the group than a child who happens to be in a group of other children. The result is that there is emphasis on the directive and referential functions (Hymes 1962), with little place for expressive and poetic. What does become important for the first time is phatic function, since the primary school teacher is forced to reassure herself that her channel of communication with her class remains open, and the swiftest way of doing this is through the use of the *very* public phatic function.

Form–Function Relationship

The speech function model employed for this research will be in the Jakobson–Hymes tradition, while such coding techniques as those used by Sinclair *et al.* (1972) and by Cook–Gumperz (1973) will be explored. But since the research proposal is for a pilot or feasibility study over say two years, it is intended to restrict the form-function relations actually studied to the language forms through which commands are realized.

Commands are widely used in schools by teachers, and it is not difficult for the trained observer to recognize a command when he hears one. Noting the reception of the utterance, the repeated elements and the consequent behaviour is enough to show that the utterance counts as a command to addresser and addressees, teacher and children. As Labov (1972) has pointed out, there are various preconditions that must be fulfilled for an utterance to count as a command. Now the questions to which we address ourselves are:

1 What differences in form are there between the nursery school and primary school commands; how heavily mitigated are they, and how often repeated? In what contexts are they given?
2 How far is there misunderstanding in the nursery school and the primary school? Can any misunderstanding be attributed to the variety of form used?
3 What responses, verbal or otherwise are there to commands in the two situations? Is the response in one more verbal than in the other?

Methodology

The methodology of the research will be anthropological with concurrent linguistic analysis. One full-time research worker will spend the first four months in full-time attendance as an observer in a Primary One class which contains both graduates and non-graduates from nursery school. He will follow the children around the school and attempt to group the kinds of demands made on them and the language involved, noting particularly what he considers to be commands and their contexts of use. Towards the end of the term a small number of tape recordings will be made, not more than one hour in all. In the second four months a similar procedure will be followed in a nursery school (preferably housed within the primary school). The final four months of the first year will be devoted mainly to data analysis. The second year will be spent similarly, but with shorter periods in the schools. The critical questions in the analysis will be: does what counts as a command in the nursery school also do so in the primary school, and for this, an appropriate grammatical description will be necessary in order to characterize sameness.

It is proposed to follow up the pilot research, if it proves viable, by a larger-scale, more experimental, project which will investigate the speech function outcomes of the differential institutional demands between nursery and primary school, hypothesizing that there is a learning problem in terms of speech function at that cross-over point between nursery and primary school.

Discussant: *Asher Cashdan*

1. *Background points*

(a) It is true that the success of the nursery school is poorly documented; nevertheless people are certainly convinced of it—as for example in the teachers' views given in Schools Council Working Paper No. 41 (1972), in Marianne Parry's recent book (1974) and so on. Teachers do think they know what they are doing, but what they are after does not emphasize cognitive development, though many researchers are after this nowadays, as apparently are politicians too.

(b) I am not too happy with the boundary Davies draws between the nursery as nurturing and Primary One (reception class in England) as pedagogical. In England at any rate I think that this sort of division is firmer between infant and junior school. But I do agree that the infant school makes a specific demand for literacy.
Similarly I feel that the distinction between the one as preoccupied with activity and the other with language is much too strong.

(c) I also have reservations about the suggestion that in the infant school the teacher is really dealing with groups even when she apparently speaks to an individual. I wonder also what proportion of class talk is in fact teacher talk. [In the open discussion it was later suggested that the distinction Alan Davies made would hold, if the comparison was made between nursery schools and the more old fashioned infant schools who had not been 'infected' by progressive ideas (Ed.).]

2. I sympathize with the idea of investigating commands. There is a strategy problem: whether it is best to go for a general coverage of all the demands made on the child, or whether one would learn more at this stage by concentrating attention on the one area. If the former, this would amount to a quite different research in which one would be studying the whole range of teacher behaviours and pupil responses in the classroom. I do agree that it is worth asking what difference there is in the demands made in the nursery as opposed to the infant classroom, or indeed if there is a real boundary. This would be of great value, among other things, in helping (as Davies suggests) to evaluate the achievements of the nursery school.

3. I would want to investigate:

(a) How much the teacher *directs* the children in either school, and how this relates to their learning. The kind of measure that interests me at the moment is that of social competence in the sense in which Burton White (1973) uses it in his studies of mothers and their young children. For White, social competence is the extent to which the child makes use of the environment around him, including those adults who can be of help to him.

(b) How much pupils understand/respond appropriately to teacher language. Difference in social class/language code may be interesting, as may be the extent to which the teacher uses language forms differently (or not) according to her view of her pupils.

4. I sympathize with the small-scale, analytical approach advocated by Alan Davies. Nevertheless, it must be emphasized that only certain kinds of generalizations will be possible if one examines commands in the context of one teacher and her class in one nursery school and one Primary One class. As Roger Brown (1973) has shown, the study of a tiny number of children can be of great profit if one is asking the right questions of the data. But certainly it would be a mistake to consider this study (as proposed) could give us more than some very initial ideas on the use of commands by 'teachers'.

Finally, I would emphasize the point that the study of commands may not tell us enough about demands. In other words, I wonder whether a preoccupation with form may inhibit important work in examining functions.

Discussion

A considerable amount of discussion centred on making explicit the methodological and pedagogical assumptions underlying this proposal and on giving it educational justification.

The position of the proposer was that the aims of the nursery school are very rarely made explicit except in vague terms of 'happiness' or 'helping children to socialize' in order to ease their transition to infant school. We need greater knowledge of what the nursery teacher actually does, in order to establish measures of success which might be relevant to teacher training.

Opinion in this area varied from the position that nursery schools are 'to supply the deficits in the environment of underprivileged children' to the view that 'nursery schools mainly provide a benign care-taking environment to relieve parents'. The distinction was made at this point between *describing* the nursery school situation and *setting up prescriptive teacher training schedules*. The two are often only distantly related and failure to distinguish between them confuses the issues under consideration. Various further additions were made to the discussion; that cognitive aims have so far been low on the list of nursery teachers' priorities and also that social learning is perhaps one of the most complex forms of cognitive skill, and that it has so far received little attention. We need to know what, if any, are the cognitive aims of nursery teachers and we also need more detailed information on the social interactions that the nursery school sets out to provide.

A further area of discussion was the effect of the boundary between nursery school and infant school. It was generally agreed that boundaries of an institutional kind affect the roles in which teachers see themselves and the tasks they set out to perform. They are therefore a useful research convenience for throwing up contrasts in teacher–child interaction. It was hypothesized that if the subject matter of 'Commands' was extended to include the whole area of 'Demands' made on the child in these two settings, interesting differences might be revealed. Is there a shift towards more specific cognitive demands as the child moves from nursery to infant school? Is there a movement from context-bound utterances to context-free utterances of greater generality? Is there a shift in the selection of functional types?

Another large topic was the more practical one of *recording methods*. Perhaps the largest problem in setting up a project along the lines of the proposed one is that of getting reliable good sound-recordings. Discussants reported various degrees of success in this respect but, by and large, the successful ventures had attempted to record only a particular teacher and one or two individual children. Attempts to record the teacher in all her interactions with the whole class, and in the hygienic, but acoustically difficult, schoolroom setting had been much less successful.

The further question was considered of additional visual information achieved by videotaping methods or stop-frame photography. Most participants considered that some form of visual recording is a necessity in order to capture the role of gesture and also to analyse functions in their situational setting. The point was made that only where a small, and well-defined, area of interaction has been delimited for consideration can one hope to note all relevant details and dispense with visual recording apparatus. Time-sampling techniques were briefly discussed, the length of sample required to pick up extended interactions etc. It was noted finally that there was a definite need for information on available hardware and associated techniques.

One final well-trodden area was that of setting up viable definitions of 'Command'. Various possibilities were considered from the extreme linguistic one of allowing only those utterances in imperative form to the much wider catch-all definition: 'any utterance of the teacher intended to bring about behaviour on the part of the children is a command'. Labov's criteria (1972), incorporating the variable social status of the participants, were mentioned:

1. The speaker must have status.
2. The addressee must have the ability to carry out the command.
3. The addressee must understand what is involved in the notion of a command.

The role of intonation in conveying the force of a command was noted as well as the mitigating effect of various polite and circumlocutory request forms.

While, in fact, much of the discussion addressed itself to hypotheses and areas for study not considered under this proposal, the wide variety of views expressed can only be taken as evidence that the study of language in the classroom is as yet in its infancy, and that there is much ground to be covered at both the theoretical and practical levels. The participants did however, seem universally in favour of the focusing of research on the classroom situation.

(d) *Analysis of Teacher–Child Interchange*

MARION BLANK

Marion Blank presented an outline of a scheme that she has developed for analysing teacher–child interchange in order:

(a) to diagnose the strengths and difficulties of the child in the cognitive realm;
(b) to identify the strengths and weaknesses of the teacher and in particular, the effectiveness with which she communicates with the child.

The scheme, which is geared to the pre-school-age child, is based upon a coding system that rates every exchange that occurs between the teacher and child in a tutorial session. (The system could be used for coding the teacher and a group of children, but such application would entail some revision in the coding categories.) Generally, for the analysis, a three- or four-minute segment of dialogue is selected. It has been found that this period of time is sufficient to capture many of the central features of the teacher–child exchange. However, if one is to get a full picture of the teacher, it would be necessary to have her engage in dialogues with a variety of different types of children (e.g. a highly active child, a quiet child, a bright child, a dull child, etc.).

The scheme codes the child on only one dimension—namely, the correctness of his response to the cognitive demands posed by the teacher. This scale covers twelve points, ranging from fully correct responses, through partially correct responses, to various types of incorrect responses. By contrast, the teacher is rated on three categories. The first is the type of cognitive demand put to the child (e.g. memory, imagery, concepts, rationale etc.). Based on test data collected, these cognitive demands can be operationally rated as ranging from simple to complex. The second category of teacher rating is that of simplification. Briefly defined, this refers to the teacher's use of simple cognitive demands that will permit her to help a child overcome a wrong response. It is hypothesized that the effectiveness with which a teacher uses simplification techniques will be a critical factor in the teacher's ability to reach a child in difficulty. The third category on which the teacher is rated is the appropriateness of her statement, request, or behaviour relative to the child's previous response. This category includes such factors as the teacher's use of praise, acknowledgement of the child's response, use of criticism etc. None of these factors is judged absolutely; all are judged on a relative basis (e.g. praise is appropriate when the child is correct, but inappropriate when the child is incorrect).

Each interchange is rated, but the performance of both teacher and child is based not on any single interchange but rather on the overall pattern that emerges. For example, the child is assessed on the types of cognitive demands he generally copes with successfully, those he copes with partially well, those which he fails totally etc. Similarly, the teacher is assessed on such factors as:

(a) the range of cognitive demands posed;

(b) the number of demands that she poses that lead the child to success relative to the number of cognitive demands posed in all. (It is hypothesized that for effective teaching the error rate should be about 30 per cent. A greater number of errors leads the child to be frustrated; a smaller number means that the child is only rehearsing what he already knows);

(c) the teacher's readiness to use simplification when the child has encountered difficulty.

As this description indicates, the scheme is a totally contingent one, in that each response of both teacher and child is rated according to his partner's immediately preceding behaviour. In general, the scale is not intended to be used on a 'one-shot' basis, but rather it is intended to be used repeatedly so as to assess such questions as:

(a) the changes in a poorly functioning child's behaviour with and without special teaching;

(b) the progress made by a teacher as she is trained to use new techniques to reach poorly functioning children.

II. GENERAL DISCUSSION

Form and Function in the Analysis of Linguistic Data

A theme which ran through all the discussions was the need for functional analyses of language behaviour as opposed to purely formal analyses. The word 'function' almost seemed to be acting as a rallying cry in the way that 'structure' did a decade ago. One group, concerned that this unanimity might be more apparent than real, attempted to clarify what was meant by the term. It immediately became apparent that there were two very general senses in which the term was being used.

In the first, function was being used to indicate a concern with the purposes that language serves within a culture, and to direct attention to the importance of taking the social context of use into account when studying performance data. From this perspective, for example, it would not be sufficient to describe responses to a picture story task as containing a certain proportion of pronouns with exophoric reference (as in Hawkins 1969), without at the same time describing the testing situation and the subject's perception of the task. The observed difference between 'middle' and 'working' class children might then be attributed to differences in the functions that the responses were realizing, stemming from differences between the two groups in their perception of what was being demanded of them.

In this first sense, function was obviously very close to 'meaning intention', another term which has achieved considerable currency in recent years. Whose interpretation of the meaning intention of an utterance was to be taken as its function, the sender's or the receiver's? When an utterance has been successful in communicating between sender and receiver it was agreed that there would be no problem, as the receiver would have correctly attributed to the sender just that meaning intention which the sender had intended to communicate. In the case of unsuccessful communication there was a problem, since the impact on the receiver of an utterance might not match the meaning intention of the sender. Nevertheless, the receiver's (incorrect) reconstruction of the sender's meaning intention was a second-order phenomenon, dependent for its existence on the reception of an utterance, which was itself the realization of the sender's meaning intention. (The problem of how meaning intentions are to be inferred is discussed in another section.)

This global view of function has been further clarified by Halliday's (1970) distinction between the three 'macro-functions' which together make up the 'meaning potential' of a language: the 'ideational', the 'interpersonal' and the 'textual'. The meaning intention of an utterance is made up of options selected within *each* of these macro-functions in the light of the speaker's perception of the communication demands of the total situation. A global categorization of function thus fails to make important distinctions, and so what should be aimed at, it was suggested, was a hierarchical ordering of function, with macro-function delineating these major areas of meaning potential, and with micro-functions, or specific options, nested within these.

The second sense in which 'function' is used is more specific, and refers to options within Halliday's *interpersonal* macro-function, e.g. the Sociological Research Unit's work on the language of control. In this sense, 'function' is closely related to 'speech act' as discussed by Austin, Searle and others.

In either sense, however, there is no agreed taxonomy of function, and so there is obviously a danger that a concentration, in analysis, on function alone may give rise to a proliferation of idiosyncratic categories that yield no genuine increase in understanding of differences in language use between individual children or groups of children.

What is required, therefore, is a form of analysis which relates language function to language form. Although there is no simple isomorphic relation between function and form, since one form can, in different contexts, realize a number of very different functions, and one function can have a variety of formal realizations, the evidence for a functional distinction must ultimately rest on formal criteria. It was suggested that it might be helpful to think of function (in the first sense, above) as 'form in a context of use'. This definition stresses the interdependence of these two ways of looking at language and indicates that it is the presence of a systematic formal distinction within a given context that is the evidence for an equivalent functional distinction.

Not all functional distinctions, in the sense of differences in intended meaning, are educationally significant however, and so the problem still remains of deciding which categories of function to attend to. A number of participants argued strongly that a useful categorization of function can only be based on a sociological or pedagogical model of teacher–child interaction within the larger framework of a hierarchy of educational objectives. The work of Halliday, Bernstein and Britton was considered helpful in this context.

Such an orientation is particularly important when it comes to selecting tasks for experimental study. Ideally these should be closely related to the skills in using language in educational contexts that teachers consider important. Many experimental tasks currently being investigated seem to be attempting to tap the development of the ability to give verbal definitions. However, the approach which is usually adopted, which involves the extraction of lexical items and their meanings from their normal context of use, may not correspond very closely to the teacher's conception of this skill. Teachers tend to stress the importance of the development of the ability to express a spatio-temporally coherent, logical theme, which involves the contributory skills of classification, grouping and handling logical relationships. It may be that competence with respect to this particular cluster of skills requires different rules for its realization within different contexts: (a) in education, in which the goals of 'abstraction' and 'explicitness' are embedded within the unique context of the classroom; and (b) in other naturalistic settings, in which implicit elements of the shared physical and social background provide a supporting framework for communication. It is possible that the characteristics that distinguish the communication styles of different cultures and sub-cultures can be represented in terms of their different modes of transmission and maintenance of such rules of realization.

Problems of Interpretation and Inference in Language Research

All studies that use language behaviour as primary data involve a substantial element of interpretation. What the researcher is usually interested in is the meanings intended by the speaker, and these can only be recovered from the acoustic data by the appli-cation of a complex set of rules about sound-meaning correspon-dences (i.e. the grammar of the language) in conjunction with expectations derived from a similar interpretation of the situa-tional context. Whilst the problems that such a procedure poses apply to all language data, they are particularly acute with respect to data collected from young children. Earlier studies of child language, in which the emphasis was on distributional analyses of form-classes, glossed over the interpretative aspect of their methodology, priding themselves on their empirical rigour in eschewing any concern with meaning. The empirical purity was illusory however, since the segmentation of the stream of sound and the subsequent assignment of these segments to form-classes necessarily relied heavily on the researcher's (implicit) attribution of a particular meaning to the utterance as a whole. Now that research on child language has become explicitly concerned with the development of meaning and meaning intentions, the prob-lems raised by the need to make interpretations can be brought out into the open.

The major problem, of course, is that of establishing the accuracy of the interpretation. In the case of adult speakers, it is possible to ask for confirmation of a particular interpretation either on the spot or when replaying the recording. This has not been found possible with young children, and so alternative procedures are needed to ensure that the enthusiasms and preconceptions of the researcher are not allowed to run riot. The younger the child, the more important these safeguards are.

Clearly the possibility of successful communication between mothers and their young children depends upon the mother's assumption that her interpretations are usually correct. However, little is known about the information upon which mothers base their interpretations, although they seem to draw upon a wide variety of cues, such as accompanying gestures and direction of gaze, habitual affective responses and sequences of behaviour, expectations set up by previous utterances, and the feedback gained from the child's subsequent acceptance or rejection of the response to his utterance. What weighting is given to these different cues, particularly when they are in conflict, and does the weighting change with situation and age? In the absence of any clear knowledge of how mothers and other adults habitually, and apparently successfully, make their interpretations, it is difficult to establish empirical criteria to guide the research worker. This should by no means be taken to imply that the protocols that are derived from recordings of child speech are highly inaccurate, but rather as a recognition of the fact that they rely very heavily on the intuitions of the research worker, which will inevitably be affected by the theoretical position that he or she adopts to the data in question.

The problems of interpretation so far discussed are common to any study that makes use of linguistic data, since they are associated with the preliminary task of making a transcription. Those studies that then go on to attempt to account for the actual form of the child's performance in terms of some theory of development, linguistic, social or other, are faced with a further problem of interpretation, as they seek to assign utterances or other forms of behaviour to theoretical categories of various sorts. Here again, it has not been found feasible to question children directly about their knowledge of the rules that underlie their behaviour, and so researchers have to rely rather heavily on inferences made from observed behaviour. But what is the relationship between observed behaviour and underlying rules; and can we justify attributing to the child control of the conceptual organization implied by the theory? (A rather extreme case of this sort is the positing of a deletion rule which is theoretically required to derive two-word utterances from underlying NP–V–NP constructions (Bloom 1970).)

Whilst it is true that the child is developing towards the adult system of organization, it does not follow that the structural description that the researcher formulates on the basis of the adult system, or even of a part of it, provides a satisfactory framework for the description of the child's behaviour at points along the way. Of course, this problem has been recognized before, and it was in an attempt to overcome it that Brown and his colleagues (1967) constructed the series of grammars of individual children at different points in their development. Even there, however, the basic framework and the set of categories employed were drawn from a theory based on adult competence. The problem is that, in so far as children think in ways that are different from the ways in which adults think, we are in danger of systematically misrepresenting their thought processes by the imposition of categorization schemes which we construct on the basis of conceptual frameworks that are evidently not available to the child.

It is, indeed, possible that the child is operating within a totally different frame of reference from the adult, organizing his behaviour in terms of idiosyncratic strategies that nevertheless happen to enable him to act and respond appropriately in a sufficiently large proportion of situations for the adult model to seem to be appropriate.

Such scepticism is probably a healthy reaction to Maureen Shields's explicitly stated assumption that the development of communicative ability is only possible if child and adult share 'a common field of interpersonal and contextual meaning' (p. 192). What is probably necessary, as argued earlier, is that the mother or other adult interacting with the child should make this assumption. But the researcher's stance should be more empirical. Almost certainly there will be some measure of correspondence between the child's and adult's conceptual organization: the researcher's task, however, is to map out the areas of mismatch as well as those of match.

The problem of inference then becomes one of research strategy: whether to start with the minimum of preconceptions about the structure of the child's world, only using categories common to adult and child when these have been empirically demonstrated, or whether to start with a descriptive model, informed by the categorization scheme employed by the adult, and assumed to be shared by the child, but which is flexible enough to incorporate alternative possibilities that are suggested by close scrutiny of aspects of the child's behaviour that do not easily fit into the adult's model.

Selection of Research Strategies

Closely related to the problems encountered when interpreting observed behaviour is the more general issue of the role of theory in the study of language and learning or, as the argument developed, of the relative merits in terms of research methodology of 'rationalism' and 'empiricism'.

How much should the researcher take into the free field situation, whether it be home or classroom, by way of explicit hypotheses, well-defined hunches or taxonomies of categories for the analysis of data? The 'rationalist' stance was that, in order to settle on which aspects of the enormously complex and constantly changing field of interaction presented by the home or classroom are to be attended to, it is necessary to formulate some hypotheses in advance. It is not enough to note differences; they must be *significant* differences, and significance can only be determined in relation to a theory, however tentative. In practice, it was argued, decisions about which hypotheses to test and what sort of analytic categories are forced on the researcher by (a) the need to establish what is actually to count as data; (b) the limited amount of information that the researcher can note down while simultaneously making observations; (c) the necessity for accurate communication between members of a research team, only some of whom will be actually involved in collecting the data; (d) economy of time and effort where immediate practical application is envisaged. In any case the researcher will inevitably be operating with a set of implicit assumptions, e.g. that particular linguistic forms are being used to realize different functions as the age of the child increases, and the only methodologically sound procedure is to make these assumptions explicit and to relate them to whatever descriptive categories are to be used before embarking on the research.

The 'empiricist' faction, defending the data reduction approach, countered with the argument that the study of language in naturalistic settings is still at the hypothesis-generating stage, and that a premature approach with firm hypotheses and preconceived categories would be to risk either a distortion of the facts or the discovery that both hypotheses and categories are inappropriate when it comes to actually describing the situation. It is a valid procedure, it was argued, to enter the classroom 'with a butterfly net' in order to catch various samples of interaction data on the basis of which hypotheses can then be constructed.

However, as the majority agreed, scientific research is rarely conducted satisfactorily from either of these extreme positions. A spiral-like procedure is the norm, in which a start is made with a period of naturalistic observation of some sort, during which intuitions and hunches are clarified into explicit hypotheses. This is followed by a period of more systematic research, whether through experimentation or structured observation of the naturalistic situation, with a view to testing the hypotheses previously generated. Inconsistencies and ambiguities discovered at this stage lead to a further stage of hypothesis formulation, which may well involve further free-ranging observation, and so to a further stage of hypothesis testing. Where an individual researcher enters the spiral will depend very much on his assessment of the validity of the work that has already been carried out in his chosen field of enquiry.

The further dichotomy between experimentation and study of naturally occurring situations was also considered. Some people were of the firm opinion that it was methodologically sounder only to carry out naturalistic studies in order to attempt to corroborate findings that had already been established in carefully structured experimental situations in which the focus was on the manipulation of specific variables. Advocates of the alternative procedure argued that it was only after studying the frequency and contexts of different behaviours in a naturalistic setting that one was in a position to determine which variables to manipulate under experimental conditions. Here again, the majority agreed that both approaches are useful and, to a considerable extent, complementary. Which approach predominates in a particular piece of research is partly determined by the topic being investigated, particularly its breadth, and partly by the preferences of the investigator.

However, both approaches are faced by problems of how far they can be generalized. With respect to the experimental approach, standardization of experimental conditions in no way guarantees that the task will be perceived in the same way by all subjects or all social classes. There is the further problem of the extent to which any experimental situation can yield generalizations which apply outside that situation. For this reason it is highly desirable that experimental findings should be validated, wherever possible, by naturalistic study of the same phenomenon.

For the naturalistic approach, the problems are largely concerned with sampling. Such studies are usually based on relatively small numbers of subjects in one particular institution or locality often chosen on the basis of availability or convenience, and the question is then of the representativeness of the particular sample. For example, how far is it possible to generalize from one teacher or mother to another, or from one school to another, or even from the Scottish to the English educational system? Numbers are not everything however, and very worthwhile research can be carried out by detailed study of a small sample, where the focus is on what children have in common rather than on the ways in which they differ.

The Measurement of Social Background

What is at issue here is the selection of appropriate indices of social background when attempting to isolate possible causative mechanisms for the observed differences between groups with respect to their development of skills in linguistic communication. The central theme of the discussion was the necessity of escaping from global measures of social class, based on occupational indices, towards more detailed measures of those aspects of the child's family background that can be directly related to the quality of linguistic interaction that takes place in the home and from which he acquires his language skills. It was stressed that the work of the SRU was already taking this direction, by attempting to map out the 'ground rules' laid down by different families in their socializing and interactional practices, and by correlating these with syntactic and semantic phenomena.

The crucial question is then whether to study differences between groups as defined by fairly crude indices of social background, or to use social background information as a starting point for the investigation of possible variations in linguistic input. It is dangerous merely to assume that differences at the former level necessarily correspond with differences at the latter level, since it is often the case that within-group variations are at least as great as between-group variations.

There was some discussion about the advisability, when using global measures of social background, of combining occupational indices with indices of educational background and attainment. There was generally held to be no *a priori* ground for considering either of these two measures to be necessarily associated with the type of linguistic input encountered by the child. Nevertheless, the problem to which many studies are directed—that of how to account for the persistent relative failure of working-class as opposed to middle-class children—requires using these cruder techniques in order initially to isolate possible real differences in children's use of language in different contexts. Only then will it be possible to investigate systematically the mechanisms linking such differences in language use with specific aspects of social background.

IQ Testing

The debate on the question of whether or not to use IQ tests demonstrated the problem to be as intractable as ever. Arguments for and against the use of IQ tests were posed forcefully. Initially, the argument centred upon the use of IQ as a controlling device in experimental investigations. However, many participants questioned the idea of treating IQ as a simple unitary quantifiable attribute, which could be treated as an independent variable; the question was further raised as to whether such a control should be for verbal or non-verbal IQ. In neither case was it felt that any adequate appraisal was available of what competences and/or skills IQ tests actually measure. Counter-arguments focused upon the necessity of being able to refute possible assertions that observed differences at a linguistic level between different groups of children are a mere function of IQ differences.

Later, however, the discussion broadened its scope to encompass the wider problem of the educational validity of IQ measures. The major argument in favour of continuing to use IQ tests is the administrative necessity of identifying both individuals and schools where an injection of educational resources might give rise to substantial benefits. However, the concept of 'under-achievement' was questioned in this context. It was maintained that for every individual there exists a biological and social potential for a certain level of intellectual and other functioning, and that this potential is frequently not fully realized. This is a different concept from the statistical one of 'under-achievement', whose logical corollary is that of 'over-achievement', which is an absurd notion. It was maintained that the notion of under-achievement can only make sense if we have a reliable measure of *potential*, and this cannot be gained by the use of a *performance* test. It was claimed that since the notion of IQ is theoretically contradictory and vacuous, and that since there should be a fair measure of correspondence between theory and educational practice, the only logical conclusion must be to abandon IQ tests completely. Their further use not only reinforces the dubious ideology of 'intelligence' testing, with its genetic overtones, but prevents us from clarifying the rationale behind the use of *any* test, standardized, Piagetian or other.

The problem of allocation of educational resources and of under-achievement was considered further. It was suggested that an effective way of assessing priority areas might be to select for special attention those schools where reading age is generally and consistently below chronological age, using literacy as the 'achievement' criterion; this might avoid the implication that those with *low* IQ are not in fact under-achieving when they do not succeed. A further suggestion was that a re-examination of the concept of 'under-achievement' might lead to a shifting of emphasis away from the learner to the school. By scrutinizing the effectiveness of allocating resources to schools, in terms of the measured success of the extra provision, it would be possible to identify 'under-achieving schools'.

Oral Language Skills and the Acquisition of Literacy

The background to this discussion was the observation that many investigations have failed to find a correlation between language development, measured in terms of the length and syntactic complexity of children's utterances, and their reading ability in the early stages of learning to read (five to eight years). This finding is rather surprising, since there are good reasons to expect that a child's skill in using spoken language should bear a fairly close relationship to his skill as a reader. Several reasons were suggested to account for the reported lack of correlation. Firstly, the particular measures used were perhaps inappropriate: the Schonell word-recognition test, in particular, although an effective predictor of progress in reading across many different types of reading scheme, is not a measure of the ability to obtain meaning from printed text, which is what reading ability is about. The concentration on measures of oral language production is perhaps also misplaced, since it is skill as a *receiver* that one might, prima facie, expect to be related to reading ability. In addition, fully appropriate measurement of both abilities would involve attention to linguistic function as well as to form.

A second possible explanation concerns the difference between fluent reading and beginning reading. Some of the contributory skills that a child has to acquire in order to be able to extract meaning from a printed text, are not very closely related to the abilities he already has with regard to spoken language, such as orientation to the top→bottom, left→right display of visual information, the construction of criterial sets of distinctive visual features for word recognition, and the precise way in which spoken language is related to print, particularly if there is a problem of dialect interference. Whilst there is some likelihood that those with well-developed oral language skills will also come to school better prepared to tackle the new medium, these skills themselves are sufficiently different from those involved in oral language to account for the initial lack of correlation that has been reported.

When the relationship between the development of reading ability and oral language has been examined in relation to social class, two types of difference have been found between middle-class and working-class groups. Firstly, there are dialect differences. Secondly, there are differences in rate of oral language development, with a delay of some six months separating the working-class from the middle-class group. Whilst work in the U.S.A. suggests that 'dialect interference' may inhibit learning to read, the developmental delay does not appear to have any significant deleterious effect.

The reported findings that there were significant relationships between spoken language ability and reading ability in older children (approximately nine years of age) led to agreement that this area of research warranted more detailed investigation, probably along the lines of isolating common factors in the different strategies of comprehension of spoken and written language.

Another potentially fruitful approach would be to examine the child's orientation towards text (spoken and written), and the types of strategies utilized by the child when error is encountered. Many children who are judged to be good readers by teachers, because when reading *with* the teacher they can 'fill' gaps in the text by reference to the context, are, when reading alone, unable to utilize this contextually-based predictive strategy. On the other hand, children utilizing probabilistic and heuristic strategies based on text may produce a greater number of actual errors, and be judged poor readers, although the errors they produce are potentially fruitful.

The concept of the 'productive error' was stressed several times in the course of discussions. There would appear to be two distinct but related notions subsumed under this heading. Firstly, from the point of view of the learning process itself, it is clear that, provided that the context is capable of providing supporting cues, either in itself or through active manipulation by the educator, errors can be productive from the point of view of the person making the error. He can, in the right circumstances, learn from 'mistakes'—and in fact much of cognitive development proceeds through the dialectical resolution of the contradictions between appearance and reality, what is expected and what is perceived, what is 'known' and what is 'seen'. It is likely that this approach is not sufficiently stressed by teachers.

Secondly, from the point of view of the scientific investigator, the 'errors' made by subjects both in experimental tasks and in naturalistic situations, can provide insight into the actual strategies formulated by children and adults when they encounter problems to be solved. There are not only 'degrees' of error, but also consistent and 'logical' errors stemming from the application of certain (often implicit) rules for the resolution of conflict. A related point is that not enough attention is paid in studies of children to the types of strategies pursued by *adults*, who are often assumed to work with exactly the same frame of reference as the experimenter.

III. SUGGESTIONS FOR RESEARCH IN LANGUAGE AND LEARNING

Introductory Paper

BARBARA TIZARD

I will try to put the research proposals which have been suggested into a context of certain questions about the relationship between language, learning, education and schools which seem to me to be implicit in this area. All the discussions at these seminars have been concerned with the processes by which language and language skills are learnt, the extent and manner to which educational processes should intervene in this learning, and the adequacy of the school as an educational medium. Much of the discussion has not in fact been concerned with education, and especially not with schools, but I think it is important to bring these aspects back to a central position, if only because I see no reason why the rest of society should support us all in tolerable comfort unless our discussions are in some way relevant to the educational needs of their children.

Perhaps I should start by a few definitions; education I take to involve some notion of teaching with intent. An educational process, by my definition, involves directed effort on the part of one person with the aim that another should acquire certain skills or bodies of knowledge. This may involve direct instruction, or, as in the case of a nursery school, it may involve structuring the environment with the deliberate aim of ensuring that the child will have certain experiences from which it is assumed he will learn. This education may involve such formal decontextualized teaching as a lesson on history, or such informal practical instruction as tying up shoe laces. In any event, it is clearly not a process which is confined to school. For example, a lot of education nowadays occurs through the medium of television; every day large numbers of children watch programmes like *Blue Peter*, which have a deliberate educational intent; and at least in middle-class families, the child's whole environment is often arranged with an avowed educational intent—the child's books, toys, outings, clothes, even his room decoration (e.g. friezes of animals or alphabets), are chosen with an overt instructional purpose. In fact, I think it is very important to remember that wherever the child finds himself in our society he is receiving education from some source. It is as important to look at the curriculum of the parents, the day nursery, the childminder and the television producers as it is to examine schools.

Equally clearly, much of what the child learns is not the result of an educational process in this sense, but either results from encounters between the child and his environment which have not been planned by an educating adult, or is the unintended product of planned encounters with the environment. The relationship between learning and education is certainly complex and one that needs further exploring. Placed in an educational environment, or confronted with a teaching situation, the child may fail to learn what was intended. Worse, he may learn what was unintended. What the child may learn from an Arithmetic lesson is as likely to be a feeling of inadequacy or confusion as a numerical skill. Indeed much of what a child learns comes from unintended teaching; for example, if you say to little girls but not to little boys 'How pretty you look' you probably have no intention of developing sex-role behaviour but none the less this is probably a more effective way of developing sex-role behaviour than by such direct teaching as saying 'little girls should concern themselves about their appearance but little boys shouldn't'. Of course, much valuable learning occurs incidentally, and since it appears to come effortlessly it is perhaps important to know under what kinds of conditions it occurs, and what kinds of learning occur in this way and what kinds require deliberate educational interventions. Thus everyone knows that a foreign language is better learned by mixing with native speakers than by formal lessons, but the crucial variables have not been isolated—is it motivation, or learning in context or simply the frequency of practice?

How, as research workers, do we see the approach to relating problems of language, learning, education and the schools? One research approach to this problem is to argue that educational procedures can only succeed if based on an adequate understanding of development. That is, an understanding of learning must precede educational recommendations. So far, it is argued, 'compensatory' education has failed because it has not been based on such an understanding and indeed it has usually been devised in more or less total ignorance of the young child's actual encounters with his environment and of his development. Some research workers believe that our first need is for a better understanding of normal developmental processes. Tom Brown would like to see a comparison between the acquisition of communicative competence in speech and writing, and a study of the considerations which determine the degree of ease with which individuals acquire one more easily than the other. Ruth Clark would like to see intensive longitudinal studies of the acquisition of language structures in individual children. Maureen Shields argues that we need to understand what social skills are developed in early childhood, and the role that language plays in this development, before making recommendations to teachers. Sinclair Rogers would like to use the transcribed tapes of teenagers talking, collated by Rutherford in York, for linguistic analysis. Of particular interest are some tapes of three teenagers on their own organizing and debating a topic. He would like to study the setting up of the debate, the discussion of the rules of the debate, the frames of reference of the speakers, the existence and nature of any meta-language, the logic of the discourse, and so on. Ewan Klein would like to see a study of the development of conversational skills. Though much work has been based on children's speech to adults, the data has rarely been considered as a *dialogue*, or an organized social interaction. Still less research has examined child–child dialogue. Things to look at might be: sequencing of conversational contributions; grasp of felicity conditions on speech acts; sharing of presuppositions that govern the appropriate use of different linguistic expressions, such as definite descriptions, demonstratives, factive verbs, etc.

In particular, one might look at the way in which pre-linguistic communicative acts of the young child develop into speech acts of asserting, questioning and requesting, and the way in which these are realized linguistically, i.e. as the sentence moods of declarative, interrogative and imperative, or indirectly, as in expressions such as 'Can you pass the salt?'. He would also like to know more about the development of the cognitive and linguistic skills involved in using counterfactuals. Current analyses of counterfactuals such as 'If Israel and Egypt were to start fighting again, a third World War would break out' claim that we evaluate their truth by considering what would happen in a 'possible world' which is pretty much the same as our actual world, except that the antecedent of the hypothetical holds in that world. Thus we need to be able to consider non-actual states of affairs. It is known that children can construct fantasy situations in play, but not how this relates to the task of using counterfactuals.

The utility of setting up a data bank for researchers in child language was also stressed by Ewan Klein. Minimally, it would consist of transcriptions from as many naturalistic recording projects as possible, classified according to age, sex, socio-economic class, native language, etc., of child. The information could be stored and reproduced quite cheaply on micro-fiche. He believes that such a scheme would encourage a healthy relationship between theory and data, since there is a fair amount of speculation about 'linguistic universals' which is, as yet, unsupported except for the most meagre evidence.

Gordon Wells and his associates argue that the most urgent need at the present time is to bring together the findings from the wide variety of investigations of child development in cognition, in language acquisition etc., in an attempt to construct a coherent theory (or competing theories) of the early stages of development, on which to base decisions about the form and content of pre-school provision. Specific research projects, in their view, ought to attempt to test hypotheses derived from such an overall theory. They have selected a number of topic areas which their own current research suggests is worth further investigation. Their first suggestion is to investigate the conditions under which patterns and strategies of communication are established in the 'pre-linguistic' stage. They see as particularly important the degree of compatibility between child and adult with respect to the purposes of communication and the interpretations by mother and child of each other's meaning intentions. At a later age, they conceptualize the communication problem in terms of the kinds of language experience needed to develop flexibility in assessing and taking account of the other's knowledge and expectations in the situation when constructing a message. What strategies do children employ to derive meaning from utterances, and how does the relationship between verbal and non-verbal communication change according to age and situation? During this meeting it has been suggested that we also need to look at the parent's end of this—what cues do they use to interpret children's utterances and how do they know when they are correct?

Wells and his associates thus see as the central task the understanding of the processes by which the child and perhaps the parent develops patterns and strategies of communication. Presumably there is an implicit suggestion that school failure is related to a relative failure or inflexibility in communication strategies.

Other research workers also believe that a better understanding of the child's language system will assist educational policy, but see as most important a direct confrontation with the problem of the nature of social-class differences in language. Although earlier crude notions of these differences have recently been refined, we have still a very inadequate understanding of their nature. Is there a difference in the frequency with which children of different social classes choose to use codes in different contexts? Or is there a developmental lag? Ken Reeder asks a similar question—are language differences between social classes attributable to cognitive differences or to differing sociolinguistic norms for the use of discourse rules in specific classes of settings? He suggests that problems in the acquisition of literacy could be attributable to difficulties in the extension to the written medium of role-taking and inferential skills, and not to fundamental differences in cognitive organization. Asher Cashdan suggests that we still need to test Labov and Bernstein in naturalistic settings, by studies of children's language in free situations such as the playground.

The assumption behind both these sets of research ideas, that is, both research suggestions concerned with the way in which language develops, and the analysis of social-class differences in language structure and usage, is that the knowledge derived from such projects would enable us to devise more effective or appropriate educational procedures. However, as a number of people have pointed out, there is not necessarily a causal connection between differences in sociolinguistic aspects of speech and educational failure—the failure could relate to other associated differences between social-class groups, e.g. with respect to motivation or the meaning given to reading at home. Some people therefore argue that we need a frontal attack on the relationship between language skills and use, the characteristics of the home, teaching methods in school, and success in acquiring literacy.

However, the step from understanding language development or sociolinguistic differences in language to devising educational procedures is a large one; such research can only be a source of ideas for educational practice, it cannot prescribe practice. Such a source is, however, badly needed. Unfortunately, there is a dearth of people willing to take the step from theory into practice. The research worker usually sees his job as finished when his research report appears in the appropriate journal, whilst the teacher rarely has the inclination or training to derive educational ideas from research reports. An important need in my opinion is to make systematic plans to bridge this gap. This implies as a minimum that research-funding bodies should allow time and money to be set aside for this purpose, and that better communication channels be established between teachers and research workers. A more fundamental approach would be to involve teachers in the research at an early stage, and research workers in the teaching process.

A third group of research suggestions was directly concerned with educational practices and the school. Chazan sees as an important need the development of better diagnostic language tools for teachers. Other research suggestions concerned the possibility that educational failure in the school may represent less a deficit in the children than a mismatch between their interests and what the school offers, or between the communication norms or teaching strategies of home and school. Thus Jimmy Britton suggested exploring ways of relating children's language experiences in and out of school to their first attempts at reading, and exploring the effect of relating dialect speakers' first steps in reading as closely as possible to their speech. He also suggested that it would be worth experimenting with the application to reading of Chomsky's conclusion that children appear to succeed in 'educing principles' from the vast range of imperfect speech which they hear. That is, it may be a mistake to restrict so closely the range of written materials used in teaching children to read. With reference to older children, he suggested cooperative exploration by linguists and subject specialists of the language processes involved in teaching and learning specific subjects, which would hopefully lead to a theoretical synthesis.

Ken Reeder suggested that school failure may be related to communication interference between the communication norms of the school and of the child's home. Further, he suggested that problems in the acquisition of literacy might be related to difficulties in the extension to the written medium of the role-taking and inferential skills which underlie spoken discourse, and that such difficulties may be attributable to sociolinguistic rather than fundamental cognitive differences. During this meeting it was suggested that we need to compare the value systems of home and school and the ways in which they are realized, as well as teachers' and mothers' teaching styles.

Several people besides Alan Davies thought that we needed a better understanding of the linguistic demands made of the child at school, and how children learn to become pupils in the linguistic sense. David Olson suggested looking at the gradual de-contextualizing of instructions by the teacher, and the children's response to it, and Asher Cashdan that we should look at the initiation of interactions in the classroom, their maintenance, context and effect in relation to the class, sex and age of the pupil. Wells and his associates would like to know more about linguistic practices in schools and nurseries, whilst both Wells and Reeder were concerned with the possible effect of teachers' judgements, expectations and attitudes on the learning and communication situations they set up for their pupils. Asher Cashdan and a number of other people raised the problem of examining teachers' perceptions of pupils and how they are transmitted to them. We also need to know, it was suggested, much more about the basis on which teachers make their judgements and what criteria, explicit or implicit, they take into account. Someone suggested that one approach would be to compare teachers' ratings of tapes of children talking with their ratings of transcribed tapes.

In fact, quite a lot of research suggestions concerned the educational process in school, but I think I'm right in saying that at the present time very little of such research is being carried out. I myself would like to make a plea for looking at the school as an *institution*: as psychologists, we tend to be concerned with individual teachers and pupils, but my experience in other fields is that the institutional framework and its goals place constraints on pupils and teachers that override differences between individuals. Much of what goes on in school is clearly not education. This is most crudely evidenced by the fact that the greater part of the child's school day is in fact spent in *waiting*, in a whole variety of situations, looking for pencils, talking to his peers, playing in the playground, etc. On the one hand the child undoubtedly *learns* a great deal at school—he is, for example, rapidly socialized into the appropriate sex-role behaviour, age-role, peer-group role, pupil-role behaviour, he effortlessly acquires peer-group values, as well as new self-concepts, usually related to his own failure, and new teacher-centred values, such as the importance of being competitive, obedient, and punctual, and what may be to him new social values, e.g. religious and nationalist sentiments.

On the other hand, the apparently avowed purpose of the school—to hand on to the child a body of explicit skills and knowledge—is often inadequately and inefficiently fulfilled. Another aspect of this paradox is that, despite the specialized nature of the school as an educational institution, and the professional nature of its staff, the teacher in school appears unable to equal the un-trained middle-class parent as an educator. Moreover, not only are schools inefficient at teaching basic skills, but they set their sights astonishingly low. We know that four-year-olds can be taught to play the violin, and two-year-olds can be taught to swim: even more remarkably two-year-olds can be taught to co-operate to fulfil a common aim. I think it is clear that if we wanted to do so, we could find ways of teaching many kinds of skills to quite young children, and that the eleven years which they do spend in schools are very ineffectively used.

I myself think that one can only conclude that our society does not in fact want to develop high levels of skill in most children, and indeed that schools are not organized with the primary aim of transmitting skills and information. This at once raises the question of what they are organized for; if we are concerned about education we should include in another seminar on language and learning a study of schools as institutions. This would involve not only looking at what children are *not* learning at school, but also looking at what functions the school *is* serving, that is, what the children are learning as well as what they are not, and whether it is what we want them to learn. This is by no means a plea for de-schooling, but a suggestion that one should as it were start from scratch, and consider what should be the characteristics of educational institutions, remembering to keep under scrutiny both the implicit and explicit teaching that goes on.

Thus many people in this seminar stressed the importance of shared activity and shared purpose in the development of communication. But in most schools there is a striking lack of shared purpose and activity between pupils and teachers. The role of the teacher and the socialization of the teacher into the teaching role has hardly been studied, but it may be a key aspect of the educational process. Most people have an extensive repertoire of behaviour and speech acts which they draw on in a very limited way when their assigned role is limited; just as the child is socialized into being a pupil, so in a more important way, the adult is socialized into being a teacher, with, in both instances, a considerable restriction on their behaviour.

Another topic which was always just below the surface in our discussions was the question of educational goals. Most of our thinking about language learning and education has been in relation to the attainment of literacy. Maureen Shields, by raising the question of the role of language in the development of social skills, drew attention to the possibility of examining cognitive structures and skills in relation to a different set of educational goals. Further discussions might well concern themselves with the relationship between educational practice and educational goals.

General Discussion

The discussion that followed concentrated on three major topics. Within each, there was general endorsement of the suggestions that Barbara Tizard had reported, and a number of further suggestions were made.

Initial Language Acquisition

Considerable emphasis was placed on the importance of studying problems and strategies of parent–child interaction, with attention to function as well as to structure, and also to the degree of congruence between adult and child intention. Reference was made to Trevarthen's (forthcoming) work on the development of pre-linguistic communication, in which it had been noted that changes in the behaviour of the child influenced the behaviour of the mother. More work was needed on the sensitivity of adults to children's communications and on the ways in which adults modify their speech to children and on the ways in which these modifications change. Does this modification result from sensitivity to changes in the child's speech production, to the apparent comprehension of the child or simply to his attentional processes as the child gets older? What are the effects that different types of modification produce, and is there an optimum type of adult speech at different stages in development? A distinction would have to be made between short and long term effects in attempting to answer this question: there was a danger of sacrificing long term advantages by concentrating too exclusively on measurable short term gain.

Another aspect of parent–child interaction that would repay further study is the ways in which the participants interpret each other's utterances—what sorts of cues they utilize and the differential importance given to different cues in different contexts. Hazel Francis reported an informal study by one of her students of the bases of her own interpretations of her child's speech, but no systematic study is apparently being carried out at present on this topic. The importance of understanding how adults interpret early utterances was referred to above, although doubt was expressed as to whether it made any difference whether these interpretations were correct or not. How children interpret adults' utterances is equally important, since this is an essential part of acquiring language. Studies of children's comprehension are beginning to investigate the influence of social and physical context, but clearly much more research with this orientation is still needed. In connection with parent–child interaction, a plea was made that the father's contribution should not be ignored.

Taking up the distinction between short and long term in assessing the effects of different types of modification in parents' speech to young children, it was pointed out, firstly, that the characteristics of the input cannot be separated from the way in which the child processes this input, and secondly, that the situation is further complicated by the fact that language is only part of a larger *interactive* social process and that predictions based on a simple linear causal model were bound to go astray. Two research strategies were suggested in response, firstly the controlled experiment and secondly a retrospective investigation of factors determining progress towards goals that were independently specified in terms of schools as institutions.

Language and Social Background

Discussion on this topic was controversial. Although several people had earlier agreed that the linguistically deprived child is no more than a myth, it was pointed out that there really is insufficient evidence on which to base conclusions. It was suggested that there was a need for replication on a larger scale, and with samples drawn from different populations, of some of the small-scale studies that had given rise to conflicting explanation of the relationship between language, social groupings and educational success, e.g. Bernstein and Labov.

Mention was made of the current work of the Sociological Research Unit in London, in which it is on the relationship between cognition and sociolinguistic coding orientation that attention is being focused rather than on social class *per se*. This led on to an argument as to the value of social class in accounting for differences between individuals in their performance on a variety of linguistic tasks. On the one hand, it was argued that social class cannot, in itself, have explanatory value since, in so far as observed differences are socially determined, this is more appropriately attributed to differences between families in the processes by which language mediates values and styles of social interaction than to ascribed class membership on the basis of the (current) occupation of one or both parents. Moreover where social class had been used as a major variable in analysis, within-class differences had been found to be as great as, if not greater than, differences between classes. On the other hand, it was claimed that social class does have value as a typifying classification, since significant correlations have repeatedly been found between social class, however assessed, and many of the social variables that can be hypothesized as having a more direct influence on linguistic performance. It is furthermore an inescapable fact of life in our society and historically built in to the structure of educational provision. The compromise was offered that social class is useful for some forms of research but that progressively we should be looking for more differentiated types of classification appropriate to specific research issues.

In the context of replication, attention was drawn to relevant data that had already been collected and was available and which could usefully be further analysed. In particular, reference was made to the transcripts that had been prepared by the Nuffield Child Language Survey at York from recordings of the talk of children at different ages,[1] and to the recordings of the spontaneous conversations of four-year-olds at home made by Tony Wootton, and to the recordings of children in the Bristol longitudinal language development study. Other useful corpora of data on children's language in different contexts and at different ages existed and it was suggested that it would be helpful for future research if such material were collected together and a data-bank established and its existence publicized.

Language and Educational Practices

This started with a discussion of the role of researchers: it often seemed to be assumed that part of their role was to act as agents of change, but would there in fact be agreement amongst researchers as to the goals towards which change should be directed? In response, it was pointed out that there are conceptually two issues here: firstly the researcher's attempt to discover and describe what value judgements are operating within schools, and secondly the researcher's own values; in practice the two are not separate, and researchers need to be quite explicit about where their own value judgements are entering into the work that they are doing. Another function that the researcher may perform is to present his description of the processes that are taking place in an institution, together with an indication of their probable effects, and to ask those responsible for the institution whether this is what they are trying to achieve.

A specific problem of this sort is the way in which teachers' attitudes can very quickly be triggered off into stereotypes by forms of language used by children. Further research is needed into the way in which these stereotypes are arrived at, and the criteria that are used, particularly since teachers make these judgements so quickly. One way of looking at this is suggested by Cazden's (1972a) notion of communicative interference: stereotypes might be built upon habitual sociolinguistic characteristics

---

[1] Available from the Nuffield Foundation.

of groups such as the realization of specific speech acts. Another technique for gaining understanding of how such stereotypes are organized is the repertory grid. From their own reports, many teachers seem to be partly influenced by some rough categorization according to social class, with an expectation apparently derived from their acquaintance with research findings, that 'working-class' children will be 'problems'. Such stereotypes were seen as a danger in that some specific characteristic of the child or his background—such as residence on a council estate or presence of a regional accent—is taken as an index that allows a stereotype to be applied to him, and, as a consequence, all other characteristics of the stereotype are attributed to him and expectations formed of his ability, which may in fact be inappropriate or at least resistant to modification in the light of change in the child. It was objected that teacher judgements are usually pretty accurate and that whilst it was an interesting question to discover how they form such judgements, this work should not be approached with the expectation of finding the 'Rosenthal effect'. Some stereotyping or categorizing is essential in dealing with others in order to guide behaviour; the value of research on this topic would be to give teachers knowledge about this extra dimension of their behaviour in relation to children, which would help them to be more effective.

The session ended with a further discussion of the dissemination of research findings, which, it was generally agreed, was an important part of the researcher's task. To rely on teachers and administrators to read research project reports is obviously unsatisfactory, and in any case most projects are restricted in scope and need to be interpreted in the light of other knowledge and the needs of the teachers concerned. One solution is to engage, with teachers, in collaborative research with the aim of leading them to be more reflective and questioning about their own experience. Although valuable, this approach is limited, however, by the kinds of investigation that can be carried out in this way, and by the number of teachers that can be involved. Even local meetings at which research findings are reported only reach a small proportion of teachers. To reach a wider audience, programmes specifically devoted to dissemination will have to be devised and a number of 'middle men', such as college lecturers and LEA advisers, will have to be found who are well enough informed to transmit and interpret recent research findings through in-service education of various kinds. Ideally, opportunities for such people to acquire this expertise would exist in centres where research is currently being carried out.

This discussion led to two recommendations that were submitted to the SSRC.

1. That a greater effort should be made to disseminate the findings of research on language and learning to teachers, and educational planners and administrators.

2. That opportunities for teachers to carry out advanced study of language and learning with respect to the native language, for example through courses leading to a Master's degree, should be provided in institutions of higher education in Britain.

A further recommendation, arising from earlier discussions, was:

3. That there should be a pooling of technical expertise acquired in attempts to carry out naturalistic studies of language use in nursery and primary schools, perhaps through a meeting sponsored by the SSRC.

PART III

5

Research on Spoken Language in the Primary School*

CLIVE CRIPER AND ALAN DAVIES

FOREWORD

The report is a personal assessment by the two main authors of the present 'state of the art' of research into and accepted knowledge of the 'language in the classroom'. It ranges far wider than the classroom itself for the obvious reasons that the way children perform there can only be understood by examining the way they behave elsewhere together with the factors which contribute to this difference. Indeed, the amount of space devoted to an analysis of the research on classroom language is quite limited since the considerable amount of work carried out does not cohere and make up a body of findings within a coherent theory or even within a handful of such theories.

The report is not written in order to present to the academic community a critical analysis of the research literature. Indeed each of the areas we have covered is worthy of a book-length review on its own account. Its purpose is to select out a number of dominant (or absent) themes in research and present to the Scottish Education Department a non-technical document, which reflects a coherent viewpoint and indicates those areas we consider most suitable for research in Scotland.

The bibliography as originally compiled for this Report (now of course expanded by additions from Parts 1 and 2) was designed so as to include the most important references for those intending to start research in the field of spoken language in the primary school, whether or not those references were reviewed in the text itself. One caveat should be entered. Child language acquisition is a vast subject and there is no clear-cut demarcation between it and the subject of this report. Most references to early acquisition have been excluded. The purpose of the bibliography is to provide the starting point for any researcher in the first stages of his critical review of the literature.

We hope, therefore, that the report will be of use in pointing up potential areas of research into spoken language in the primary school.

---

* Originally prepared as a report to the Scottish Education Department in 1974.

ACKNOWLEDGEMENTS
The theoretical sociolinguistic orientation underlying this report is
derived from C. Criper, and H. Widdowson, Sociolinguistics and
Language Teaching in P. Allen and S. P. Corder (eds.), *The Edinburgh
Course in Applied Linguistics* Vol. II (1975) O.U.P. London.

We would like to acknowledge in particular the help of Myint Su in
the bibliographic search, together with Ethel Jack, Caroline Tutton
and Lillias Wylie. Extremely helpful comments have been received from
our colleagues Keith Brown, Tony Howatt and Henry Widdowson.

Introduction

This report contains a critical survey of research in the area of
spoken language in the primary school and concludes with the
recommendations for new openings in research.

We start from the fact that much of the work on language in
education has begun from the standpoint of educational failure.
Language has been seen as a cause of failure but at the same time
as open to remedial action. There are two contrasted viewpoints
on why language can cause failure in school. One argument runs
that some children are lacking in the essential words and structures necessary for them to think and argue: therefore they must be
given the words and structures and drilled in them until they can
use them freely. The counter-argument is that these children
already have the structures and most of the words and are just as
capable of thinking and arguing amongst their peers as anyone
else. Where they differ is in the use of the language which teachers
and others believe to be suitable for school. According to this
argument, their use of language and their attitudes are not inferior, just different, and society needs to recognize these differences. The teacher's job is therefore to make children use their
existing language structures and words appropriately in different
contexts.

We go on to look at the different remedial programmes set up in
Britain and the USA with the intention of compensating for
various kinds of deprivation. Even our brief examination shows
that the aims of the programmes are both extremely varied and
frequently vague and unrealistic.

Since attitudes to language and language use may be relevant
to performance in the school we go on to examine the research
in this area. We examine the way that language is often used
as a means of making stereotyped judgements about others and

conclude that there is prima facie evidence that teachers may be influenced in the way they classify and treat children by the accents and dialect features that they hear. Children likewise are influenced by their families and by their peers in the attitudes and values about language that they hold, with a resultant effect on what kind of language they are prepared to learn to use in school.

The implication of differing attitudes towards the language of teachers and of peers is that different varieties of language are spoken in different domains of society. We therefore examine some of the research on social dialect differences, and in particular look at the effect of the contexts of the playground, the home and the peer group on children's usage.

Language in the classroom forms one particularly important domain. We have therefore examined the large amount of educational research on classroom interaction or microteaching, case studies of schools and classrooms as social institutions, and the more limited work specifically aimed at studying the structure of the verbal interaction between teachers and pupils. We conclude that the theoretical models underlying the analysis of classroom verbal interaction are still very primitive.

Perhaps for this reason it is not clear from the literature whether or not children do need to be taught the spoken language at all. Indeed the assumption seems to be that they do not. This would appear to be the reason for the scarcity of existing normal (not remedial) teaching programmes for the spoken language. Those in favour of such programmes have so far restricted themselves to a number of unconnected suggestions rather than concrete syllabuses.

In conclusion we give the assumptions underlying our recommendations for research and then list a number of suitable areas for research.

I: EDUCATIONAL FAILURE

Causes

Many factors, alone or in combination, have been considered to be responsible for educational failure. On the one hand, they include 'environmental' factors such as the home, the peer group, and the school; on the other they include what were often considered to be the genetic or individual factors of intelligence, motivation and language. It should be noted that the last three factors are only in part determined genetically or by the individual personality. They must also be considered socially determined.

It is interesting, if sad, to notice how, in accordance with the intellectual fashions of the day, a single factor has been picked out as dominant in causing educational failure. During the period of the 1920s–1940s intelligence was thought to be the key factor. In the 1950s and 1960s it appears as if the home was considered the dominant factor and this is certainly the message we are left with by the Plowden Report. The SED Report of Primary Education in 1965 may be said to have focused on the school as dominant. Since the late 1960s language has been coming to the forefront as the prime factor.

It is not surprising that language should be seized on as the overriding factor, since it enters into most human behaviour, social and cognitive, forms a large part of the schooling process and appears isolatable and hence can be acted on alone in any educational intervention programme.

The reason for the unsuccessful search for the cause of educational failure is the excessive weight that has been heaped in turn on the chosen factor. Educational failure could never and cannot now be attributed primarily to any of the above quoted factors. It can only be caused by the interplay of this or another set of factors. We can only recommend and hope, therefore, that linguistics is not treated as the easy practical answer to failure as this would inevitably lead to total disillusion setting in and the useful, but limited, work in language programmes which could be done, being halted.

Theories of Educational Disadvantage through Language
In many government reports reference is made to groups or categories of children who are at a disadvantage compared with most other children when going to school. Their chances of success are much lower. The cause of their greater likelihood of failure is then said to be deprivation. This may be some form of social deprivation, or, as is most relevant here, language deprivation. This means that children are said either not to have enough language or not to have the right bits.

Now deprivation for a Pakistani immigrant child, born in Pakistan and brought to Britain during the primary school years is obvious. He doesn't have English and needs to learn it.

Deprivation, however, for a Glasgow child, born in Glasgow and speaking a local (and class) dialect is more problematic. The argument runs that he suffers from language deprivation since he does not speak the kind of language used in the school. What then can account for his language deprivation? There are two alternative answers which we shall discuss under the headings of deficit and difference; they stand for a whole set of attitudes towards deprivation in general and social differentiation in particular.

Let us take the *deficit* theory first. According to the proponents of this theory, amongst whom have been many educators, language deprivation is due to a linguistic deficit. The view is held that the language code known and used by the so-called deprived children is markedly inferior when compared with the standard variety. It is the structure of the language or dialect code of these children which is regarded as demonstrably inadequate since it does not contain enough sophisticated categories for thinking and arguing, those being two basic components of education. Bereiter *et al.* (1966) are the much quoted source of statements in this mode, e.g. their report that the four-year-old Negro children they were working with had speech forms that were nothing more than a series of emotional cries and hence their decision to treat the children 'as if the children had no language at all'. In a famous or infamous quotation they state 'the language of culturally deprived children . . . is not merely an underdeveloped version of standard English, but is a basically non-logical mode of expressive behaviour.'

Put in a less abrasive manner the argument can be paraphrased thus. Children who have only a limited vocabulary and a restricted repertoire of grammatical structures are at risk in school. They are at risk because those missing words and structures are needed for thinking and arguing. Therefore these children should be taught lots of words and practise lots of structures.

The *difference* supporters claim that there is no documented case where it has ever been shown that one dialect code is logically inferior to another and that all claims that this occurs are based on very superficial contrastive studies of surface structure. They claim that there is no evidence that children are without the linguistic tools for arguing and thinking, two basic components of their normal life at home or with their friends. Furthermore they assert that within Britain or the USA there are many subcultures with different norms and associated forms of behaviour. No arbitrary sets of norms such as those associated essentially with the middle-class values of the schools can be defined as 'good', causing children to be judged as normal or deficient by the degree to which they do or do not conform to this standard. Difference supporters argue the case for equal regard for all culturally different groups.

Measurement of Language Deprivation

Before we can safely join in the argument over 'deficit' versus 'difference' we need to establish that there *are* differences in the language categories of children. How can we measure these differences?

The first distinction we need to make (which is unfortunately not always adhered to in the interpretation of research results) is between competence and performance. It is essential that there be no mixing or confusion between a child having the essential linguistic knowledge (competence) and his making use of it in some particular way (performance). Related to this is the distinction between production and comprehension. Because a child does not produce a particular kind of grammatical construction or lexical item, it cannot necessarily be assumed that he does not comprehend it.

The next important distinction to be made is between linguistic competence and what is now commonly called communicative competence. The knowledge that makes a performance as speaker or hearer possible is not knowledge of language alone but also of the sociolinguistic rules that relate speech (and its interpretation) to social variables such as sex, age, status, setting, etc.

Finally we wish to draw attention to the differences which are involved when one is specifically examining connected speech and not isolated sentences, i.e. discourse. Firstly there is a level of structure higher than the sentence involved. Secondly a distinction needs to be made between the linguistic forms used in an utterance and the function that the utterance is actually fulfilling in the context of the discourse. That is, one cannot interpret what a child means or is trying to say purely by an examination of the language forms that he uses.

Most of the research on deprivation needs to be closely examined in terms of the distinctions we make above before we can accept the conclusions given. For example, in his early work Bernstein's hypothesis appeared to be that there was a correlation between social class and the use of elaborated/restricted codes in particular experimental situations. The hypothesis was crude and the measuring tools were crude. Unfortunately many researchers elsewhere have latched on to this stage of Bernstein's development and not a later one. Subsequently there has been a plethora of studies 'proving' that lower-working-class and middle-class children have access to restricted and elaborated codes respectively.

Much, if not most, of this work is essentially trivial and cannot bear the conclusions placed upon it. In the first place the situation in which the children are asked to produce language is usually a formal interview one or a formal classroom one. What is produced there is determined not solely by a child's linguistic knowledge (competence) but by his judgement of what is appropriate for that context.

Secondly, work of this kind must be judged on whether the right linguistic units have been chosen. Cazden (1972a) mentions the three most frequent types of measures used in the descriptions of child language. Firstly, there is the mean length of utterance. In itself this is not of inherent interest. It is used as an indirect measure of complexity and does not of itself say anything about what a child can or cannot do with language. Secondly there have been attempts to draw up weighted scales to measure complexity. However, syntactic complexity is not something that linguists and psychologists are agreed it is possible to measure in any valid way. Additionally, this is an area in which dialect differences can distort a measure based on the structure of standard English. Finally frequency counts of linguistic features are used. Some such counts can be uninformative in that they pick out individual parts of the grammar and do not treat them as part of a system. They are also sometimes treated as if they were unrelated to the contexts in which they are measured. They can quite legitimately be used, of course, where the items chosen are known to be socially most significant and where inferences from the performance data are not used to make statements about the linguistic knowledge of the children. Investigation into both language knowledge (competence) and performance is needed but the two must not be mixed up.

Programmes for the Disadvantaged
Eventually the argument (and there is a great deal of it in the literature) comes back to the pragmatic question asked by Angel (1972):

I want to know what to do differently for the Mexican American

child from what I do for the Anglo child when I am teaching him
2 + 2 = 4.

Substitute lower-working-class and middle-class for Mexican
American and Anglo and we have a question relevant to the Scottish or British scene.

The viewpoint underlying Angel's question is that the educational system has norms and imposes them through certificates and
examinations etc. The issue is said to become a completely
practical one, of how to do something for those who are likely to
fail in schools. What the cause is, may be left unresolved. This is
where the Programmes for the Disadvantaged come in, or in the
UK the Educational Priority Areas action research.

The trouble with leaving causes unresolved is, of course, that it
just doesn't work. Unless the causes are known how can the effects
be changed? What can be done meaningfully for the disadvantaged child unless you know what is causing that disadvantage?
This is exactly where the language programmes have foundered
and where, so far as has been reported, the EPAs have also come
to grief.

What all language programmes have in effect done, is to compensate in some way for what is regarded as non middle class about
the working class. In other words to do that socially tainted thing
—intervene. Starting pragmatically they have accepted one or
other version of class differences and have attempted to compensate for this. We may guess that it is hoped that, working as they
do on disadvantaged children's language, the programmes will
have an effect on children's cognitive development.

For such a pragmatic approach it does not matter whether
language is merely the means to an end (development of cognition)
or the end in itself. What such programmes do, then, is accept a
view of class or other status differences and attempt some compensating action.

Practical Action in Language Programmes—USA
Many many language programmes have been assembled;
already in 1965 the National Council for Teachers of English
publication *Language Programs for the Disadvantaged* (Corbin and
Crosby) was able to detail a whole series of interventions. As we
have hinted, after the initial euphoria in the USA in the mid
1960s at the height of the NDEA period there has followed a
stage of scepticism. The reason for this is the lack of agreement

about what is intended, what is the criterion of desired performance, and what 'advantage' is. Baratz (1972) summarizes the kinds of approach by these programmes:

Speech and language programs have been devised that focused on the language abilities of preschoolers, elementary and secondary students, dropouts, and adult 'new careers' people.

The preschool programs are best represented by the intervention programs known generally as 'head start'. The programs were developed on a deficit model, and most program directors believed that they were teaching these children language (not a second language). These programs were generally of two types:

(a) Enrichment—here it was presumed that the language of the black child was underdeveloped due to lack of stimulation, poor mothering etc., and the program was designed to compensate for this. The children learned about neighbourhood workers, the friendly policeman, colors, nursery rhymes etc. The best of the middle-class nursery school was presented to these children.

(b) Academic—the now famous Bereiter and Engelmann approach. These intervention programs were not based on underdevelopment of skills but rather on a presumed absence of the skills. These programs attempted to teach the children language arts and mathematical skills through formalized instruction.

Since one of the avowed purposes of these early childhood intervention programs was to 'improve language skills' (tacitly defined in these programs as teaching the child to speak standard English), one would have to say the programs were a failure in that there are no data to indicate that following a preschool intervention program, these children were more proficient speakers of standard English.

While accepting the general gloom of this review, it does seem relevant to note that Baratz's equation of 'improve language skills' and 'more proficient speakers of standard English' is not necessarily acceptable. It all depends how that improvement/proficiency was assessed. It looks as though fairly standard tests of attainment were used in so far as any evaluation was carried out, and these are not necessarily valid tests of language skills 'improvement'.

Halsey (1972) in his description of the EPA plan raises the question of whether 'the whole (USA) compensatory education movement has not in fact been a series of "paper programmes" founded on inadequate assumptions and poorly articulated theory.' He maintains 'such programmes have set themselves unrealistic objectives. This problem is particularly marked where vague non-educational goals are put forward—for example "breaking the poverty cycle"; and in general, the more extensive and varied the programme, the more likely it is to have such objectives. Thus "umbrella" programmes such as Headstart almost inevitably become associated with broad objectives as a way of including the varied components of such programmes.' On the other hand 'the more intensively the programme is geared to such intellectual development as language skills, the more substantial the gains that have been achieved. The work of Bereiter and Engelmann is among the best known in this field, but several other research studies have shown considerable gains in children's ability at the end of the programme, for example the Early Training Project in Nashville, the work of Deutsch and his associates at the Institute for Developmental Studies in New York, the various pre-school projects run at Ypsilanti, Michigan, by Weikart and his colleagues, the individual tutorial scheme carried out by Marion Blank in New York, and many others.'

Halsey sums up the American experience in compensatory education as a movement that began with a specific educational problem and spread into a socio/political issue. Educational solutions were, it was felt, not enough.

Practical Action in Language Programmes—UK
The British Educational Priority Area scheme was intended to be an approach on a wider social front. 'All four projects were concerned to devise action programmes which would be effective in producing institutional change' (Halsey 1972). The Scottish project (in Dundee) had a similar intention. As part of their National Pre-School Experiment the EPA teams made use of the American Peabody Language Development Kit and concluded 'in general the PLDK groups improved more over the year on all three tests thus supporting the view that the PLDK assists language development' (Morrison, Swatt and Lee 1974).

Further experiments in the development of pre-school language kits are described in the EPA Report (Vol. 1, Chapter 8, Halsey 1972). The most fully described is the individual language programme used in the West Riding Project. What is particularly significant about this programme is that its effects tend to be maintained into the primary school. The individual language programme appears to make much use of face to face language contact between teacher and pupil in which the teacher uses questioning to help the child's thinking.

The conclusion of the EPA (Vol. 1) report on language is:

'there is a firm case to be made for extensive language programmes, but here again it is important that these are imbued with a high sense of social purpose, and that reading and writing are exercised on socially relevant material.'

The Dundee Project describes one such programme developed by the Project. Their programme may, they say, be viewed as a curriculum made up of smaller 'playsems' within larger themes. (Playsem is a coinage from play and seminar.) As far as we can see this is a situational type programme in which the purpose is to link context (e.g. the body) to relevant language items. Such a programme differs from a highly behavioural one of the Bereiter/ Engelmann type (known in Second Language circles as 'pattern practice') where there is no attempt at indicating situation. The Dundee conclusion, based on analysis of data from various standardized tests, including language ones, is that nursery schooling produces the most dramatic rise of test scores but that their language programme might well be able to achieve similar results much more cheaply. It is interesting, however, that in their conclusion the Dundee reporters make no statements about the need for or value of language programmes either in the pre-school or in the primary school.

Summary
Definitions of the linguistically deprived or the linguistically different must ultimately come from sensitive measures of children's language performance. The measures may then be treated either as indirect measures of the children's knowledge of the language code or of their knowledge of how to use language appropriately.

A large proportion of the work done in the area correlates a social measure, e.g. social class, with syntactic or lexical forms. This is legitimate if often uninformative. Conclusions, however, are often drawn which purport to make statements about the children's knowledge of language. This is unjustifiable if it is assumed that what children perform is all they are capable of performing. What they do perform is what they, with their own set of values and attitudes, judge to be appropriate.

Language programmes for the disadvantaged differ in the assumptions they make about what linguistic knowledge or skills are known by the group they set up as the target (or normal) group and the one which is said to need additional language training. We consider that it is not surprising that such programmes have fallen or are falling into disrepute since quite excessive and unjustified hopes have been placed on them as *the* answer to failure in the school. In addition we are without adequate descriptive tools to describe and hence compare actual language in use.

The emphasis, we feel, should be on both the study of normal language interaction and language programmes for 'normal' teaching programmes. What is needed is more knowledge of the range of skills possessed and practised by different groups of children in different situations before we can pronounce definitely on whether there is language deficit. However, we would not subscribe to the views of the (over-) committed difference supporters. The values rewarded by schools are the ones rewarded outside in society and in the absence of any revolutionary changes in society, maximum effort should be made to enable all children to gain equal benefit from the skills that the schools can offer.

II. ATTITUDES

Introduction
From what has been said about the differing values held by teachers and pupils, it may already be obvious that the attitudes of teachers towards their pupils and vice versa are crucial to understanding the extent to which learning is going on in any particular school. More than any other activity, learning is hard to force: there must be a willingness, if not eagerness on the part of the individual to learn, otherwise no amount of teaching of drills will change his behaviour easily.

Norms of Behaviour
In the UK, regional accents have all become in effect social accents. Regional dialects have been regarded similarly as socially inferior to some form of standard, in England usually a modified Received Pronunciation, in Scotland a Standard Scots (Speitel, in Davies 1975). It is simplest to use the term dialect to cover all such variations both regional and social and including accent. The fact that the variation may be lexical in the case of some Scots, accentual in the case of others and grammatical in the case of, for example, some West Indians, is irrelevant from the point of view of attitudes towards such variation. The attitudes of teachers and pupils to dialect differences remain important. In effect each

group or category may set up norms of behaviour and speech and recognize these as correct. Problems thus arise in schooling when the norms of teachers do not coincide with the norms of the pupils they teach, resulting in forcible attempts to impose what they consider to be 'good' or 'correct' English.

The pressures to conform or to refuse to conform come from the way that language is so frequently used as a way of demonstrating group membership. To change from a dialect form to speak educated Scots English may be interpreted as the abandonment of the values of, and identification with, the community one has been brought up in for that of some 'educated' elite. As Labov (1968) points out refusal to speak the language thought to be appropriate for school may appear unconventional to the teacher or the educational administrator but in practice may be following the norms set by a group of peers. A common way of speaking serves to give a group a sense of identity and a means of distinguishing themselves from other groups. Thus any attempt to describe the language of classrooms must take into account not only the range of the different code systems used by or available to the participants but also the social factors which determine the individual's view of what is appropriate language behaviour. Since communicative competence is what we are interested in then it is the social factors affecting language performance that must be examined in most detail.

Stereotypes
While it is possible to talk of 'norms' or attitudes attributable to groups of people as a whole, it is still necessary to account for the way in which these group norms affect the individual and his choices. Stereotypes are conventional pictures of how groups of people behave which may or may not have some truth in them. We all use stereotypes as a model for predicting the behaviour of others in situations where we have no personal information about them. Thus teachers may have a stereotyped picture of those who are 'too unintelligent to succeed' or pupils of middle-class teachers as posh and well-groomed agents of authority. Many such stereotypes are triggered off by the use of language whether through accent differences, grammatical or lexical ones. They remain extremely resistant to modification since they frequently affect the way that people perceive. Actions which confirm the stereotypes are noticed while actions contradicting them are frequently not noticed.

Lambert and his associates have produced a mass of experimental work in this area (Lambert 1972) which dominates the field. They have developed 'the matched guise' technique to assess indirectly a speech community's view of itself (or other communities). Speakers who can operate in two speech varieties found in a community record a passage in each variety. These samples are then mixed up and presented to a panel of judges drawn from the same community with a request to evaluate the voices on a number of scales, e.g. intelligence, self-confidence, good looks, likeability. It has been found repeatedly that the *same* speakers have been evaluated more favourably when using one speech variety than when using the other even though the judges were unaware that any speaker had performed in both varieties. In other words the way in which a person evaluates speech is a measure of his stereotype attitude towards the users of that speech.

Labov (1966) has tried to identify the particular features which serve as critical ones for a listener in differentiating a speaker's social status. Whereas in Lambert's experiments the variable that was changed was the speech variety as a whole, in Labov's work in New York he varied particular features in the speech, e.g. presence/absence of voiced/voiceless dental fricatives in words like *thing* (e.g. thing—ding—ting). He succeeded in identifying a limited number of features which appear crucial for the evaluation of speech in New York.

Williams and Naremore (1969a, b) and Williams (1970) examined forty children's speech tapes taken from the Detroit Dialect study. They found firstly that high/low social status was correlated with many of the linguistic indices of the samples, e.g. hesitation, pause phenomena, syntactic elaboration, non-standard characteristics and then that in turn these linguistic features correlated with judgements of status by teachers about the children. Thus they suggest that on hearing a very small portion of a child's speech a sterotype is elicited and *this*, rather than the detailed listening to the child, is then the basis for further judgements.

Roles
Often stereotypes are held about the way in which people playing certain roles should behave, e.g. teachers, headmasters, pupils. The assumption is, so to speak, that a group or society is made up of a number of sets of related positions, each of which is associated

with a role. In this approach the positions and the roles are independent of any individual who may fill them. The implication of this for attitudes of teachers to pupils and vice versa is of course that they see one another as role occupiers, i.e. as 'teacher' or as 'pupil' and not as individuals. More important from our point of view is that, as is well-known, role-simulating in the classroom seems both possible and efficacious in releasing pupils from the stereotype they cast themselves and others in. What this indicates in terms of pupils' language ability is that when they are able to break away from their own role bondage (admittedly into another's) they exhibit a far wider range of language ability, both speaking and listening than when they are only 'pupils'. It is always important to distinguish between what children do do and can do.

Pupil Performance

There is a wide measure of agreement that teacher attitudes are important in influencing the performance of pupils. A much-quoted book, *Pygmalion in the Classroom,* by Rosenthal and Jacobson (1968) reported that children who had been chosen randomly and who had then been pointed out to their teachers as 'spurters' did better and gained more in IQ than those who were not so chosen. Criticisms of the research have been made by Thorndike (1968) and Snow (1969). Other reports have indicated similar findings even though the proof cannot be considered conclusive. Thus Barker Lunn (1970) suggests that the fall-off in reading performance of children of lower social-class origin in comparison to that of higher social-class children might be partially due to teachers' lower expectancies for them. Burstall (1970) showed that the children who scored low in oral French after two years' French teaching were not randomly scattered over the whole sample of schools but concentrated in a small number where teachers expressed negative attitudes.

Rosenthal and Jacobson (1968) defined the self-fulfilling prophecy implied in the work above as ' . . . how one person's expectation for another person's behaviour can quite unwittingly become a more accurate prediction simply for its having been made.'

Much of this prediction is derived from the stereotypes associated with particular speech varieties which we have already mentioned. Williams (1970) puts it thus ' . . . in a situation (1) speech types serve as social identifiers, (2) these elicit stereotypes held by ourselves and others (including one of ourselves), (3) we tend to behave in accord with these stereotypes and thus (4) translate our attitudes into a social reality.' Speech thus can act as an index of the stereotypes that we had.

The general direction of the hypothesis from the use of speech to judge status, the influence of the judgement on the teachers' behaviour and the subsequent effect on the pupils' performance is borne out elsewhere, in part in Heider, Cazden and Brown (1968) and in Lawton (1968).

Lambert has addressed himself to the problem of the relationship between speech characteristics and the classroom in two articles. Frender, Brown and Lambert (1970), having controlled for age, verbal and non-verbal intelligence, found that lower class pupils who received better grades had a distinctly different speech style from others with poor grades, and concluded that 'how a child presents himself through his speech . . . may very well influence teachers' opinions and evaluations of him'. In 1971 Lambert reported on an experiment exploring the influence of speech style on the formation of teachers' expectations of pupil behaviour in relation to other cues such as appearance, drawings, composition. The results showed that boys with good voices were always evaluated significantly more favourably than those with poor voices, though other of the variables were also important, e.g. appearance. What is not dealt with in these studies is *how* teachers' attitudes affect students' performances.

Experimental Work in the UK
Experimental work in Britain on attitudes to speech has been rather limited. Strongman and Woozley (1967) asked university students from two different regions to evaluate Yorkshire and London varieties. Cheyne (1970) used both matched and unmatched guises of speakers of English and Scottish varieties and had them evaluated by judges in Glasgow and London. He found that the Scots were consistently rated lower on a social status rating. However, since there is little information about the actual dialect used for testing it is somewhat difficult to draw any useful conclusions about attitudes to Scots speech.

Giles (1970, 1971) experimented in a slightly different way by presenting twelve- to seventeen-year-olds from Somerset and South Wales with a wide range of accents and asking them to rate the aesthetic, communicative and status content of the voices that they heard. Unlike the previous studies he specifically asked for attitudes to be expressed about the accents themselves and not the speakers using those accents. Besides generally supporting the conclusions of previous works, his studies suggested that accent loyalty was also an important factor in determining the kind of judgements made. In other words people's judgements tend to differ according to where in the country they come from themselves.

One recent study which has touched on attitudes to language of both teachers and pupils is that of Macaulay and Trevelyan (1973). This is really a pilot study into a number of language related topics within the city of Glasgow. Interviews with a number of teachers are reported and extracts given. It is difficult to summarize any conclusions, but the kind of opinions sought were on whether or not schools should try to change accents, whether children liked the Glasgow accent or not, whether bi-dialectalism was associated with school/community differences, middle-class/working-class differences or just individual differences, the problem of lack of fluency and confidence in speaking.

Children's Attitudes
Macaulay and Trevelyan also quote from statements made by ten- and fifteen-year-olds about their attitude to different varieties of speech in Glasgow, but the main emphasis falls not so much on the school as on the likely effects for employment. The researcher who has placed most stress on the importance of pupils' values and attitudes in explaining the differences between performance in school and performance in the home or in the community is Labov. In his study of New York English (1966) he emphasized the importance of the peer group influences on a child's linguistic development, suggesting that from the age of entry into school the influence of the home and local community begins to diminish. Somewhere between the ages of five and twelve the influence of the peer group becomes dominant—which suggests how little time the school has for presenting its values as important where they are in conflict with a particular peer group. Both this study and the developments from it (Labov *et al.*, 1968) provide well documented evidence for the presence of linguistic norms which are quite contrary to those of the school middle-class society. Labov's underlying thesis is that there is no 'linguistic deprivation', no lack of intelligence on the part of speakers of Nonstandard Negro English, no lack of logic in the code of Nonstandard Negro English. He asserts that there is basically one reason why speakers

of nonstandard English do not copy the model of language that they are bombarded with both through the media and in years of schooling: not everyone subscribes to the values represented by the essentially middle-class environment. The evidence points strongly to the overwhelming influence of the peer group as providing an opposing and stronger set of linguistic (and other) norms. He shows for example that the adult population in Harlem mostly acknowledge the norms of the educated middle class even if they do not themselves use language in the same way. The linguistic influence of the home is thus much weaker than that of the peer group for a number of years. Reading failure in the schools is particularly attributed to this clash between the attitudes of children and the attitudes of the school. Labov's work in this area, as in so many others is rich in methodological suggestions and in hard data and is unequalled in its attempts to prove and measure the importance of attitudes and norms in affecting linguistic performance.

There is one example of an attempt to determine whether children in Scotland on entering primary school are able to perceive different accents and whether they use such information to make social judgements. Bratt (1974) found that the responses of five-year-old children to examples of different Scottish dialects differed from the responses of adult judges in that many showed no differences in their responses while others did perceive significant differences on the aesthetic dimension (i.e. whether they sounded nice or not). It would appear as if at the age of five children are only just beginning to make social evaluations based on speech variety.

Conclusion
We have tried to present attitude as a crucial factor in the school language situation. Two areas seem to us critical ones for research and relevant to the situation in Scotland.

The first concerns norms and correctness. Teachers' attitudes towards and responses to pupils' dialect and substandard forms are largely a matter of hearsay. What seems to us interesting is just how much correction of children's spoken language goes on in classrooms, how systematic it is, and how far it represents norms maintained in the teacher's own speech.

The second concerns the influence on speech of the peer group. This research is much more difficult to organize methodologically than the first but probably more important if our argument as to peer group influence is accepted. Role playing, role simulation, the use of video could all be used for such an investigation since what is necessary is to make use of the children themselves as informants.

III. DOMAINS OF LANGUAGE USE

Multilingualism is the norm in most societies. Yet at the same time in any stable situation there are strong conventions about which language or which dialect is appropriate to different 'domains' in the society. Thus frequently some particular domain (or area of social life) is associated with a particular language. This is most obvious in a bilingual situation where, for example, Punjabi or Welsh may be the sole language of the home and English the vehicle used for all contacts outside the home. The situation in a monolingual society (e.g. the one that most Scots live in) may not provide a vivid language contrast between home and other domains, but the contrast is no less real. Typically, the family is associated with one language variety (dialect) and the school with another. Where these varieties are associated with quite distinct domains of use, a speaker need have no difficulty in keeping the language systems apart.

One problem which arises from the identification of a language variety with a domain is the status of the 'variety' and the way in which it is or is *not* different from the language used in other situations. Some linguists have attempted to identify a number of separate 'registers' or varieties on the grounds that there are formal differences between them, and these differences are correlated with some signifiant factor in the social situation (e.g. Halliday, McIntosh and Strevens 1964). Thus in English the 'schoolroom register' is different from the 'legal register', is different from the 'scientific register' and so on. The effect of this approach is to represent the varieties as different linguistic codes in terms of grammar, etc.

A more fruitful approach to register differences is to regard them as being different uses of the same code. It is our view that English has a single common code and that different groups of people may use that code differentially for different purposes, that is language differs functionally as well as formally. Thus the same language may be used to convey information in some situations or by some people whereas in other situations its main function is to serve as a means of identifying someone with his reference group, e.g. family or peer group. Examples are difficult to provide here because children's peer group usage changes so quickly. Perhaps this school example will make the point: The teacher passes a pupil in the playground and says 'How are you?' which demands the response 'How are you?' in the teacher's peer group; but the pupil replies: 'Not very well today.' Such functional differences may well be much more widespread, as e.g., Bernstein has suggested in his later work, and may lead to lack of comprehension or just general muddle far more readily than differences in grammar, phonology or vocabulary.

The Home

Every educational report in recent years has underlined the importance of the home: 'one of the strongest threads running through much educational research is the general agreement on the important role played by the home in affecting progress and adjustment at school' (Newson, Newson and Barnes in Butcher and Port 1973). This being so, it is remarkable how little is known about the use of language in the home in a monolingual situation; it is assumed that in bilingual societies the mother tongue only is used at home—though the extent of bilingual switching at home is not well known.

The fact is that it is very difficult to investigate the language of the home. The home is no more uniform than the more professional domains, e.g. the church, medicine or the school are.

Furthermore, the belief in the potency of the home influence is already in question in view of evidence such as Labov's (1966 and see above) as to the superior influence of the peer group over all other influences for those at school. Hence, of course, the increasing interest in the home at the pre-school stage.

Bernstein and his fellow workers have reported on the influence in the home of the mother on the pre-school child. Robinson and Rackstraw (1967) for example contrasted the way that middle or working-class mothers of five-year-old children said they would answer their children's questions and reported that their findings bear out the restricted/elaborated linguistic code hypothesis. The middle-class mothers, it was concluded, were more likely to answer the question: to give more information and to give more accurate information than the working-class mothers. They were more likely to use compound arguments and analogies, and to give a greater variety of causal and purposive answers. Similarly Bernstein and Henderson (1969) report their findings that in terms of everyday tasks middle-class mothers 'socialize' their young children in more overtly verbal ways than do working-class mothers. It is concluded that as a consequence the working-class child learns skills in terms only of an undertanding of the operations they entail, while the middle-class child learns both the operations and the principles on which they are based. Bernstein is at pains to point out that his researches, especially these more recent ones on child-socialization, are concerned with *kinds of home* and *types of family* and not with such crude indices as social class; though, of course, his findings do correlate with social class. Cook–Gumperz (1973) has looked interestingly and closely at the home from this point of view and examined in some detail *how* young children are socialized by their mothers and reports that there are class differences between mothers' methods of social control in general and also between specifically verbal means.

Bernstein and his colleagues have posited two types of families, positional and person-oriented. The way each type trains its children in interpersonal behaviour is different and it leads to differences in their language behaviour and communication. Positional families (in practice mainly working class) train their children to respond to fixed status features (such as father, mother, age or sex of child) of the speaker or listener. In person-oriented families (equated to the middle class) the child learns to respond to the unique features of the speaker or listener. He is trained to react to the person as an individual rather than to his formal status. Person-oriented families use more verbal explanations and allow the child more opportunities to express himself in words than do positional families.

Other researchers have worked on the theoretical basis of Bernstein's ideas about the influence of the home on the language of children and their conclusions have sometimes been contradictory: Hawkins (1969) presented five-year-old middle-class and working-class children with pictures and asked them to tell a story. Hawkins concluded that the working-class child's use of language is context bound since the pictures would be needed to make full sense of the story while the middle-class child's story could be understood free of the context of the pictures. The

working-class child's language is full of implicit meanings while
the middle-class child makes verbally explicit his thinking about
the pictures. The middle-class child's use of nouns (boy, ball) in
preference to pronouns (he, it) suggests that there are possibilities
of expanding his structures through modification.

American reports by Slobin (1968), Baldwin and Frank (1969),
Phillips (1970) and Snow (1971) all point to a simplifying process
by mothers on their normal language use when talking to young
children. Mothers gradually make their speech less simple as the
child's speech becomes more complex. As Cazden (1971) points out
few people have actually collected data on the infant's language
environment. Friedlander (1970) has done so, analysing the
source of all utterances in the home directed towards the child.
Brandis and Henderson (1970) have stressed the importance of
the mother's attitude variable as against the social class variable
in terms of the mother's influence on the child's language proficiency. Wells's (1974) account of his research is methodologically
interesting inasmuch as it provides a fine sampling technique of
investigating a whole range of children's language use in the home.
What inevitably emerges from these studies (as from very many
others in the area of language acquisition tangential to this
report) is the obvious importance of the mother–child relationship
in the development of the child's language. This may be because
of what Friedlander calls the most intimate one-to-one encounters
between parent and child, such as the bath, dressing and feeding
(1970).

However, this relationship and the dominance of the home
begin to diminish as soon as the child starts school. It is not,
however, the school influence which takes the place of the home:
it is the peer group.

Peer Group
The rich verbal culture of the playground is revealed by Opie and
Opie (1959) who report on the verbal art of children playing
with words and rhymes. These rhymes are made up of new
sequences, the components of which are selected from existing bits.
Bernstein (1960) suggests that children's speech is essentially a
group possession and use of it forges a social tie between the child
and his peer group. The child is then made free to use the daring or
savage terms of this playground language since he is using it as a
member of the group and is not held responsible as an individual.
The Opies (op. cit.) conclude that in spite of the onslaught of mass

media such as television and film 'the oral lore of children remains traditional in form and content'. Creber (1972) points to the need for teachers to accept playground English since it 'is the language the children encounter in their home or street'. Labov collected speech samples from street gangs in Harlem including those of boys eight to nine years old. His main subjects, however, were older boys. Labov and his colleagues compared the language behaviour of Negro boys belonging to peer groups with that of isolated individuals who do not belong to any group (termed 'lames' by Labov) and with that of white boys of similar age and background. The interviews were recorded in situations which, unlike the home and the school, were free from the domination of adults.

To belong to a peer group means conforming to its rules and set of values and attitudes towards things like fighting, working, drugs, violence, family, etc., which may be totally different from those of the school. What is meant by 'good' and 'bad' values in a peer group is ingrained in its members, and to understand any verbal interaction, reference must be made to these values.

The dominant family structure pattern in the peer group studied was lack of a father as head of family. The absence of male authority may or may not be part of the reason for the power exerted by the peer group over other obligations.

Labov refers to the wide variety of verbal skills in the NNE (Negro Nonstandard English) community which seems to have developed away from the school and to be unknown to teachers. As with other values, the standards by which a person is judged as a good and skilful speaker are not the same as those which govern elsewhere, and developing a high skill in the vernacular is irrelevant to a boy's performance at school. Success in this street community is not connected with school learning. This may be partly a reason for failure to learn to read and speak in standard English, since good street speakers are not necessarily good speakers at school.

Labov states that in each group there are vocabularies and ways of talking which are specific to that group and which help to identify a particular speaker as belonging to a particular group. But the 'focal concerns' of all groups are similar—such as conversational topic and activity revolving around gang fights, the sentiment of 'all for one and one for all' and 'smarts'—the use of language and mental agility to excel over and manipulate others. In a way similar to the children from whom the Opies collected their data, Labov's subjects possess a rich, elaborate and highly-developed oral culture exemplified, e.g. by 'toasts'—long oral epic poems unknown in white society and 'soundings'—ritual insults, through which members display their skill and inventiveness.

The study of the language of the *lames* highlighted the difference of their language from the language of peer group members. Because they have been kept apart from participating in the street culture by parents or other elders, they accept certain values which peer group members reject. They are more open to adult influence and respond more favourably to school teaching or improvement programmes. Their grammar deviates from NNE grammar at various points and is closer to that of the white working-class boys studied in the project. Labov also reports that they resemble older people in that they, like older people, are abandoning certain NNE characteristics, in shifting towards SE (Standard English) patterns. They also show a greater awareness of the 'wrong' NNE forms judged according to SE norms. This was revealed in what are called 'classroom correction' tests, where pupils are asked to correct sentences written in NNE.

The peer group's hold on members relaxes with age. Throughout adolescence, learning of middle-class norms through exposure to formal education goes on together with the exposure to and the acquisition of SE forms. The classroom correction tests show a general rise in score with the increasing age of the students taking them. While being a fully committed member of a group, however, there is resistance to school and standards other than those that govern their sub-culture. Toughness and masculinity are associated with their vernacular and thus resistance to SE is greater in boys than in girls, and girls show better reading and general educational achievement than boys. This characteristic is also noted by others. Bernstein speaks of a marked difference between boys and girls in large working-class positional families. Girls are not tied to the 'activity-oriented, group-dominated peer group structure of the boys' and their language use is more individualized and oriented towards roles they play in the family, such as mothering or intervening between parents and siblings. The work on social relations in school referred to in Section IV (below) is relevant here, particularly Hargreaves (1967) and Nash (1973). Hargreaves concluded that while school values are essentially middle class, two pupil subcultures differed in their acceptance/rejection of these values. Nash reports similar results.

Bilingualism

Little need be said in this report on bilingualism, but we do wish to point out that the consistent findings that used to be quoted (e.g. Saer 1923, Jones and Stewart 1951, Lewis 1959) on the superiority in verbal intelligence of monolinguals over bilinguals are now attributed to the unsatisfactory nature of the samples used for these researches, the fact that the bilingual samples belonged typically to socially and/or economically disadvantaged groups or to groups (e.g. recent immigrants) existing in socially and politically unstable situations. As far as can be seen now, stable bilinguals who are non-disadvantaged belong to the same population in terms of IQ tests as monolinguals.

Peal and Lambert (1962), having reviewed the prior research, carried out an experiment which tried to contain all the errors that they attributed to earlier research. They tested monolingual and bilingual ten-year-old pupils in a Montreal school, all being from comparable socio-economic and home backgrounds. Their conclusions were that (1) bilinguals were better than monolinguals in verbal and non-verbal intelligence tests; (2) bilinguals had a greater flexibility of mind and superior concept formation; (3) bilinguals were further ahead in school.

It is to be expected that a bilingual will tend to use one language rather than the other in specific domains. One piece of research on this aspect of bilingualism is reported by Fishman *et al.* (1968), in a series of papers entitled *Bilingualism in the Barrio*. One report is relevant to us as the subjects were thirty-four schoolchildren in a Puerto Rican neighbourhood in Jersey City, USA, aged between six and twelve. The purpose of the research was to measure the degree of bilingualism, i.e. proficiency in the two languages and the relative use of each language in different domains such as school, home, church, etc. The assumption was that individuals are more proficient and likely to converse in one language than another depending on the contexts they find themselves in. The children were interviewed separately and each interview was tape recorded. Four domains were selected—family, neighbourhood, religion and education—and the children were asked (1) to what extent they would use Spanish and English with bilingual interlocutors in each of the settings; (2) to name first in Spanish and then in English within forty-five-second periods as many objects as they could think of connected with the kitchen, church, school and neighbourhood, these being taken as representative of the four domains. In the first test, the children reported using more Spanish in the home and neighbourhood than in the contexts of religion and education. The author concludes that the scores from the second test agreed in general with this result, the greatest difference in scores between Spanish and English words being in the domain of education and the least in that of family.

The implication of such 'switching' among bilinguals is, of course, that for them domains have a kind of reality, and switching helps to establish (for them and for the analyst) the boundaries between one domain and another. There is, indeed, a pecking order between statuses so that a 'headmaster' may be thought of as superior to, say, an uncle. If an African child whose uncle is also his headmaster switches from the home language to English when addressing the uncle/headmaster, then that is thought reasonable evidence for arguing that the school and the home are viewed by such a child as belonging to different domains.

Bidialectalism

In some areas of Scotland, mostly parts of the Hebrides, children demonstrate the vividness of language switching between the domains of home and school inasmuch as they are bilingual in English and Gaelic. But most Scottish children are not bilingual in this sense. They do, however, still exhibit similar switching between domains though in a less dramatic way, viz. between one dialect of English and another. Of course there are some homes (usually middle-class ones) in which this particular switching, as between the home and the school, may not take place, simply because for these children the language of *these* domains does not vary. It may indeed be that one effect of education is to make the child forget his home dialect. Bilingualism may survive education; bidialectalism may not. Of course most bidialectals, including the educated ones, do retain their capacity to switch for certain domains.

Studies of bidialectalism commonly report on the adverse effects of being bidialectal. These adverse effects may arise from mistaken ambiguity (e.g. Creber 1972) or from hurtful attitudes from the socially superior group to the others' language (e.g. Baratz 1969). Labov demonstrates in his work on NNE the logical equivalence of NNE and Standard English. At the same time the two dialects are kept separate, so much so that an expression in SE cannot be repeated word for word by a speaker of NNE (Labov 1968). Labov's conclusion is that NNE interferes with written SE patterns 50 per cent of the time, even though in oral-testing situations the use of SE is favoured. (Notice the effect of the oral-testing situation and therefore the argument in favour of gathering data in as naturalistic a situation as possible.) Labov also reports that his classrooms correction tests were valuable as a diagnostic tool in investigating how much interference is caused by dialect in the writing of SE. If a pupil does not recognize an error (according to SE rules) he will not hesitate to write it.

We recommend that the crucial area in which to develop research in the field of Domains of Language Use is the peer group. In view of Labov's highly suggestive language data or Hargreaves's and Nash's more sociological conclusions we maintain that this is a very important area to develop research work in Scotland. We know a good deal about classroom language and while we know little about the language of the home it seems as if we know almost nothing about group language and, more important, peer group attitudes to language and maintenance/shift of language. Further, it looks from the evidence as though in the top primary –early secondary years, the influence of the peer group—on language as on other values—is paramount.

IV: CLASSROOMS

The observation of school and classroom behaviour covers such a wide range of purposes and techniques that the results cannot easily be summarized. Perhaps the work can be grouped into three main categories on the basis of the main topics and interests of the researchers.

Social Relations in Schools

In Britain there have recently been a number of case studies of single schools. While differing to some extent in their aims and methods they have all been concerned with the analysis of social relationships amongst small groups within schools, and their effect on the schooling process. Hargreaves (1967), Lacey (1970), Ford (1969) and King (1969) have all made studies of schools in England. Hargreaves (1967) provides a good example of the kind of ethnographic description arising from this work. He spent a year as a participant observer in a secondary modern school and used a variety of methods of data collection—observation, informal chats, interviews, questionnaires, orientation tests, sociometric tests, and the analysis of school records. He gives a valuable description of the development of pupil subcultures emerging over time as a result of the interplay between the formal structure, e.g. class organization and the informal structure; pupil interaction and friendship patterns. The norms and values through which the school was organized were essentially middle class and it was shown clearly how two pupil subcultures differed in their acceptance/rejection of these values. Nash (1973) reports the result of similar work in Scotland observing primary schools and the initial changeover to secondary school. He uses the same range of techniques, and the theme that runs through his report is that teachers' perceptions of their pupils are closely correlated with the children's ability and behaviour. He showed that children were aware of how they are seen by their teachers even though classes were not streamed. He showed that the teachers normally saw their pupils in terms of their personality rather than their academic ability.

The interest of this work is twofold: firstly in its exploration of the clash of values (see below) within the school which may lead to pupils refusing to adopt the school norms and to use language in the way that teachers expect and secondly in its observations on actual classroom interaction and language use which are the first steps to an understanding of how teacher attitudes and judgements actually affect the performance of their pupils. It must be pointed out that these observations are not systematic in the sense of trying to attribute all verbal and other interchanges to a particular system of classification. They, like Jackson (1968), are a first attempt in Britain to bring a more anthropological approach to the school.

Interaction Analysis
Purposes: Unlike the previous approach, those who pursue what we may group together as Interaction Analysis are primarily concerned with trying to produce theoretical schemes for systematically analysing the verbal interaction between teachers and pupils. Interest in such work started in the USA in the 1940s and burgeoned rapidly during the 1960s. There appear to be four main purposes: (1) to describe current classroom practice; (2) to train teachers; (3) to monitor instructional systems; (4) to investigate relationships between classroom activities and student growth. The actual uses to which such descriptive systems have been put overlap but it can be seen that the majority are concerned with

providing a vocabulary and a measuring instrument which can be used to describe to teachers or would-be teachers either what should be going on in the classroom or what they themselves are doing and consequently how they may improve their techniques.

The number of observational systems which have been set up are enormous; an anthology of ninety-two systems is to be found in Simon and Boyer (1967, 1970).*

Perhaps the underlying aim of much of the work in the area has been how to measure the 'classroom climate' and compare this with an ideal climate which is currently thought to be educationally sound. Thus educational ideology currently holds that teachers should not emphasize their authority over their pupils by imposing their opinions, but should consider their role as one of providing the context in which children can learn themselves. Consequently many observational systems have been concerned with measuring what Flanders (see below) calls the ratio between the teachers' 'indirect and direct influence' as seen in the verbal interchanges in the classroom. From a similar ideological background come the enquiries into the types of questions used by teachers or the relative amount of time in which teachers and pupils are speaking.

Flanders' Analysis: A brief description of the scheme set up by Flanders (1960, 1970) will give some idea of both the aims and the problems associated with observing instruments of this kind. Forty-six hours' classroom work in Mathematics and Social Studies were studied. Observers were trained to code verbal utterances at three-second intervals according to a ten-item classification scheme.† The ratio of the number of tallies in categories 1–4 (Indirect Influence) to the number of categories 5–17 (Direct Influence) gave a measure of the teachers' kind of influence (I/D ratio), which could be used either to compare one teacher with another or the same teacher in different situations. He found that the I/D ratio varied according to the following factors: (1) subject matter being taught; (2) age and maturity of students; (3) the teachers' preferred style of teaching and (4) the nature of the learning activities. He went on to correlate the I/D ratios with student attitudes and achievement. His results showed that student

---

* See also: Amidon and Hough (1967), Sinclair *et al.* (1972), Weick (1968), Biddle (1967), Meux (1967), Kliebard (1966), Medley and Mitzel (1963) and Withall (1962).

† See table at foot of following page.

achievement is higher in the classes of teachers who used more indirect influence and that teachers who use more direct influence do not vary their behaviour in different situations as much as the 'indirect' teachers.

There are a number of points which should be noted about a Flanders type analysis:

1. The sampling of the interaction is done on a time basis and not on the basis of any structural units of classroom discourse.
2. The aim is to *measure* what might be called the 'classroom climate' (dominative/integrative, teacher-centred/learner-centred, direct/indirect influence, etc.)
3. Language is the measure used, in part because it is the aspect of the lesson that is easiest to record and to separate from other aspects of the total communication or interaction going on.
4. Language is not in itself of interest to the researchers and hence they tend to ignore the problems of assigning structure to the discourse and of relating the linguistic forms occurring to the meaning attributed to the interaction by both participants and observer. How pupils understand what is meant from the linguistic forms used is not discussed.

Other American Studies: Some observation systems have concentrated on particular aspects of classroom behaviour, for example the logical operations performed by teachers and pupils (Smith *et al.* 1964, Smith and Meux 1967) or modes of thinking (Taba, Levine and Elzey 1964). Yet others have had a purely descriptive bias, sometimes even attempting to describe quantitatively as much as

Teacher talk	Indirect influence	1. accepts feelings
		2. praises or encourages
		3. accepts or uses ideas of students
		4. asks questions
	Direct influence	5. lecturing
		6. giving directions
		7. criticizing or justifying authority
Student talk		8. student talk—response
		9. student talk—initiation
		10. silence or confusion

Flanders' Classification Scheme for Classroom Interaction

possible of what goes on in the classroom (Cornell *et al.* 1952, Medley and Mitzel 1958a, 1958b, 1959). Such blunderbus instruments are unlikely to be of much use in providing insights either into what is going on in the classroom generally or in the area of verbal interaction in particular. Survey instruments generally are of most use only when the items to be examined have been carefully chosen and their meaning or significance known.

One further American study is worth mentioning. Bellack *et al.* (1966) is the first attempt to try to provide a hierarchical structure of the lesson in terms of such units as *pedagogical moves, teaching cycles,* and *categories of meaning.* Their approach is to treat the teaching situation as a 'game' involving a number of players who can respond with a limited number of moves. Consequently the discourse of the classroom is seen as a combination of allowable moves. These pedagogical moves are defined by their function in total discourse and are called *structuring, soliciting, responding* and *reacting.* Utterances also convey meaning within the discourse and hence are analysed in terms of the kinds of meaning communicated.

Speech Functions: Bellack's work was done without the advantage of the recent interest in language functions. Hymes (1962) took up Jakobson (1960) and his analysis of the 'functions of language' and further developed it. They and many others since, were concerned in providing a typology of the purposes for which language was customarily used in differing situations and in differing societies. They used categories such as expressive, directive, contact, metalinguistic, contextual. Halliday (1969) uses a different set of categories (which do not exactly correspond to the Hymes-Jakobson ones) to describe the stages through which children pass in their use of language, e.g. instrumental, regulating, interactional, personal. This last typology has proved extremely stimulating to teachers and educationists.

Nevertheless it and other speech function typologies remain just that—typologies. As with all typologies in science, they can become more and more differentiated in a (false) hope of making them more precise. In other words a typology will *never* fit the real world exactly. They can be profitably used to bring order into an undifferentiated mass and they can draw our attention to opposing tendencies.

Some British Studies: While the speech function typologies of Hymes, Halliday and others have not been used as a means of classifying successive utterances or parts in a discourse into mutually exclusive categories, they have been used as either direct or indirect models for looking at classroom lessons and trying to analyse in what ways teachers and pupils are using language. Barnes, Britton and Rosen (1971), C. and H. Rosen (1973), Creber (1972), Barnes (1973) all subject the lesson to concentrated scrutiny in an attempt to get behind the form of the lesson to describe what is the function of parts of the interaction, e.g. teachers' questions. It would be fair to say that most of this work is aimed at descriptions of the 'classroom climate' but in a quite different way from Flanders and the other interactionists described above. Barnes's analysis, for example, deals with the analysis of: the teachers' questions into factual, closed/open reasoning, open and social ones; pupils' behaviour in terms of initiation of exchanges, types of response, understanding, etc.; the language of instruction in terms of the presence or absence of vocabulary and grammatical differences in differing subjects; the presence of examples of language outside the range of the children and so on. The method of most of this work can be said to be insightful observation and its aim that of drawing teachers' attention to the often unconsidered results of the way that they operate verbally in the classroom.

Speech Acts: Interest in speech functions arises out of awareness that language is being used differently in different contexts and that these differences cannot be gauged directly from the linguistic forms present. A different kind of approach to the same problem derives from the interest of philosophers and theoretical linguists and sociolinguists in notions of 'speech acts'. Commands and refusals, for example, are acts or actions, they are things that are done; declarations, interrogatives, imperatives, on the other hand, are linguistic categories, they are things that are said. Discourse analysis is thus concerned with analysing the rules which show how things are done with words and how one interprets these utterances as actions: relating what is said to what is done and vice versa. The theory of discourse analysis is in its infancy. The little work that has been done in this area derives mostly from studies carried out by sociologists (particularly of the ethno-methodological brand) perhaps because sociological, non-linguistic categories such as roles, rights and obligations have to be taken into account. (Cicourel 1968, Turner 1974, Labov 1970.)

This work is clearly related to the more impressionistic analysis of Barnes and others but differs in its emphasis on laying bare the rules governing the relationship between linguistic items and their interpretation as acts or actions. Children both need to and do acquire rapidly a set of such rules to enable them to respond appropriately to the teacher in front of them but little or nothing is known of this process. Both the developmental aspect and the systematic study and description of the rules underlying the interpretation of linguistic items merit far more work. The total absence of descriptions of the role of intonation and other paralinguistic features in defining speech acts is particularly noticeable and regrettable.

Overall Structure of Discourse: There is one further aspect of discourse analysis which should be mentioned. It is not enough to treat particular speech acts in isolation. That is, to understand what is going on in the classroom it is insufficient to describe the general rules which hold if an utterance is to be heard as, for example, a valid command. Classroom language is not made up of isolated utterances but can be considered to be structured discourse thus providing the context in which speech acts are to be analysed.

Sinclair *et al.* (1972) have carried out a three-year project aimed primarily at establishing what this larger structure of the classroom is and how it relates to the smallest meaningful unit, the speech act. They worked from tape-recorded lessons and set up a hierarchy of discourse units (defined linguistically not pedagogically). The highest was the lesson, which comprised a number of transactions, in turn comprising exchanges. These exchanges consisted of moves which were made up of a number of (speech) acts. With this hierarchy they analysed a number of class periods and came out with statements on the co-occurrence rules that operate with some of the types of units. What they have tried to provide is a tentative way of describing the customary structure of verbal interaction between pupils and teachers. Crudely speaking, each of the units and their realizations is defined in terms of how they can or cannot combine together to form a larger unit and how they are made up of different kinds of smaller units. The work is interesting but should be considered tentative rather than definitive, both in terms of its approach to discourse (one only of many) and in terms of its results.

It is safe to say that the study of classroom discourse has barely begun and it is an area in which research in Scotland could make a substantial contribution.

V. TEACHING MATERIALS

Materials used for spoken language instruction in the primary school are of two kinds: they are either to teach a skill or to remedy a fault. Since both have as an aim a notional language proficiency they are essentially the same thing.

Why Teach Spoken Language?

It follows that it is not very easy to distinguish between language programmes devised to remedy/compensate for disadvantage among some children and those of the more straightforward syllabus type designed to advance all children in a particular skill. Spoken language is a special case in that there is no consensus as to (a) what is the required skill and (b) whether children entering school already possess it. (Reading, on the other hand, is very different.)

We may ask whether there should be any general spoken language programme designed for all children. It is possible to find a few examples of special group programmes (and we are not taking into account programmes designed for children with physical defects, e.g. stammers), e.g. the Gahagans' *Talk Reform* (1970). This is an attempt by careful planning and daily practice to make more use of the classroom situation to exercise spoken language. It neither attempts the Bereiter–Engelmann pattern practice nor the other Headstart method of enriching experience. It simply brings in more daily use of the spoken language. As far as the results can be interpreted they suggest that the scheme works.

'Normal' Syllabuses

We might have discussed the Gahagans' work under our summary of language programmes for the disadvantaged, but it seems a useful link with 'normal' programmes. Frequently, normal syllabuses are often less explicit models of what goes on overtly in disadvantaged syllabuses. The Birmingham *Concept 7–9* (Schools Council 1974) is an interesting example of a programme that has itself made just that transition. It was designed as a language deprivation programme (for West Indian dialect speakers) but has come to be valued and used for 'normal' children. The only difference in other words between West Indian dialect speakers and 'normals' is one of speed in getting through the programme.

Language Variety

In the same spirit it could be maintained that what disadvantaged children lack is control of/knowledge of/skill in language variation. But it is also argued (see Doughty, Pearce and Thornton 1971) that this skill is exactly what 'normal' children also need. While there seem to be no programmes designed specially for the primary school as the *Language in Use* (Doughty, Pearce and Thornton 1971) materials have been for the secondary school, there are suggestions (e.g. Ashworth 1973) that such materials could be of value in the primary school.

Listening Tests

The Birmingham Oracy Project (Wilkinson, Stratta and Dudley 1974) on the other hand, was a research programme which had designated aims and was not, like *Language in Use*, a collection of ideas. The aim of the project was to investigate communication skills in speech and eventually concentrated on listening comprehension. The authors speak of 'the developing of an awareness of the features and functions of spoken language', and 'see the test materials as exemplifying features and functions of the spoken language which should be part of the knowledge of every teacher or teacher in training. The role of the (test) questions is then as pointers to aspects of language.' The authors maintain that the most important outcome of their research lies in the backwash effect of their tests rather than in the tests themselves. This is in line with the (official) Schools Council Foreword to the Report which is at pains to play down the test origin and rationale of the Project. From our point of view this is a pity. The fact is that, as the authors probably rightly point out, 'of their kind the tests would seem to be unique in the English-speaking world'. We consider the construction of such tests a very necessary contribution to the encouragement of the spoken language in schools. In themselves they do not contribute to teaching materials and what is now necessary is the development of materials for programmes in spoken language which will certainly benefit from the findings and use of these tests.

Reading

This is no place to discuss reading programmes, but it is relevant to note that the two best known programmes of recent years, i.t.a.

and *Breakthrough to Literacy* (Mackay *et al.* 1970), have both made deliberate attempts to take certain aspects of the spoken language into account, i.t.a. the sound-symbol relation and Breakthrough the wholistic nature of the sentence/utterance/phrase. There are arguments that reading materials do not go far enough to relate the syntax of the child's speech to the syntax of his early readers. Reid (1972) argues that the syntax of the written sentence in beginning readers needs to be closer to the common pattern of spoken syntax so that the child will be helped to move from one language mode to another. It is interesting that Shields and Steiner (1973) report a likely relation between working-class children's utterance length (at age three to five) and their slowness in acquiring literacy. Once again there is the classical correlation problem since while spoken language and reading may be related it is by no means clear that they are so in this experiment. More important is the argument about the crucial difference which persists through school between the functions served by speech and by writing. It may be that a deliberate manipulation of spoken language is needed in order to prepare children for the special functions served by writing.

Such materials as those in the *Language in Use* series are essentially examples of different kinds of texts. The choice of such texts is usually based on some kind of content analysis (i.e. what the text is about). Thus the onus is on the teacher who makes use of these materials to explain to his pupils why *linguistically* they are different. As far as we can see no help is given to the teacher to do this. Here, then, in these *Language in Use* materials we have an idea which is obviously fruitful for teacher training but not very far developed for the classroom itself.

Many Suggestions

It looks suspiciously as if we are left with spoken language materials for the primary school at an inchoate stage—many suggestions, few materials. Some suggestions even undermine the need for materials since their main point is that it is incumbent on the teacher and essential in the classroom to draw out spoken language spontaneously. Hence comes their opposition to the Peabody Language Development Kit or similar programmes, an attitude understandable in the normal classroom but much less so in the special case of a disadvantaged class. While writers such as Wilkinson (1971) and Ashworth (1973) suggest the working out of an idea like Halliday's function scheme sketched in *Relevant*

Models of Language (Halliday 1969), these are more properly suggestions for informing teachers in training with language descriptions rather than suggestions for the content of classroom materials. It may be that materials writers could make use of such suggestions as Halliday's (which has been widely quoted) as a way of arranging a language programme, but they would still be faced with the task of relating language forms in their programme to the various functions they regard as goals. Perhaps the most fruitful use of such suggestions remains at the suggestion stage, as a means of generating ideas in the teacher's mind.

Whatever may be said officially about the need for developing and teaching the spoken language in the primary school, it looks to us as though in practice speech is regarded as something that develops in 'normal' children without intervention. Hence the lack of speech programmes. Further, as we noted above, it is considered that speech can only develop 'normally' in the classroom by allowing it to happen spontaneously. We would expect all the effort therefore to be on creating and developing opportunities and situations in which speech can take place. What spoken language programmes there are for normal children are therefore of the *language variety* kind, rather like *Language in Use* (see above). The Oracy tests present a variety of demands in their assumed syllabus, but are not in themselves materials. The Gahagans' *Talk Reform* (Gahagan and Gahagan 1970) comes nearest to a syllabus but is intended for disadvantaged children. The only spoken language syllabus for 'normal' children we have found is *Teach Them to Speak*.

Shiach's language development programme, containing two hundred detailed lessons, *Teach Them to Speak* (Shiach 1972) is intended to help 'teachers develop the oral language skills of their pupils'. This is rarely done, he says and therefore his book is intended as a contribution 'towards filling this glaring gap (not just at primary level) in what is taught and learned in our schools.' Shiach assumes his programme will be equally suitable for a wide range of children, viz:

1. the normal class of first-year and second-year infants;
2. some groups of slower learning children . . .;
3. some groups . . . educationally subnormal;
4. some groups . . . severely subnormal;
5. partially hearing children;
6. immigrant children;
7. preschool playgroups and nurseries.

It seems unlikely that any one programme would be equally suitable for so many populations. What is disappointing about Shiach's book is that he follows his sensible introductory rationale with detailed lesson plans which seem more suited to developing written language than spoken language. He does emphasize oral grammar work but the content of that work seems unnecessarily sentence bound (i.e. by written language forms).

From the point of view of 'the best practice' the Rosens report that the primary school classroom today in England is a place where a great deal of talk of all kinds goes on (Rosen and Rosen 1973). Mrs Rosen indicates also the importance of the connection between such free talk and the process of beginning to read: 'the introductory stages are supported by talk'. In similar vein the Breakthrough team stress the importance of talk in assisting with reading, 'reading matter for children should, from the beginning, be linked to their own spoken language.' Certainly such a wholistic approach makes a great deal of sense as Tough (1973a) points out, but we are left wondering whether talk is just ordinary talk since it is clear that the best practice referred to by the Rosens does not take place in all classrooms. What seems necessary is detailed assistance with the kind of talk that is useful both for itself, for help with related activities like reading and for the development of the child's whole personality.

(The Bullock committee completed their report on all aspects of English after this Report was presented. Bullock, HMSO, 1975.)

Recommendation
Our recommendation for research in this area is not as direct as in some of the earlier sections in this report. Materials need to be firmly linked to some research area in attitudes, domains or classroom interaction. Indeed the production of materials in one of these research areas would be of immediate practical benefit since it would shape the research in an applied way. Of the topics we have touched on under materials the Oracy research seems of most interest. While it was not in itself strictly a materials project, it did produce measures which are very necessary in indicating areas and setting goals for syllabus construction. In particular these tests (still unpublished) seem from their preliminary description (Wilkinson *et al.* 1974) to make a start towards charting that unknown area of children's reception of the paralinguistic cues available in discourse (e.g. intonation).

Coda: Vocabulary

We have realized quite late, that there is a remarkable gap in the literature. It is not that we have missed it but that it is just not there. What is missing is vocabulary. It is as if researchers some ten years ago were so convinced by the argument that language is not only vocabulary—and so guilty that they appeared to have confused the two—that all work on children's vocabulary just came to a complete halt. Bruner (in Davies 1975) makes much the same point about the disappearance of vocabulary in psychological research. A useful summary of basic word lists was provided by Burroughs (1957) but only a year later Brown (1958) was sounding the death knell of vocabulary investigations: '. . . . the sequence in which words are acquired is not determined by the cognitive preferences of children so much as by the naming practices of adults.' It seems about time that this total embargo on vocabulary studies was lifted.

VI. CONCLUSION AND RECOMMENDATIONS

In this report we have attempted to draw together what we consider to be the main trends in research into spoken language in so far as it impinges on the primary school. Little work has been done on spoken language in the primary school itself and we have therefore used our own judgement in deciding which work in other areas is particularly relevant, for example by including the research into the classroom interaction in the secondary school while omitting the substantial work on language acquisition in the early years of childhood.

In making recommendations for future research it is as well that the most important of our assumptions should be made explicit. They should be recognized as being no more than personal prejudices (this constituting no grounds for either accepting or rejecting them) referring essentially to techniques of study and data collection. The most important of them are:

Replication of Studies

Research follows intellectual fashions and frequently results in massive replication of findings. Bernstein's early work and findings on the relationship between social class and linguistic forms used by children in (often) formal contexts has been repeated too many times to mention. Few replications have brought anything more than confirmation, with no further insights or explanations. Bernstein himself in the meantime has gone on to reformulate the whole hypothesis in terms of family types and sociolinguistic codes. Similarly the attempt to provide a coding system for sampling classroom interaction on a time basis has been repeated a myriad of times without any theoretical reformulation, the result being rather profitless.

Having said that, we must point out that many ideas currently being taken over derive from 'single-shot' research which has not been replicated in other situations and proved valid. Examples of this kind that we have discussed are Sinclair *et al.*'s classroom discourse and Labov's peer group work. In these instances what are needed are repeated studies in different situations.

Our view is, therefore, that the first consideration in mounting a research project should *not* necessarily be originality and uniqueness. Of equal importance is adequate (but not excessive) replication.

Case Studies and Surveys
It is necessary to consider two different strategies for tackling research in this area. Which is more suitable—case studies or surveys? On the one hand highly detailed analyses of limited situations with homogeneous groups may not yield results which can be generalized. On the other hand large scale investigations are liable to skate over individual or group differences and over contexts. Thus 'grand counts of linguistic features used by five-year-olds across a range of contexts each explicitly intended to encourage rather different speech styles . . . can obscure social class differences within contexts' (Robinson 1972). We agree with the conclusions that Robinson draws as to the advantages of case studies, namely that it seems safer to get to close grips with a strictly delimited problem using a homogeneous group of subjects and then collate both the problems and the ideas these suggest. We acknowledge that, if there are general laws governing the use of spoken language, then they will be manifested as much with a few subjects as with many. We feel that there are dangers in setting up a very large scale research project in this field at the present stage when knowledge is limited. A conservative piecemeal strategy is more likely to provide cumulative knowledge and less likely to result in disillusion at the limited educational pay-off which will follow. The survey can come into its own at a second

stage when it is wished to examine more widely throughout Scotland (or a part of it) the extent of a behaviour, attitude or problem.

Naturalistic Observation and Experimentation

Related to our preference for the case study approach initially is another preference for naturalistic observation where possible. Psychologists and social psychologists have traditionally operated experimentally by trying to limit the variables that they need to take into account. This can only be done by removing their subjects from their normal environment and putting them in a more or less laboratory setting. As our earlier discussion showed there are differences between what people can say and what they do say in particular contexts. Just as zoologists have recently made advances in the detailed and painstaking observation of animals in their natural habitat, so we are inclined to advocate more such studies in the use of the spoken language.

Relevance of Research in Spoken Language to Education

The lack of materials on spoken language is enough to make us question firstly whether there is any 'problem' of spoken English in the schools and secondly whether research will provide any answers. Our viewpoint can be summed up by saying that there will be no quick and direct pay-off from the research suggested to educational policy or practice. It is not yet clear if or how results could be incorporated into materials for the classroom. That said, the value of having information on the rules underlying spoken language and its interpretation for teacher-training purposes should not be underestimated.

Language Disadvantage and Normal Language

We do not regard the arguments in this area as profitable. We acknowledge that there are code differences and functional differences in the use to which the code is put. It is also true that certain linguistic skills are valued and rewarded at school while others are not. We feel that attempts to identify failure or deficit in the spoken language should not form the focus of research, at any rate in the immediate future. Knowledge of the range of linguistic behaviour and attitudes must come first.

Age of Subjects

We feel strongly that the answer to the educationists' quest for the causes of educational failure is not to be found by directing research at children of earlier and earlier years. Current theoretical interest in child language acquisition has led to answers about a child's language abilities being sought further and further back in his life. We maintain that most of the problems in the study of primary-school children's spoken language arise out of the development of their ability to use language appropriately in context. Research should therefore be directed at the primary school and at the changeover points: nursery/primary and primary/secondary.

Recommended Areas of Research

Teacher Prescriptivism: We recommend that research be mounted to examine the norms that teachers have about what language is appropriate for the primary-school classroom and the means by which these norms are conveyed to the children. Conflicting reports are received about present-day attitudes of teachers to Scottish dialects and accents. The work would therefore examine which particular features of the local variety are received unfavourably by teachers and the ages at which they attempt to impose their own norms. Such a study would combine an examination of attitudes to language and an observational study of classroom behaviour. It would not be dependent upon a full scale study of the local dialect usage first.

Initially work could be carried out in a limited number of schools in order to provide a number of case studies. As a second stage a wider survey in classrooms could be carried out to test the preliminary conclusions.

Children's Perception and Judgements of Accent and Dialect: In a related area further information would be useful about the development of children's perception and judgements of accent and dialect. Systematic information on the developmental aspect is quite lacking.

Children's Language Outside School: We have pointed out that for practical reasons there have been very few observational studies of children's use of language either in the home or in the company of their peers. Yet much unsupported discussion circles round whether children are being asked to perform verbally in a totally different way from the way they perform at home or with their peers. The little observation on the language of the home that is reported is on younger children acquiring language. Bernstein's work on the influence of the family requires fieldwork support.

Of more importance, if the work of Labov is to be supported, is the influence of the peer group. His pioneering work badly needs to be repeated. It can only be done by an anthropological type field study run in conjunction with linguistic work and this is a time-consuming task. However, research is the only way of finding out whether by the end of the primary school and beginning of secondary school the peer group is in fact more influential than the family in providing a rival set of norms and values to that of the school. We would stress the difficulty of the work and the long term nature of it, but feel it is essential if 'peer group influence' is not to remain an unknown quantity.

Classroom Discourse: Sinclair *et al.*'s research on the discourse structure of classroom interaction has been extremely useful but it can only be considered to be a first step towards a linguistic description. Further work along these lines in Scotland will be useful.

However, we suggest that an alternative strategy should be followed. The fundamental theoretical issue is how language function is related to linguistic form. It is possible to start the research at the opposite end from Sinclair and concentrate on investigating the rules underlying the way in which a particular speech act, e.g. command, elicitation may be realized. The approach advocated is essentially a narrow one in the sense that a series of limited problems can be chosen for study. While they are discrete in themselves the knowledge gained in tackling them will be cumulative and will provide a more solid base for future studies on the larger discourse structure of the classroom. In addition we feel that it is worthwhile to investigate the way in which children gradually acquire the communicative rules necessary for interpreting their teachers' linguistic forms correctly. Language acquisition has so far been studied primarily in terms of the acquisition of the linguistic code and little work has been done on the way communicative rules are acquired. We would further point to the advantages in making comparisons at cross-over points in the child's career. The nursery/primary-school changeover may be a particularly useful contrast to examine.

Intonation: One particularly important area connected with the above is the study of intonation and other linguistic and para-linguistic features in controlling the interpretation of speech acts. Little work has been done on the study of intonation in discourse and in view of its extreme importance we would strongly recommend further research.

Materials: We recommend that research into the production and use of spoken-language materials should not be mounted at this stage. We would like to see a link up between the researches outlined above and in-service teacher training with materials production arising naturally from that link. Of most significance is likely to be the discourse work on form/function relations, i.e. alternative linguistic means of expressing particular speech acts. This would link up with the work on listening comprehension tests already developed by the Birmingham Oracy Project.

Overall Strategy

We do not recommend that a single very large scale project should be set up, but that instead a somewhat more flexible approach be followed by funding a number of smaller but related research projects. If planned within the kind of strategy suggested here the results would be additive and it would be easier to get such research off the ground quickly.

While not being directly related to the topic of this report it is worth pointing out that the absence of any major systematic or published sociolinguistic work on language use in Scotland means that the background information for the research we have recommended is not available. However, research into spoken language in the primary school should not wait on this more fundamental work.

Summary of Recommendations

We recommend the following four research areas as being of most immediate relevance to the Scottish primary school:

1. Teacher prescriptivism.
2. The study of form/function relations in a narrow area, e.g. commands, with particular reference to their development from nursery to primary and primary to secondary school.
3. The use and interpretation of intonation.
4. An anthropological type study of peer group language behaviour.

Bibliography

NOTE

Titles which are followed by a code number and 'available from EDRS' can be ordered from:

ERIC Document Reproduction Service
PO Drawer O
Bethesda
Maryland 20014
USA

AMIDON, E., and HOUGH, J. (eds.), (1967), *Interaction Analysis: Theory, Research and Applications*, Addison-Wesley, Reading, Mass.

AMIDON, E., and HUNTER, E. (1966), *Improving Teaching: the Analysis of Classroom Verbal Interaction*, Holt, Rinehart and Winston, New York.

AMMON, P. R. (1973), *Syntactic Elaboration in the Speech of Lower Class Black and Middle Class White Preschool Children* ED 081 493 (available from EDRS).

AMMON, P. R., and AMMON, M. S. (1971), 'Effects of Training Black Preschool Children in Vocabulary Versus Sentence Construction', *Journal of Educational Psychology* **62**/5, p. 421.

ANDERSON, S., MESSICK, S., and HARTSHORNE, N. (1972), *Priorities and Directions for Research and Development Related to Measurement of Young Children* (Princeton, New Jersey: Educational Testing Service).

ANGEL, F. (1972), 'Social Class or Culture? A Fundamental Issue in the Education of Culturally Different Students' in Spolsky, B. (Ed.), *The Language Education of Minority Children*, Newbury House, Rowley, Mass.

ANISFIELD, E., and LAMBERT, W. E. (1964), 'Evaluational Reactions of Bilingual and Monolingual Children to Spoken Languages', *Journal of Abnormal and Social Psychology* **69**, p. 89.

ARNOLD, H. (1973), 'Why Children Talk: Language in the Primary Classroom', *Education for Teaching* **91**.

ASHWORTH, E. (1973), *Language in the Junior School*, Edward Arnold, London.

ATKINS, D. C. et al. (1967), *Preliminary Evaluation of a Language Curriculum for Preschool Children* Final Report ED 021 618 (available from EDRS).

BAILEY, B. (1968), 'Some Aspects of the Impact of Linguistics on Language Teaching in Disadvantaged Communities', *Elementary English* **45**, p. 570.

BALDWIN, A. L., and FRANK, S. M. (1969), *Syntactic Complexity in Mother–Child Interactions* ED 035 454 (available from EDRS).

BALDWIN, T. L., MCFARLANE, T., and GARVEY, J. (1971), 'Children's Communication Accuracy Related to Race and Socio-economic Status', *Child Development* **42**/2, p. 345.

BALES, R. F. (1951), *Interaction Process Analysis*, Addison-Wesley, Reading, Mass.

BAR–ADON, A. (1971), *Child Bilingualism in an Immigrant Society: Implications of Borrowing in the Hebrew 'Language of Games'* ED 061 809 (available from EDRS).

BARATZ, J. C. (1968), 'Reply to Dr Raph's Article on Speech and Language Deficits in Culturally Disadvantaged Children', *Journal of Speech and Hearing Disorders* **33**, p. 299.

BARATZ, J. C. (1969a), *Beginning Readers for Speakers of Divergent Dialects* ED 034 664 (available from EDRS).

BARATZ, J. C. (1969b), 'Language and Cognitive Assessment of Negro Children: Assumptions and Research Needs', *American Speech and Hearing Association* **11**, p. 87.

BARATZ, J. C. (1969c), 'A Bidialectal Task for Determining Language Proficiency in Economically Disadvantaged Negro Children', *Child Development* **40**, p. 889.

BARATZ, J. C. (1969d), 'Linguistic and Cultural Factors in Teaching Reading to Ghetto Children', *Elementary English* **46**, p. 199.

BARATZ, J. C. (1972), 'Educational Considerations for Teaching Standard English to Negro Children' in Spolsky B. (ed.), *The Language Education of Minority Children*, Newbury House, Rowley, Mass.

BARATZ, J. C., and SHUY, R. W. (eds.), (1969), *Teaching Black Children to Read*, Center for Applied Linguistics Washington, D.C.

BARATZ, S. S., and BARATZ, J. C. (1970), 'Early Childhood Intervention: the Social Science Base of Institutional Racism', *Harvard Educational Review* **40**, p. 29.

BARKER-LUNN, J. C. (1970), *Streaming in the Primary School*, National Foundation for Educational Research in England and Wales, Slough.

BARNES, D. (1969), 'Language in the Secondary Classroom' in Barnes, D., Britton, J., and Rosen, H. *Language, The Learner and the School*, Penguin, Harmondsworth.

BARNES, D. (1971), 'Classroom Contexts for Language and Learning in "The Context of Language" ', *Educational Review*, Birmingham.

BARNES, D. (1973), *Language in the Classroom*, Educational Studies: a Second Year Course, E262: Language and Learning, Block 4, Open University.

BARNES, D., BRITTON, J., and ROSEN H. (1971), *Language, the Learner and the School*, Rev. Ed., Penguin, Harmondsworth.

BAVERY, E. A. (1968), *A Study of Selected Aspects of Oral and Written Language of Fifth Grade Pupils* ED 033 959 (available from EDRS).

BELLACK, A. A. (Ed.), (1963), *Theory and Research in Teaching*, Teachers College Press, Columbia University.

BELLACK, A. A., *et al.* (1966), *The Language of the Classroom*, Teachers College Press, Columbia University.

BEM, S. (1970), 'The Role of Comprehension in Children's Problem Solving', *Developmental Psychology* **2**, pp. 351–8.

BENNETT, J. V. *et al.* (1972), *Research Report on Some Effects of an Experimental Language Development Program on the Performance of Aboriginal Children in their First Year at School* ED 074 857 (available from EDRS).

BENTAL, L. M. (1972), 'Language Difficulties in Teaching Mathematics', *Forward Trends* **16**, p. 98.

BEREITER, C. (1965), 'Academic Instruction and Preschool Children' in Corbin, R., and Crosby, M. (eds.) *Language Programs for the Disadvantaged*, Champaign, Ill.: National Council of Teachers of English.

BEREITER, C., and ENGELMANN, S. (1966), *Teaching Disadvantaged Children in the Preschool*, Prentice-Hall, New Jersey.

BEREITER, *et al.* (1966), 'An Academically Oriented Preschool for Culturally Deprived Children' in Hechinger, F. M. (ed.) *Preschool Education Today*, 1966, Doubleday, Garden City, N.Y.

BERGER, P. L., and LUCKMANN, T. (1966), *The social Construction of Reality*, Allen Lane, Penguin Books.

BERLIN, B., and KAY, P. (1970), *Basic Color Terms*, University of California Press, Berkeley.

BERNSTEIN, B. (1960), 'A Review of the Lore and Language of Children' by Opie, I., and Opie, P., in Bernstein, B. *Class, Codes and Control*, Vol. I, Routledge and Kegan Paul, 1971, London.

BERNSTEIN, B. (1961a), 'Social Class and Linguistic Development: a Theory of Social Learning' in Halsey, A. H., Floud, J., and Anderson, C. A. (eds.), *Economy, Education and Society*, Free Press of Glencoe.

BERNSTEIN, B. (1961b), 'Social Structure. Language and Learning', *Educational Review* **3**, p. 163.

BERNSTEIN, B. (1964), 'Elaborated and Restricted Codes: Their Social Origins and Some Consequences', *American Anthropologist* **66**:6/2, p. 55.

BERNSTEIN, B. (1969), 'A Critique of the Concept of Compensatory Education' in Rubenstein, D., and Stoneman, C., *Education for Democracy*, Penguin, Harmondsworth.

BERNSTEIN, B. (1970a), 'Education Cannot Compensate for Society', *New Society* **26** (Feb), p. 344.

BERNSTEIN, B. (1970b), 'Social Class, Language and Socialisation' in Giglioli, Pier Paolo (ed.), *Language and Social Context* Penguin, Harmondsworth.

BERNSTEIN, B. (1971), *Class, Codes and Control*, Vol. 1, Routledge and Kegan Paul, London.

BERNSTEIN, B. (ed.), (1973), *Class, Codes and Control*, Vol. 2, Routledge and Kegan Paul, London.

BERNSTEIN, B. (1976), *Class, Codes and Control*, Vol. 3, Routledge and Kegan Paul, London.

BERNSTEIN, B. and BRANDIS, W. (1970), 'Social Class Differences in Communication and Control in Brandis W., and Henderson D., *Social Class, Language and Communication*, Routledge and Kegan Paul, London.

BERNSTEIN, B., and HENDERSON, D., (1969), 'Social Class Differences in the Relevance of Language to Socialization' in Bernstein, B. (ed.), *Class, Codes and Control*, Vol. 2, Routledge and Kegan Paul, London, 1973.

BERNSTEIN, B. and YOUNG, D. (1967), 'Social Class Differences in the Conceptions of the Uses of Toys' in *Sociology*, 1 no. 2, May, and in Brandis W., and Henderson D., op cit (1970).

BEVER, T. (1970), 'The Cognitive Basis of Linguistic Structures', in J. R. Hayes (ed.), *Cognition and the Development of Language*, New York, Wiley.

BIDDLE, B. J. (1967), 'Methods and Concepts in Classroom Research', *Review of Educational Research* 37/3, p. 337.

BLANK, M., and SOLOMON, F. (1968), 'A Tutorial Language Programme to develop Abstract Thinking in Socially Disadvantaged Pre-School Children', *Child Development* 39, p. 379.

BLANK, M., and SOLOMON, F. (1969), 'How Shall the Disadvantaged be Taught?', *Child Development* 40, p. 47.

BLOOM, L. (1970), *Language Development: Form and Function in Emerging Grammars*, M.I.T. Press, Cambridge, Mass.

BLOOM, L., (1971), 'Why Not Pivot Grammar?', *Journal of Speech and Hearing Disorders* 36, pp. 40–50.

BLOOM, L. M. (1973), *One word at a time*, Mouton, The Hague.

BOGGS, S. T. (1969), *Language Use in the Classroom* Final Report ED 038 419 (available from EDRS).

BOWERMAN, M. (1973), *Early syntactic development*, Cambridge University Press.

BOWLBY, E. J. M. (1969), *Attachment and Loss*, Vol. I: *Attachment;* Vol. II: *Separation: Anxiety and Anger*, Hogarth Press and Institute of Psychoanalysis.

BRAINE, M. (1971), 'The Acquisition of Language in Infant and Child' in C. Reed (ed.), *The Learning of Language*, Appleton-Century-Crofts, New York.

BRANDIS, W., and HENDERSON, D. (1970), *Social Class, Language and Communication*, Routledge and Kegan Paul, London.

BRATT, M. F. (1974), *Evaluative Reactions to Speech Varieties in five-year-old Children*, M. Litt, Thesis, University of Edinburgh.

BRITTON, J. (1970), *Language and Learning*, Penguin, Harmondsworth.

BRITTON, J. (1973), 'Schools and the Mother Tongue', *Ideas* 24.

BROTTMAN, M. A. (Ed.), (1968), *Language Remediation for the Disadvantaged Preschool Child*, Monographs of the Society for Research in Child Development 33 (8, whole No. 124).

BROWN, G. (1976), Discussion of Spiegel's Paper on 'Dialect' in Davies, A., (ed.) *Problems of Language and Learning*, Heinemann, London.

BROWN, R. (1958), 'How Shall a Thing be Called?', *Psychological Review* **65,** p. 14.

BROWN, R. (1968), 'The Development of Wh-Questions in Child Speech', *Journal of Language and Learning*, Heinemann, London.

BROWN, R. (1973), *A First Language*, Allen & Unwin, London.

BROWN, R., and BELLUGI, U. (1964), 'Three processes in the Acquisition of Syntax', *Harvard Educational Review* **34,** 133–51.

BROWN, R., CAZDEN, C., and BELLUGI, U. (1968), 'The Child's Grammar from 1 to 3' in J. P. Hill (ed.) *Minnesota Symposia on Child Psychology*, Vol. 2, University of Minnesota Press. Minneapolis.

BRUNER, J. (1971), *The Relevance of Education*, George Allen & Unwin, London.

BRUNER, J. (1975), 'Language as an Instrument of Thought' in Davies, A., (ed.) *Problems of Language and Learning*, Heinemann, London.

BRYNGELSON, B., and GLASPEY, E. (1962), *Speech in the Classroom*, Scott, Foresman, Chicago.

BRYSON, J., and Stern, C. (1969), *Competence versus Performance in Young Children's Use of Complex Linguistic Structures* ED 029 687 (Available from EDRS).

BULLOCK, A., (1975), *A Language for Life:* Report of the Committee of Inquiry appointed by the Secretary of State for Education and Science (H.M.S.O.).

BURNISTON, C. (1962), *What is Spoken English? Can It Be Examined in General Education?*, English Speaking Board, London.

BURNISTON, C. (1968), *Creative Oral Assessment: Its Scope and Stimulus*, Pergamon Press, London.

BURROUGHS, G. E. R. (1957), *A Study of the Vocabulary of Young Children*, University of Birmingham, School of Education.

BURSTALL, C. (1970), 'French in the Primary School: Some Early Findings', *Journal of Curriculum Studies* 2/1, p. 48.

BUTLER, J. (1973), 'Toward a New Cognitive Effects Battery for Project Headstart'. Paper prepared for the U.S. Office of Child Development under contract with the Rand Corporation, October 1973.

CAIRNS, R. T. (1973), 'The Nature of the Slow Learner', *Teaching English*.

CAMPBELL, R., and WALES, R., (1970), 'The study of Language Acquisition' in J. Lyons (ed.), *New Horizons in Linguistics*, Penguin, Harmondsworth.

CANE, B., and SMITHERS, J. (1971), *The Roots of Reading*, National Foundation for Educational Research in England and Wales.

CARPENTER, S. (1974), 'The Mother's Face and the Newborn', *New Scientist* **61**, p. 890, 21 March 1974.

CARTER, H. (1974), 'Reading and Writing, Talking and Listening' in *Dialogue*, School Council Newsletter 17 (Schools Council).

CARTER, J. L. (1967), *The Long Range Effects of a Language Stimulation Program upon Negro Educationally Disadvantaged First Grade Children* Final Report ED 013 276 (available from EDRS).

CASHDAN, A. *et al.*, (1972), *Language in Education: A Source Book*, Routledge and Kegan Paul, London.

CAZDEN, C. B. (1965), *Environmental Assistance to the Child's Acquisition of Grammar* (Doctoral Dissertation, Harvard University).

CAZDEN, C. B. (1966), 'Subcultural Differences in Child Language: an Inter-disciplinary Review', *Merrill–Palmer Quarterly* **12**, p. 185.

CAZDEN, C. B. (1968a), 'The Acquisition of Noun and Verb Inflections', *Child Development* **39**, p. 433.

CAZDEN, C. B. (1968b), 'Some Implications of Research on Language Development for Preschool Education' in Hess, R. D., and Bear, R. M. (ed.), *Early Education*, Aldino, Chicago.

CAZDEN, C. B. (1970a), *Language Programs for Young Children: notes from England and Wales* ED 040 763 (available from EDRS).

CAZDEN, C. B. (1970b), 'The Neglected Situation in Child Language Research and Education', in Williams, F. (ed.) *Language and Poverty*, Markham, Chicago.

CAZDEN, C. B. (1971), 'Evaluating Language Learning in Early Education' in Bloom, B. S., Hastings, T., and Madaus, C. (eds.), *Handbook on Formative and Summative Evaluation of Student Learning*, McGraw-Hill, New York. pp. 345–98.

CAZDEN, C. B. (1972a), *Child Language and Education*, Holt, Rinehart and Winston, New York.

CAZDEN, C. B. (ed.), (1972b), *Language in Early Childhood Education*, National Association for the Education of Young Children, Washington, D.C.

CAZDEN, C. B. (1972c), Review of M. H. Moss: *Test of Basic Experience* (*TOBE*), Monterey, Cal., CTB/McGraw-Hill, 1970 in Buros, O. K. (ed.), *The Seventh Mental Measurements Yearbook*, Vol. I, Gryphon Press, Highland Park, N. J., pp. 33–4.

CAZDEN, C. B. (1972d), 'Some Questions for Research in Early Childhood Education' in Stanley, J. C. (Ed.), *Preschool Programs for the Disadvantaged: Five Experimental Approaches to Early Childhood Education*, The Johns Hopkins Press, Baltimore, pp. 188–99.

CAZDEN, C. B. (1973), 'Problems for Education: Language as Curriculum Content and Learning Environment', Daedalus, Summer, pp. 135–48.

CAZDEN, C. B. (1974), 'Two Paradoxes in the Acquisition of Language Structure and Functions' in Bruner, J. S., and Connolly, K. J. (eds.), *The Development of Competence in Early Childhood*, Academic Press, New York.

CAZDEN, C. B., and BARTLETT, E. (1973), Review of Gahagan, D. M., and Gahagan, G. A., *Talk Reform: Explorations in Language for Infant School Children*, Sage Publications, Beverly Hills, Cal., 1970, in *Language in Society* 2, pp. 147–60.

CAZDEN, C. B., JOHN, V. P., and HYMES, D. (eds.) (1972), *The Functions of Language in the Classroom*, Teachers College Press, New York.

CHAZAN, M., COX, T., JACKSON, S., and LAING, A. F. (in press), *Studies of Infant School Children*, Vol. 2—Deprivation and Development, Basil Blackwell, Oxford (for Schools Council).

CHEYNE, W. M. (1970), 'Stereotyped Reactions to Speakers with Scottish and English Regional Accents', *British Journal of Social and Clinical Psychology* 9, p. 77.

CHOMSKY, N. (1957), *Syntactic Structures*, Mouton, The Hague.

CHOMSKY, N. (1965), *Aspects of the Theory of Syntax*, M.I.T. Press, Cambridge, Mass.

CHOMSKY, C. (1972), 'Stages in Language Development and Reading Exposure', *Harvard Educational Review* 42, pp. 1–33.

CICIRELLI, V. et al., (1969), *The Impact of Head Start: an Evaluation on the Effects of Head Start on Children's Cognitive and Effective Development*. Vols. I and II, Westinghouse Learning Corp, Bladensburg, Md.

CICOUREL, A. V. (1968), 'The Acquisition of Social Structure: towards a Developmental Sociology of Language and Meaning' in Douglas, J. (ed.), *Understanding Everyday Life*, Routledge and Kegan Paul, London.

CICOUREL, A. V. (1973), *Cognitive Sociology*, Penguin, Harmondsworth.

CLARK, R., HUTCHESON, S., and VAN BUREN, P. (1974), 'Comprehension and Production in Language Acquisition', *Journal of Linguistics* 10/1, p. 39.

CLARK, E. (1970), 'How Young Children Describe Events in Time', in Flores d'Arcais, G., and Levelt W. (Eds.), *Advances in Psycholinguistics* North Holland, Amsterdam.

CLARK, E. (1973), 'What's in a Word? On the Child's Acquisition of Semantics in his First Language', in Moore T. (ed.), *Cognitive Development and the Acquisition of Language*, Academic Press, New York.

CLARK, MARGARET (1975), 'Language and Reading: Research Trends' in Davies, A. (ed), *Problems of Language and Learning*, Heinemann, London.

CLARK, R. (1974), 'Performing without Competence', *J. Child Language* 1, pp. 1–10.

CLAYPOLE, B. (1966), 'Developments in the Testing of Spoken English within the State School Educational System', *Speech and Drama*, Autumn,

COHEN, D. (1968), 'Children and their Primary Schools', *Harvard Educational Review* 38, p. 329.

COHN, W. (1967), 'On the Language of Lower Class Children' in Keach, E. T., Fulton, R., and Gardner, W. E. (eds.), *Education and Social Crisis*, Wiley, New York.

CONVILLE, M. P. (1969), 'Language Improvement for Disadvantaged Elementary School Youngsters', *Speech Teacher* **18**, p. 120.

COOK, J. (1971), *An Inquiry into Patterns of Communication and Control Between Mothers and their Children in Different Social Classes*, Ph.D. Thesis, University of London.

COOK-GUMPERZ, J. (1973), *Socialization and Social Control: a Study of Social Class Differences in the Language of Maternal Control*, Routledge and Kegan Paul, London.

CORBIN, R, and CROSBY, M., *Language Programs for the Disadvantaged*, National Council of Teachers of English, Champaign, Ill.

CORNELL, F. G., LINDVALL, C. M., and SAUPE, J. L. (1952), *An Exploratory Measurement of Individualities of Schools and Classrooms*, Bureau of Educational Research, University of Illinois, Urbana.

COSIN, B. *et al.*, (1971), *School and Society*, Routledge and Kegan Paul, London.

COULTHARD, R. M., and ROBINSON, W. P. (1968), 'The Structure of the Nominal Group and Elaboratedness of Code', *Language and Speech* **11**/4, p. 234.

COWE, E. G. (1967), *A Study of Kindergarten Activities for Language Development* ED 030 659 (available from University Microfilms, A Xerox Co, 300 N. Zeeb Road, Ann Arbor, Michigan 48103).

CREBER, J. W. P. (1972), *Lost for Words: Language and Educational Failure*, Penguin, Harmondsworth.

CREBER, J. W. P. (1973), 'Language Difficulties, an Introduction', *English in Education* **7**/2.

DALE, P. S., and KELLY, D. (1972), *Language Use and Social Setting: a Suggestion for Early Education* ED 071 757 (available from EDRS).

DAVIES, A. (ed.), (1975), *Problems of Language and Learning*, Heinemann, London.

DAVIS, A. (1965), *Social Class Influence upon Learning*, Harvard University Press, Cambridge, Mass.

DE LAGUNA, G. (1927), *Speech: Its Function and Development*, Indiana University Press, Bloomington, Ind.

DE VILLIERS, P., and DE VILLIERS, J. (1972), 'Early Judgements of Semantic and Syntactic Acceptability by Children', *Journal of Psycholinguistic Research* **1**, pp. 299–310.

DENNER, B. (1970), 'Representational and Syntactic Competence of Problem Readers', *Child Development* **41**/3, p. 881.

DEPARTMENT OF EDUCATION AND SCIENCE (1972), *Education: A Framework for Expansion (Command 5174)*, (London: H.M.S.O.).

DESTEFANO, J. S. (1972), *Some Parameters of Register in Adult and Child Speech* ED 077 022 (available from EDRS).

DEUTSCH, M. *et al.* (1964), 'Communication of Information in the Elementary School Classroom', Institute for Developmental Studies, New York Medical College.

DEWART, M. (1972), 'Social Class and Children's Understanding of Deep Structure in Sentences', *British Journal of Educational Psychology* **42**, p. 198.

DICKIE, J. P. (1968), 'Effectiveness of Structured and Unstructured (traditional) Methods of Language Training' in Brottman, M. A. (ed.) *Language Remediation for the Disadvantaged Preschool Child*, Monographs of the Society for Research in Child Development 33 (8, Whole No. 124).

DONALDSON, M. (1972), *Cognitive Development in Preschool Children, Comprehension of Quantifiers*, Final Report to S.S.R.C.

DONALDSON, M., and BALFOUR, G. (1968), 'Less is More: a study of Language Comprehension in Children', *British Journal of Psychology* **59**, pp. 461–472.

DONALDSON, M., and LLOYD, P. (1971), 'Sentence and Situations: Children's Judgements of Match and Mismatch'. Paper presented at Psycholinguistics conference, Paris.

DONALDSON, M., and WALES, R. (1970), 'On the Acquisition of some Relational Terms' in J. Hayes (ed.), *Cognition and the Development of Language*, Wiley, New York.

DOOLITTLE, M. T. (1968), *A Survey of Teacher Practices and Preferences Related to Oral Language Instruction in the Public Elementary Schools of West Virginia* (available from University Microfilms, 300 N. Zeeb Road, Ann Arbor, Michigan, 48106).

DOUGHERTY, M. S. (1971), *A Comparison of Oral Language Patterns of Two Groups of Selected First Grade Negro Children as Measured by Loban's Analysis Techniques* (available from University Microfilms, Dissertation Copies, Post Office Box 1764, Ann Arbor, Michigan 48106).

DOUGHTY, P. S., PEARCE, J. J., and THORNTON, G. M. (1971), *Language in Use*, Edward Arnold, London.

DOUGHTY, P., and THORNTON, G. (1973), *Language Study, the Teacher and the Learner*, Edward Arnold, London.

DOUGLAS, J. W. B. (1964), *The Home and the School*, MacGibbon and Kee, London.

DOWNING, J. (1968), 'The Implications of Research on Children's Thinking for the Early Stages of Learning to Read' in Douglass, M. P. (ed.), *Claremont Reading Conference 32nd Yearbook*, Claremont University Center.

DOWNING, J. (1969), 'Children's Concepts of Language in Learning to Read', *Educational Research* **12**, p. 106.

DUNN, HORTON and SMITH (1968), The Peabody Language Development Kits', American Guidance Service, Circle Pines, Minn.

EDELMAN, M. (1968), 'The Contextualisation of Schoolchildren's Bilingualism' in Fishman, J. A., et al. (eds.) *Bilingualism in the Barrio*, U.S. Department of Health, Education and Welfare 525–537.

EDUCATIONAL TESTING SERVICE (1973) *Circus: Comprehensive Assessment in Nursery School and Kindergarten*. Proceedings of a symposium presented at the American Psychological Association Convention, Montreal, Quebec, 21 August, 1973.

EMIAS, P., SIQUELAND, E., JUZCZYK, P., and VIGORITO, J. (1972), Speech Perception in infants, *Science* **171**, 303–306.

ENGELMANN, S., OXBORN, J., and ENGELMANN, T. (1969), *Distar Language*, I, Science Research Associates Chicago.

ENTWISTLE, D. R., and GARVEY, C. (1972), 'Verbal Productivity and Adjective Usage', *Language and Speech* **15**/3, p. 288.

ENTWISTLE, D. R. and GREENBERGER, E. (1968), *Differences in the Language of Negro and White Grade-School Children* **1**, 2 ED 019 676 (available from EDRS).

ERIC (1968), *Early Childhood Selected Bibliographies Series Number 2 Language* ED 022 538 (available from EDRS).

ERIC (1968), *Language Development in Disadvantaged Children: an annotated bibliography* ED 026 414 (available from EDRS).

EVERTTS, E. L. (ed.) (1967), *Dimensions of Dialect* ED 030 632 Champaign, Ill. National Council of Teachers of English.

FEATHERSTONE, H., 'Assessing Language Development among Headstart Children'. Paper prepared for the U.S. Office of Child Development under contract with Rand Corporation, November 1973.

FELDMAN, C.' and SHEN, M. (1969), *Some Language-Related Cognitive Advantages* of Bilingual Five Year Olds ED 031 307 (available from EDRS)

FINDLEY, W. G. (1964), 'Language Development and Dropouts' in Schreiber, D. (ed.) *The School Dropout*, National Education Association, Washington, D.C.

FISHBEIN, H. D., and OSBORN, M. (1971), 'The Effects of Feedback Variation on Referential Communication in Children, *Merril Palmer Quarterly*, **13**, pp. 242–50.

FISHBEIN, H. D., LEWIS, S., and KEIFFER, K. (1972), 'Children's Understanding of Spatial Relations Co-ordination of Perspectives, *Dev. Psych.*, **7**, 21–3.

FISHMAN, J. A., *et al.* (eds.), (1968), *Bilingualism in the Barrio*, 2 vols., U.S. Department of Health, Education and Welfare, Office of Education.

FLANDERS, N. A. (1960), 'Teacher Influence, Pupil Attitudes, and Achievement' Final Report, Co-operative Research Project, No. 397, U.S. Office of Education, University of Minnesota.

FLANDERS, N. A. (1965), *Teacher Influence, Pupil Attitudes and Achievement*, Co-operative Research Monographs, No. 12, U.S. Office of Education, U.S. Government Printing Office.

FLANDERS, N. A. (1970), *Analysing Teaching Behaviour*, Addison-Wesley, Reading, Mass.

FLAVEL *et al.* (1968), *The Development of Role Taking and Communication Skills in Children*, Wiley, New York.

FLAVELL, J. H. (1974), 'The Development of Inferences About Others' in Theodore Mischel (ed.), *Understanding Other Persons*, Blackwell, Oxford.

FLEMING, J. T. (1973), *Research Review and Critique: Teacher Behaviour and Children's Oral Language/Speaking*, 1966–1972 ED 077 006 (available from EDRS).

FODOR, J., BEVER, R., and GARRETT, M. (1974), *The Psychology of Language*, McGraw-Hill, New York.

FORD, J. (1969), *Social Class and the Comprehensive School*, Routledge and Kegan Paul, London.

FOREIT, K. G. and DONALDSON, P. (1971), 'Dialect, Race and Language Proficiency: Another Dead Heat on the Merry Go Round', *Child Development* **42**, p. 1572.

FOX, S. E. (1970), *Syntactic Maturity and Vocabulary Diversity in the Oral Language of Kindergarten and Primary School Children* (available from University Microfilms, Dissertation Copies, Post Office Box 1764, Ann Arbor, Michigan 48106).

FRANCIS, H. (1969), 'Structure in the Speech of a $2\frac{1}{2}$-year old', *British Journal of Educational Psychology* **39**, pp. 291–302.

FRANCIS, H. (1972), 'Sentence Structure and Learning to Read', *British Journal of Educational Psychology* **42**, p. 113.

FRANCIS, H. (1974a), 'Social Class, Reference and Context', *Language and Speech* **17**, pp. 193–8.

FRANCIS, H. (1974b), 'Social Background, Speech and Learning to Read', *British Journal of Educational Psychology* **44**, pp. 290–9.

FRENDER, R., BROWN, B., and LAMBERT, W. E. (1970), 'The Role of Speech Characteristics in Scholastic Success', *Canadian Journal of Behavioural Science* **2**, p. 299.

FRIEDLANDER, B. Z. (1970) 'Receptive Language Development in Infancy', *Merrill-Palmer Quarterly* **16**, p. 7.

FRIEDLANDER, B., JACOBS, A., DAVIS, B., and WHETSTONE, H. (1973), 'Time-sampling Analysis of Infants' Natural Language Environments in the Home', *Child Development* **43**, pp. 730–40.

FRIEDMAN, P. (1973), 'Relationship of Teacher Reinforcement to Spontaneous Student Verbalisation within the Classroom', *Journal of Educational Psychology* **65**/1, p. 59.

FRY, C. L. (1966), 'Training Children to Communicate to Listeners', *Child Development* **37**, p. 675.

FRY, C. L. (1969), 'Training Children to Communicate to Listeners who have varying Listeners' Requirements', *Journal of Genetic Psychology* **114**, p. 153.

GAHAGAN, D. M., and GAHAGAN, G. A. (1970), *Talk Reform: Explorations in Language for Infant School Children*, Routledge and Kegan Paul, London.

GAHAGAN, G. A., and GAHAGAN, D. M. (1968), 'Paired Associate Learning as Partial Validation of a Language Development Program', *Child Development*, **39**, p. 1119.

GALLAGHER, J. J., and ASCHNER, M. J. (1963), 'A Preliminary Report on Analyses of Classroom Interaction', *Merrill-Palmer Quarterly* **9**, p. 183.

GARDNER, B., and GARDNER, R. (1971), 'Two-way Communication with an Infant Chimpanzee' in A. Schrier and F. Stollnitz (eds.), *Behaviour of Non-human Primates*, Vol. 4, Academic Press, New York.

GARNER, J., and BING, M. (1973), 'Inequalities of Teacher-pupil contacts, *British Journal of Educational Psychology* **43,** 3, 234–43.

GARVEY, C., and MCFARLANE, P. (1970), 'A measure of Standard English Proficiency of Inner-City Children', *American Educational Research Journal* **7,** p. 29.

GARVEY, C., and DICKSTEIN, E. (1972), 'Levels of Analysis and Social Class Differences in Language', *Language and Speech* **15**/4, p. 375.

GERBER, S. E., and HERTEL, C. H. (1969), 'Language Deficiency of Disadvantaged Children', *Journal of Speech and Hearing Research* **12,** p. 270.

GETZELS, J. W., and THELEN, H. A. (1960), 'The Classroom Group as a Unique Social System', in Henry, N. B. (ed.), *Fifty-Ninth Yearbook of the National Society for the Study of Education*, Chicago.

GILBERTS, R. A. *et al.*, (1971), *Teacher Perceptions of Race, Socio-economic Status and Language Characteristics* ED 052 131 (available from EDRS).

GILES, H. (1970), 'Evaluative Reactions to Accents', *Educational Review* **22,** p. 211.

GILES, H. (1971), 'Our Reactions to Accent', *New Society* 14 October.

GILES, H. and POWESLAND, P. F. (1975), *Speech Style and Social Evaluation*, Academic Press, London.

GINSBURG, H. (1972), *The Myth of the Deprived Child*, Prentice-Hall, New Jersey.

GLANTZ, M. M., and COHEE, M. C. (1941), 'Oral Language in the Primary Grades' in *Language Arts in the Elementary School, 20th Yearbook*, Bulletin of the Department of Elementary School Principals, 20, p. 259, National Education Association, Washington, DC.

GLEITMAN, L. and GLEITMAN, H., and SHIPLEY, E. (1973), 'The Emergence of the Child as Grammarian', *Cognition* **1,** 137–64.

GOLUB, L. S., and FREDERICK, W. C. (1971), *Linguistic Structures in the Discourse of Fourth and Sixth Graders* ED 058 322 (available from EDRS).

GORDON, S. B. (1970), *Ethnic and Socio-economic Influences on the Home Language Experiences of Children* ED 043 377 (available from EDRS).

GUMPERZ, J. J., and HERASIMCHUK, E. (1972), *The Conversational Analysis of Social Meaning: a Study of Classroom Interaction* (mimeographed Berkeley, University of California).

GUMPERZ, J. J., and HERNANDEZ, E. (1972), 'Bilingualism, Bidialectism and Classroom Interaction' in Cazden, C., John, V. P., and Hymes, D., *The Functions of Language in the Classroom*, Teachers College Press, New York.

GUPTA, W., and STERN, C. (1969), *Comparative Effectiveness of Speaking Versus Listening in Improving the Spoken Language of Disadvantaged Young Children* ED 029 689 (available from EDRS).

HAKES, D. (1973), 'The Emergence of Linguistic Intuitions in Children'. Grant proposal, University of Texas, Austin.

HAKES, D. (1970) Reflections on 'Pivot Grammar', *Cognition*.

HAKULINEN, A., LEWIS, B., and TAYLOR, S. (in press), *Seven year old Children and the Contextual Use of Language*, Routledge and Kegan Paul, London.

HALL, V. C., TURNER, R., and RUSSEL, W. (1973), 'Ability of Children from 4 Subcultures and 2 Grade levels to Imitate and Comprehend Crucial Aspects of Standard English: a test of the different language explanation', *Journal of Educational Psychology* **74**/2, p. 147.

HALL, W., and FREEDLE, R. O. (1973), 'A Developmental Investigation of Standard and Non-standard English among Black and White Children', *Human Development* **16**/6, p. 440.

HALLIDAY, M. A. K. (1968), 'Language and Experience', *Educational Review* **20**/2.

HALLIDAY, M. A. K. (1969), 'Relevant Models of Language' in Wilkinson, A. M. (ed.) *The State of Language*, University of Birmingham, School of Education.

HALLIDAY, M. A. K. (1970), 'Language Structure and Language Function' in J. Lyons (ed.), *New Horizons in Linguistics*, Penguin.

HALLIDAY, M. A. K. (1973), *Explorations in the Functions of Language*, Edward Arnold, London.

HALLIDAY, M. A. K. (1975), *Learning How to Mean*, Edward Arnold, London.

HALLIDAY, M. A. K. and HASAN, R. (1976), *Cohesion in English*, Longman, London.

HALLIDAY, M. A. K., MCINTOSH, A., and STREVENS, P. D. (1964), *The Linguistic Sciences and Language Teaching*, Longman, London.

HALSEY, A. H. (ed.) (1972), *Educational Priority: EPA Problems and Policies*, Vol. 1, H.M.S.O. London.

HAMMER, E. F. (1969), *A Comparison of the Oral Language Patterns of Mature and Immature First Grade Children* (available from University Microfilms, Dissertation Copies, Post Office Box 1764, Ann Arbor, Michigan 48106).

HARGREAVES, D. H. (1967), *Social Relations in a Secondary School*, Routledge and Kegan Paul, London.

HARGREAVES, D. H. (1972), *Interpersonal Relations in Education*, Routledge and Kegan Paul, London.

HARRISON, B. (1974), 'Language, Schools and the Working Class', *Forum* **16**, p. 50.

HARVEY, B. (1968), *The Scope of Oracy: Teaching Spoken English*, Pergamon Press, London.

HASAN, R. (1967), 'Grammatical Cohesion in Spoken and Written English, Nuffield Programme in Linguistics and English Teaching (Paper 7), London.

HAWKINS, P. R. (1969), 'Social Class, the Nominal Group and Reference', *Language and Speech* **12**, 125–35.

HAWKINS, R. B. (1969), 'A Speech Program in an Experimental College for the Disadvantaged', *Speech* **18,** p. 115.

HEIDER, E. R. (1968), *Style and Effectiveness of Children's Verbal Communications within and between Social Classes* (Doctoral dissertation, Harvard University).

HEIDER, E. R., CAZDEN, C. B., and BROWN, R. (1968), 'Social Class Differences in the Effectiveness and Style of Children's Coding Ability', *Project Literacy Report* **9,** Cornell University.

HENDERSON, D. (1971), 'Contextual Specificity, Discretion and Cognitive Socialisation with Special Reference to Language' in Bernstein, B. (ed.), *Class, Codes and Control*, Vol. 2, Routledge and Kegan Paul, London, 1973.

HENDERSON, D. (1970), 'Social Class Differences in Form–Class Usage among five-year-old children' in Brandis, W., and Henderson, D. (eds.) *Social Class, Language and Communication*, Routledge and Kegan Paul, London.

HESS, K. M., and MAXWELL, J. (1969) *What to do about Nonstandard Dialects: a review of the literature* ED 041 027 (available from EDRS).

HESS, R. D., and SHIPMAN, V. C. (1965), 'Early experiences and the socialisation of cognitive modes in children', *Child Development* **36** (3), 869–86.

HESS, R. D., and BEAR, R. M. (Eds.), (1968), *Early Education*, Aldine Press, Chicago.

HICKER, J. (1973), 'Spoken English in the Primary School', *Use of English* **24,** p. 301.

HITCHMAN, P. J. (1966), *Examining Oral English in Schools*, Methuen, London.

HORNER, V. M., and GUSSOW, J. D. (1972), 'John and Mary: a Pilot Study in Linguistic Ecology' in Cazden, C. B., John, V. P., and Hymes, D. (eds.), *The Function of Language in the Classroom*, Teachers College Press, New York.

HOUSTON, J. G., and PILLINER, A. E. G. (1974), 'The Effect of Verbal Teaching Style on the Attainment of Educational Objectives in Physics', *British Journal of Educational Psychology* **44**/2, p. 163.

HOUSTON, S. (1969), 'A Sociolinguistic Consideration of the Black English of Children in Northern Florida', *Language* **45,** p. 599.

HOUSTON, S. H. (1970), 'A Re-examination of Some Assumptions about the Language of the Disadvantaged Child', *Child Development* **41,** p. 947.

HOYT, F. S. (1906), 'The Place of Grammar in the Elementary School Curriculum', *Teachers College Record* **7,** p. 1.

HUBBELL, R. D. (1969), *An Exploratory Study of Selected Aspects of the Relationship between Family Interaction and Language Development in Children* (available from University Microfilms, A Xerox Co., 300 N. Zeeb Road, Ann Arbor, Michigan 48103).

HURLEY, O. L. (1967), *Linguistic Analysis of Verbal Interaction in Special Classes for the Mentally Retarded*, ED 020 597 (available from EDRS).

HUTTENLOCHER, J., EISENBERG, K., and STRAUSS, S. (1968), 'Comprehension: Relation Between Perceived Actor and Logical Subject', *Journal of Verbal Learning and Verbal Behaviour* **7**, 527–30.

HUTTENLOCHER, J., and STRAUSS, S. (1968), 'Comprehension and Statements Related to the Situation it Describes', *Journal of Verbal Learning and Verbal Behaviour* **7**, 300–4.

HYMES, D. (1962), 'The Ethnography of Speaking' in Gladwin, T., and Sturtevant, W. C. (Eds.), *Anthropology and Human Behaviour*, Anthropological Society of Washington, Washington.

JACKSON, P. (1968), *Life in Classrooms*, Holt, Rinehart and Winston, New York.

JAKOBSON, R. (1941—English translation, 1968), *Child Language, Aphasia and Phonological Universals*, Mouton, The Hague.

JAKOBSON, R. (1960), 'Closing Statement: Linguistics and Poetics' in Sebeok, T. (ed.), *Style in Language*, M.I.T. Press, Cambridge, Mass.

JENSEN, A. R. (1969), 'How Much Can We Boost IQ and Scholastic Achievement?', *Harvard Educational Review* **39**, p. 1.

JESTER, R. E. (1970), *Relationship Between Teachers' Vocabulary Usage and the Vocabulary of Kindergarten and First Grade Students*, Final Report ED 051 429 (available from EDRS).

JOHN, V. P., and MOSKOVITZ, S. (1968), *A Study of Language Change in Integrated Homogeneous Classrooms*, Project Report No. 2, Yeshiva University, New York,

JOHNSON, R. L., and CROSS, H. S. (1968), 'Some Factors in Effective Communication', *Language and Speech* **11**/4, p. 259.

JONES, A., and MULFORD, J. (eds.), (1971), *Children Using Language: an Approach to English in the Primary School*, Oxford University Press.

JONES, A. R. (1970), *Oral Facility in Bilingual and Monoglot Children*, Pamphlet No. 18 (University College of Wales).

JONES, P. A. (1972), 'Home Environment and the Development of Verbal Ability', *Child Development* **43**, p. 1081.

JONES, P. A., and MCMILLAN, W. B. (1973), 'Speech Characteristics as a Function of Social Class and Situational Factors', *Child Development* **44**/1, p. 117.

JONES, W. R., and STEWART, W. A. (1951), 'Bilingualism and Verbal Intelligence' *British Journal of Psychology* **4**, p. 3.

JONES, W. R. et al., (1957), *The Educational Attainment of Bilingual Children in Relation to their Intelligence and Linguistic Background*, University of Wales Press, Cardiff.

JORDAN, M., and ROBINSON, W. P. (1972), 'The Grammar of Working and Middle Class Children Using Elicited Imitations', *Language and Speech* **15**/2, p. 122.

KASDON, L. M. (1967), *Language Experience Approach for Children with Non-standard Dialects* ED 016 588 (available from EDRS).

KATZ, J. (1966), *The Philosophy of Language*, Harper & Row, New York.

KEACH, E. T., FULTON, R., and GARDNER, W. E. (eds.), (1967), *Education and Social Crisis*, Wiley, New York.

KEAN, J. M. (1967), *A Comparison of the Classroom Language of Second and Fifth Grade Teachers* ED 018 777 (available from EDRS).

KEDDIE, N. (ed.), (1973), *Tinker, Tailor: . . . The Myth of Cultural Deprivation*, Penguin Education, Harmondsworth.

KEISLAR, E. R. and PHINNEY, J. (1970), *An Experimental Game in Oral Language Comprehension* ED 038 171 (available from EDRS).

KELLNER, H. (1970), 'On the Sociolinguistic Perspective of the Communicative Situation', *Social Research* **37**, pp. 71–8.

KING, R. (1969), *Values and Involvement in a Grammar School*, Routledge and Kegan Paul, London.

KINZEL, P. F. (1964), *Lexical and Grammatical Interference in the Speech of a Bilingual Child*. Studies in Linguistics and Language Learning, Vol. 1 ED 029 273 (available from EDRS).

KLEIN, J. (1965), *Samples from English Cultures*, Routledge and Kegan Paul, London.

KLIEBARD, H. M. (1966), 'The Observation of Classroom Behaviour' in Hitchcock, C. (ed.), *The Way Teaching Is*, Association for Supervision and Curriculum Development and Center for the Study of Instruction, Washington.

KNIEF, L. M. (1972), *Linguistic Development among Mexican-American and Anglo Primary Students in the Public Schools*, Final Report ED 037 480 (available from EDRS).

KOHLBERG, L., and MAYER, R. 'Development as the Aim of Education', *Harvard Educational Review*, 1972, **42**, pp. 449–96.

KOHLERS, P. A. (1966), 'Reading and Talking Bilingually', *American Journal of Psychology* **79**, p. 357.

KORNFELD, J. (1972), 'Some Theoretical Issues in the Acquisition of Phonology', Proc. 7th Chicago Linguistic Society.

KRAUSS, R. M., and GLUCKSBERG, S. (1969), 'The Development of Communicative Competence as a Function of Age', *Child Development* **40**/1, p. 255.

KRAUSS, R. M., and ROTTER, G. S. (1968), 'Communication Abilities of Children as a Function of Status and Age', *Merill-Palmer Quarterly* **14**, p. 161.

KRAUSS, R. M., VIVEKANANTHAN, P. S., and WEINHEIMER, S. (1968), '"Inner Speech" and "External Speech" Characteristics and Communication Effectiveness of Socially and Non-Socially Emoded Messages', *Journal of Personality and Social Psychology* **9**, p. 295.

LABOV, W. (1964), 'Stages in the Acquisition of Standard English' in Shuy, R. W. (ed.), *Social Dialects and Language Learning*, National Council of Teachers of English, Champaign, Ill.

LABOV, W. (1966), *The Social Stratification of English in New York City*, Center for Applied Linguistics, Washington.

LABOV, W. (1968), 'The Nonstandard Negro Vernacular: Some Practical Suggestions', *Position Papers from Language Education for the Disadvantaged* Report No. 3, NDEA. (National Institute for Advanced Study in Teaching Disadvantaged Youth.)

LABOV, W. *et al.*, (1968), *A Study of the Nonstandard English of Negro and Puerto Rican Speakers in New York City*, Vol. 2, Columbia University, New York.

LABOV, W. (1970), 'The Study of Language in its Social Setting', *Studium Generale* 23/1, p. 30.

LABOV, W. (1970), 'The Logic of Non-standard English' in Frederick Williams (ed.), *Language and Poverty*, Markham, Chicago.

LACEY, C. (1970), *Hightown Grammar: The School as a Social System*, Manchester University Press, Manchester.

LACONTE, C., and LACONTE, R. (1969), *Writing English in Primary Schools* ED 041 008 (available from EDRS).

LAMBERT, W. E. (1972), 'The Effects of Speech Style and other Attributes on Teachers' Attitudes Toward Pupils' in Lambert, W. E., *Language, Psychology and Culture*, Stanford University Press, California, 1972.

LAMBERT, W. E. (1972), *Language, Psychology and Culture*, Stanford University Press, California.

LAVATELLI, C. S. (ed.), (1967), *Problems of Dialect* ED 025 300 (available from EDRS).

LAVATELLI, C. S. (ed.), (1971), *Language Training in Early Childhood Education*, University of Illinois Press (for ERIC Clearinghouse on Early Childhood Education).

LAWTON, D. (1964), 'Some Class Language Differences in Group Discussions', *Language and Speech* 7, p. 182.

LAWTON, D. (1968), *Social Class, Language and Education*, Routledge and Kegan Paul, London.

LAWTON, D. (1973), *Language, Social Class and the Curriculum* in Butcher, H. J., and Pont, H. B. (eds.), *Educational Research in Britain 3*, University of London Press, London.

LEAVERTON, L. (1971), *Dialectal Readers—Rationale, Use, and Value* ED 060 701 (available from EDRS).

LEE, L. (1966), 'Developmental Sentence Types: A Method for Comparing Normal and Deviant Syntactic Development', *Journal of Speech and Hearing Disorders* 31, p. 311.

LEGUM, STANLEY E. *et al.*, (1969), *Social Dialects and their Implications for Beginning Reading Instruction*, Southwest Regional Laboratory for Educational Research and Development, Inglewood, California.

LEHMAN, E. K. (1966), *A Study of Certain Language Skills of Kindergarten Children* ED 029 880 (available from University Microfilms, A Xerox Co., 300 N. Zeeb Road, Ann Arbor, Michigan 48103).

LEOPOLD, W. (1939), *Speech development of a bilingual child*, Vol. 1, Northwestern Univ. P., Evanston.

LEVINSON, E. J. (1971), 'The Modification of Intelligence by Training in the Verbalisation of Word Definitions and Simple Concepts', *Child Development* **42**, p. 1361.

LEWIS, D. G. (1959), 'Bilingualism and Non-verbal Intelligence: a Further Study of Test Results', *British Journal of Educational Psychology* **29**, p. 17.

LEWIS, R. (1973), 'Speaking in the Primary School', *Speech and Drama* **22/2**, p. 8.

LINDSAY, M. R. (1969), *A Descriptive Exploration of the Growth and Development of Spontaneous Oral Vocabulary of Elementary School Children* ED 052 189 (available from University Microfilms, Dissertation Copies, Post Office Box 1764, Ann Arbor, Michigan 48106).

LINN, G. B. (1965), *A Study of Several Linguistic Functions of Mexican American Children in a Two-Language Environment* ED 065 263 (available from R and E Research Associates, San Francisco, California 94112).

LLOYD, D. (1967), 'Subcultural Patterns which Affect Language and Reading Development' in Keach, E. T., Fulton, R., and Gardner, W. E. (eds.) *Education and Social Crisis*, Wiley, New York.

LOBAN, W. D. (1963), *The Language of Elementary School Children*, Research Report No. 1, National Council of Teachers of English, Champaign, Ill.

LOBAN, W. D. (1966a), *Language Ability, Grades Seven, Eight and Nine*, US Government Printing Office, Washington, D.C.

LOBAN, W. D. (1966b), *Problems of Oral English*, National Council of Teachers of English, Champaign, Ill.

LOBAN, W. (1967), *Language Ability—Grades 10, 11 and 12* Final Report ED 014 477 (available from EDRS).

LOBAN, W. (1970), *Stages, Velocity and Prediction of Language Development: Kindergarten Through Grade Twelve* Final Report ED 040 198 (available from EDRS).

LOVELL, K., HEALEY, D., and ROWLAND, A. D., 'Growth of Some Geometrical Concepts' in Sigel, I. E., and Hooper, F. H. (eds.), *Logical Thinking in Children, Research Based on Piaget's Theory*, Holt, Rinehart and Winston, New York, 1968, pp. 140–157.

LUCAS, E. (1972), 'Language in the Infants' Playground', *Multiracial School* **1/3**, p. 18 and **2/1**, p. 20.

LUNZER, E. A. *et al.*, (1973), 'Internal and External Determinant Factors affecting Cognitive Behaviour of Children in their First Year of Schooling', International Soc. for the Study of Behavioural Development, Biennial Meeting, Ann Arbor.

MACAULAY, R. K. S. and TREVELYAN, G. D. (1973), *Language, Education and Employment in Glasgow*, A Report to the SSRC, Vols. 1 and II.

MCCONNELL, F., HORTON, K. B., and SMITH, B. R. (1969), 'Language Development and Cultural Disadvantage', *Exceptional Children* **35**, p. 597.

MCDADE, D. F. (1967), 'Language, Intelligence and Social Class', *Scottish Educational Studies* **1**/1, p. 34.

MACKAY, D. and THOMSON, B. (1968), *The Initial Teaching of Reading and Writing: Some Notes toward a Theory of Literacy*, Programme in Linguistics and English Teaching Paper No. 3, University College and Longman, London.

MACKAY, D. *et al.*, (1970), *Breakthrough to Literacy: Teachers' Manual*, Longman, London.

MCKEE, P. (1939), *Language in the Elementary School*, Houghton Mifflin, Boston.

MACNAMARA, J. (1972), 'Cognitive Basis of Language Learning in Infants', *Psychological Review* **79**, pp. 1–13.

MCNEILL, D. (1970), *The Acquisition of Language: the Study of Developmental Psycholinguistics*, Harper & Row, New York.

MCNEILL, D. (in press), 'Sentence Structures in Chimpanzee Communication, in Bruner, J., and Connolly, K. (eds.), *Competence in Infancy*, Academic Press, New York.

MARASCUILO, L. A., and LOBAN, W. (1969), *An Empirical Study of the Dominating Predictive Features of Spoken Language in a Representative Sample of School Pupils: a Multivariate Description and Analysis of Oral Language Development* ED 038 424 (available from EDRS).

MARATOS, M. P. (1973), 'Decrease in the Understanding of the Word "Big" in Preschool Children', *Child Development* **44**, pp. 747–52.

MARSHALL, J., and WALES, R. (1974), 'Pragmatics—Biology or Culture?' in special issue, Cherry, C. (ed.), *Theory and Decision* (Riedel, Dordrecht, Holland).

MARSHALL, R. C., and CULLINAN, W. L. (1971), 'Effects of Reward Schedule Changes on Children's Speech Fluency', *Language and Speech* **14**/4, p. 341.

MASANGKY, Z. S. *et al.*, (1974), 'The Early Development of Inferences about the Visual Percepts of Others', *Child Development* **45**, 357–366.

MASSAD, C. E. (1968), *A Comparative Study of Language Aptitude and Intelligence in 6th-Grade Children from Low-Socioeconomic and Middle-Socioeconomic Levels* ED 020 291 (available from EDRS).

MATTLEMAN, M. (1966), *An Evaluation of the Effects of an Enrichment Program on Six Year Old Children* ED 012 369 (available from EDRS).

MEAD, G. H. (1934), *Mind, Self and Society*, University of Chicago Press.

MEDLEY, D. M. (1967), *The Use of Orthogonal Contrasts in the Interpretation of Records of Verbal Behaviours of Classroom Teachers*, (paper presented at a symposium of the American Psychological Association).

MEDLEY, D. M., IMPELLITTERI, J. T., and SMITH, L. H. (1969), *Coding Teachers' Verbal Behaviour in the Classroom: a manual for users of OS AR 4V* (Mimeo) City University of New York, Division of Teacher Education, New York.

MEDLEY, D. M., and MITZEL, H. E. (1958a), 'Application of Analysis of Variance to the Estimation of the Reliability of Observations of Teachers' Classroom Behaviour', *Journal of Experimental Education* **27**, p. 23.

MEDLEY, D. M., and MITZEL, H. E. (1958b), 'A Technique for Measuring Classroom Behaviour', *Journal of Educational Psychology* **49**, p. 86.

MEDLEY, D. M., and MITZEL, H. E. (1959) 'Some Behavioural Correlates of Teacher Effectiveness', *Journal of Educational Psychology* **50**, p. 239.

MEDLEY, D. M., and MITZEL, H. E. (1963), 'Measuring Classroom Behaviour by Systematic Observation' in Gage, N. L. (ed.) *Handbook of Research on Teaching*, Rand McNally, Chicago.

MEUX, M. D. (1967), 'Studies of Learning in the School Setting', *Review of Educational Research* **37.**

MICKELSON, N. I., and GALLOWAY, C. G. (1969), *Cumulative Language Deficit among Indian Children* ED 030 864 (available from EDRS).

MINISTRY OF EDUCATION, (1945), *Language Teaching In Primary Schools* (Welsh Department Pamphlet No. 1).

MITTINS, W. H. (1969), 'What is Correctness?' in Wilkinson, A. M. (ed.) *The State of Language*, University of Birmingham, School of Education.

MITTLER, P., ed. (1970), *The Psychological Assessment of Mental and Physical Handicaps*, Methuen, London.

MOFFETT, J. (1968), *Teaching the Universe of Discourse*, Houghton Mifflin, New York.

MONAGHAN, A. D., 'Children's Contacts: Some Preliminary Findings', unpublished term paper, Harvard Graduate School of Education, 1971.

MOORE, D. R. (1971), *Language Research and Preschool Language Training*, in Lavatelli, C. S. (ed.), *op. cit.*

MORRISON, C. M. (ed.) with SWATT, J., and LEE, T. R. (1974), *Educative Priority: EPA A Scottish Study*, Vol. 5, H.M.S.O., London.

MUMA, J. R. (1967), *Frequency of Aspect in Oral and Written Verbal Samples by Children* ED 015 202 (available from EDRS).

NAREMORE, R. C. (1969), *Teachers' Evaluational Reactions to Pupils' Speech Samples*, doctoral dissertation, University of Wisconsin.

NASH, R. (1973), 'Clique Formation among Primary and Secondary School Children', *British Journal of Sociology* **24**, p. 303.

N.C.T.E. (1966), *Problems in Oral English: Kindergarten through Grade 9.* NCTE Research Report No. 9 National Council for the Teaching of English, Champaign, I.

N.C.T.E., *Classroom Practices in Teaching English 1968–1969: a Sixth Report of the NCTE Committee on Promising Practices* ED 029 020 (available from EDRS).

NELSON, K. (1973), *Structure and Strategy in Learning to Talk*, Monograph Society for Research in Child Development, Vol. 38, No. 149.

NEWSON, J., NEWSON, E., and BARNES, P. (1973), 'Child Rearing Practices' in Butcher J. H., and Pont, H. B. (eds.) *Educational Research in Britain*, University of London Press, London.

NOEL, D. L. (1953), 'A Comparative Study of the Relationship Between the Quality of the Child's Language Usage and the Quality and Types of Language used in the Home', *Educational Research* **47**, p. 61.

NOLEN, P. S. (1972), 'Reading Nonstandard Dialect Materials: a Study at Grades 2 and 4', *Child Development* **43**, p. 1092.

OLIM, E. G., HESS, R. D., and SHIPMAN, V. C. (1967), 'The Role of Mothers' Language Styles in Mediating their Preschool Children's Cognitive Development', *School Review* **75**, p. 414.

OPIE, I., and OPIE, P. (1959), *The Lore and Language of School Children*, Oxford University Press, London.

OSBORN, J. (1968), 'Teaching a Teaching Language to Disadvantaged Children' in Brottman, M. A. (ed.) *Language Remediation for the Disadvantaged Preschool Child*, Monographs of the Society for Research in Child Development 33 (8, Whole No. 124).

OSSER, H. *et al.*, (1969), 'The Young Child's Ability to Imitate and Comprehend Speech: a Comparison of Two Subcultural Groups', *Child Development* **4**, p. 1063.

PALMER, F. H., CAZDEN, C. B., and GLICK, J., 'Evaluation of Day Care Centers: Summative and Formative' in Grotberg, E. H. (ed.) *Day care: Resources for Decisions*, U.S. Office of Economic Opportunity, Office of Planning, Research and Evaluation, 1971, pp. 442–57.

PANCRATZ, R. (1967), 'Verbal Interaction Patterns in the Classrooms of Selected Physics Teachers' in Amidon, E. J., and Hough, J. B. (eds.) *Interaction Analysis: Theory Research and Application*, Addison-Wesley, Reading, Mass.

PARRY M., and ARCHER H., (1974), *Preschool Education*, the report of the Schools Council project on preschool education 1969–71, Macmillan Education Ltd, London.

PEAL, E., and LAMBERT, W. E. (1962), 'The Relation of Bilingualism to Intelligence' in Gardner, R. C., and Lambert, W. E. *Attitudes and Motivation in Second Language Learning*, Newbury House, Rowley Mass., 1972.

PEISACH, E. C. (1965), 'Children's Comprehension of Teacher and Peer Speech', *Child Development* **30**, p. 467.

PERINE, M. H. (1976), *Using Tapes and Human Recorders in Recording Children's Dictated Composition* ED 017 513 (available from EDRS).

PHILLIPS, J. R. (1970), *Formal Characteristics of Speech Which Mothers Address to Their Young Children*, unpublished doctoral dissertation, The Johns Hopkins University.

PIAGET, J. (1928), *Language and Thought in the Child*, Routledge & Kegan Paul.

PIAGET, J. (1963) 'La Langue et les Operations intellectuelles', in *Problemes de Psycho-linguistique*, Presses Universitaires de France, Paris.

PIDGEON, D. A. (1970), *Expectation and Pupil Performance*, National Foundation for Educational Research in England and Wales, Slough.

PLOWDEN REPORT, THE, (1967), *Children and their Primary Schools*, Vols 1 and 2, H.M.S.O., London.

PLUMER, D. (1969), *Parent-Child Verbal Interaction: a Naturalistic Study of Dialogue Strategies*, Interim Report (Harvard Graduate School of Education).

PLUMER, D. (1971), *Verbal Interaction and Verbal Ability: research and practice* ED 053 129 (available from EDRS).

POLITZER, R. L., and HOOVER, M. R. (1972), *The Development of Awareness of the Black Standard/Black Nonstandard Dialect Contrast Among Primary School Children: a Pilot Study*. Research and Development Memorandum No. 83 ED 062 464 (available from EDRS).

POLITZER, R. L., and RAMIREZ, A. G. (1973), *An Error Analysis of the Spoken English of Mexican-American Pupils in a Bilingual School and a Monolingual School*, Research and Development Memorandum No. 103, ED 073 879 (available from EDRS).

PRIDE, J. B. (1969), 'Analysing Classroom Procedures' in Fraser, H., and O'Donnell, W. R. (eds.) *Applied Linguistics and the Teaching of English*, Longman, London.

PRINGLE, N. L. K. (1965), *Deprivation and Education*, Longman, London.

QUAY, L. C. (1971), 'Language Dialect, Reinforcement and the Intelligence Test Performance of Negro Children', *Child Development* **42**, p. 5.

QUIGLEY, H. (1971), '*Nursery Teachers' Reactions to the Peabody Language Development Kit*,' *Br. J. Educ. Psych.* **41**, 155–62.

RACKSTRAW, S. J., and ROBINSON, W. P. (1967), 'Social and Psychological Factors Related to Variability of Answering Behaviour in Five-year-old Children', *Language and Speech* **10**, p. 88,

RAMSEY, K. I. (1970), *A Comparison of First Grade Negro Dialect Speakers' Comprehension of Material Presented in Standard English and in Negro Dialects* ED 049 261 (available from University Microfilms, A Xerox Co., Dissertation Copies, Post Office Box 1764, Ann Arbor, Michigan 48106.)

RANKIN, E. (1969), *Report of Problems Relating to the Teaching of the Mother Tongue: Scotland*, UNESCO First Language Learning Seminar, Hamburg.

REID, J. F. (1972), 'Children's Comprehension of Syntactic Features Found in Some Extension Readers' in Reid, J. F. (ed.), *Reading Problems and Practices*, Ward Lock, London.

REMICK, H. (1973), *Maternal Speech to Children During Language Acquisition* ED 072 863 (available from EDRS).

REYNOLDS, N. J. and RISELY, T. R. (1968), 'The Role of Social and Material Reinforcers in increasing the talking of a Disadvantaged Child', *Journal of Applied Behavioural Analysis* **1**, p. 253.

RICHARDS, L. W. (1972), *A Study of the Effect of Systematic Practice of Standard English Sentence Patterns on Reading Achievement: Attitudes toward Reading and Oral Responses of fifth Graders* ED 070 055 (available from University Microfilms, Dissertation Copies, Post Office Box 1964, Ann Arbor, Michigan 48106).

RIEHM, C. L. (1969) *The Effects of Increased Pupil-Teacher Verbal Interaction on Oral Language Development in Disadvantaged First Grade Children* ED 056 007 (available from University Microfilms, Dissertation Copies, Post Office Box 1764, Ann Arbor, Michigan 48106).

RILEY, J. E. (1968), *The Influence of Bilingualism on Tested Verbal Ability in Spanish and English* Final Report ED 026 935 (available from EDRS).

RITTER, K. W. (1972), *The Challenge of Speech Communication in the Elementary Classroom* ED 067 715 (available from EDRS).

ROBINSON, W. P. (1968). 'Language and Education in the Primary School', *Aspects of Education* **7**, p. 67.

ROBINSON, W. P. (1971), 'Social Factors and Language Development in Primary School Children' in Huxley, R., and Ingram, E. (eds.), *Language Acquisition: models and methods*, Academic Press, New York.

ROBINSON, W. P. (1972), 'Where Do Children's Answers Come From?' in Bernstein, B. (ed.), *Class, Codes and Control*, Vol. 2, Routledge and Kegan Paul, London, 1973.

ROBINSON, W. P. (1973), *The Question Answer Exchange between Mothers and Young Children*, S.S.R.C., Final Report.

ROBINSON, W. P., and CREED, C. D. (1968), 'Perceptual and Verbal Discriminations of "Elaborated" and "Restricted" Code Users' in Bernstein, B. (ed.), *Class, Codes and Control*, Vol. 2, Routledge and Kegan Paul, London, 1973.

ROBINSON, W. P. and RACKSTRAW, S. J. (1967), 'Variations in Mothers' Answers to Children's Questions', *Sociology* **1**, p. 259.

ROSCH, E. (1973), Natural Categories, *Cognitive Psychology*, 328–50.

ROSE, S. *et al.*, (1973), *The Development of a Measure to Evaluate Language Communication Skills of Young Children* ED 076 665 (available from EDRS).

ROSEN, C. (1971), 'Classroom Encounter' in Jones, A., and Mulford, J. (eds.) *Children Using Language*, Oxford University Press, Oxford.

ROSEN, H. (1972), *Language and Class: a Critical Look at the Theories of Basil Bernstein*, Falling Wall Press, Bristol.

ROSEN, C., and ROSEN, H. (1973), *The Language of Primary School Children*, Penguin, Harmondsworth.

ROSENTHAL, R., and JACOBSON, L. (1968), *Pygmalion in the Classroom: Teacher Expectation and the Pupil's Intellectual Ability*, Holt, Rinehart and Winston, New York.

RUDDELL, R. B. (1965), 'The Effect of Oral and Written Patterns of Language Structure on Reading Comprehension', *Reading Teacher* **18**, p. 270.

RUDDELL, R. B., and GRAVES, B. W. (1968), *Socio-ethnic Status and the Language Achievement of First-Grade Children* ED 031 475 (available from EDRS).

RYANS, D. G. (1961), 'Some Relationships between Pupil Behaviour and Certain Teacher Characteristics', *British Journal of Educational Psychology* **52,** p. 82.

RYSTROM, R. (1968), *The Effects of Standard Dialect Training on Negro First-Graders Learning to Read*, Final Report ED 029 717 (available from EDRS).

SAER, D. J. (1923), 'The Effects of Bilingualism on Intelligence', *British Journal of Psychology* **14,** p. 25.

SANSOM, C. (1965), *Speech and Communication in the Primary School*, A. and C. Black, London.

SAVIN, H. B. (1972), 'What the Child Knows about Speech when He Starts to Read' in *Language by Ear and by Eye; the Relationships between Speech and Reading*, M.I.T. Press, London.

SCHAERLAEKENS, A. M. (1974), *The Two-word Sentence in Child Language Development*, Mouton, The Hague.

SCHAFFER, H. R. (1971), *The Growth of Sociability*, Penguin, London.

SCHMIDT-MACKEY, I. (1971), *Language Strategies of the Bilingual Family* ED 060 740 (available from EDRS).

SCHOLNICH, E. K., and ADAMS, M. J. (1973), 'Relationships between Language and Cognitive Skills: Passive-voice Comprehension, Backward Repetition and Matrix Permutation, *Child Development* **44,** pp. 741–6.

SCHOOLS COUNCIL, Working Paper No. 41 (1972), *A Study of Nursery Education*.

SCHOOLS COUNCIL (1974), *Concept 7–9*, E. Arnold, London.

SCHOOLS COUNCIL PRESCHOOL LANGUAGE PROJECT, THE, *Listening to Children Talking*, the Institute of Education, University of Leeds, September. 1972

SCOTTISH EDUCATION DEPARTMENT (1965), *Primary Education in Scotland*, H.M.S.O., Edinburgh.

SCOTTISH EDUCATION DEPARTMENT, (1972), *The Teaching of English Language*, Bulletin No. 5, Central Committee on English.

SCRIBNER, S., and COLE, M. (1973), 'Cognitive Consequences of Formal and Informal Education', *Science*, **182,** 553–9.

SCRIVNER, W. M. (1969), *Defensible Assumptions Concerning Oral Language* ED 039 234 (available from EDRS).

SEALEY, L. G. W., and GIBBON, V. (1972), *Communication and Learning in the Primary School* ED 071 780 (available from Schocken Books, 200 Madison Avenue, New York, N.Y.).

SEMPLE, S. W. (1964), *The Problem of Bilingualism in the Schools of Wales and Scotland* (Publications of the Department of Research: University of Toronto).

SERRANO, R. G. (1971), *The Language of the Four Year Old Chicano* ED 071 791 (available from EDRS).

SHANTZ, C. U., and WILSON, K. E. (1972), 'Training Communication Skills in Young Children', *Child Development* **43/2,** p. 693.

SHAPIRO, E. (1973), 'Educational Evaluation: Rethinking the Criteria of Competence, *School Review*, **81,** pp. 523–49.

SHIACH, G. M. (1972), *Teach them to Speak*, Ward Lock Educational, London.

SHIELDS, M. M. (1972), 'Saying It Without Sentences: the Role of Grammatical Abbreviation in the Speech of Young Children', *English in Education* **6** (3).

SHIELDS, M. M. (1974), 'The Development of the Modal Auxiliary System', *Birmingham Educational Review* **26** (3).

SHIELDS, M. M., and STEINER, E. (1973), 'The Language of Three to Five year olds in Preschool Education', *Educational Research* **15,** p. 97.

SILVAROLI, N. J., and WHITCOMB, M. W. (1967), *A Comparison of the Oral Language Patterns of Three Low Socio-economic Groups of Pupils entering First Grade* ED 032 943 (available from EDRS).

SIMON, A., and BOYER, E. G. (1967), *Mirrors for Behaviour: an Anthology of Classroom Observation Instruments*, Vols. I–VI, Research for Better Schools, Philadelphia.

SIMON, A., and BOYER, E. G. (1970), 'Mirrors for Behaviour' *Classroom Interaction Newsletter*, Special Edition, 2 Vols., Philadelphia.

SINCLAIR DE ZWART, H. (1967), *Acquisition du Langage et du Développement de la Pensée*, Dunod, Paris.

SINCLAIR DE ZWART, H. (1969), 'Developmental Psycholinguistics' in Elkind, D., and Flacell, J. H. (eds.), *Studies in Cognitive Development*, Oxford University Press, New York.

SINCLAIR, DE ZWART H. (1971), 'Piaget's Theory and Language Acquisition' in *Piagetian Cognitive Developmental Research and Mathematical Education*, NCTM, Washington.

SINCLAIR, J. MCH., et al., (1972), *The English Used by Teachers and Pupils*, SSRC Report, University of Birmingham.

SKOCZYLAS, R. V. (1972), *An Evaluation of Some Cognitive and Affective Aspects of a Spanish-English Bilingual Education Program* ED 066 990 (available from EDRS).

SLOBIN, D. I. (ed.), (1967), *A Field Manual for Cross-cultural Study of the Acquisition of Communicative Competence* (second draft), University of California, ASUC Store, Berkeley.

SLOBIN, D. I. (1968), 'Questions of Language Development in Cross-Cultural Perspective'. (Paper prepared for symposium on Language Learning in Cross Cultural Perspective, Michigan State University.)

SLOBIN, D. I. (1972a), 'Cognitive Pre-requisites for the Development of Grammar' in Slobin & Ferguson, op. cit.

SLOBIN, D. I. (1972b), 'Seven Questions about Language Development' in Dodwell, P. (ed.) *New Horizons in Psychology* **2,** Penguin, Harmondsworth.

SLOBIN, D. I., and FERGUSON, C. (eds.), (1973), *Studies of Child Language Development*, Holt, Rinehart & Winston, New York.

SMITH, A. B. (1969), *The Development of Connative and Denotative Meaning in*

Middle and Lower Class Children. (Master's Thesis, University of Alberta, Edmonton.)

SMITH, B. O., *et al.*, (1964), *A Tentative Report on the Strategies of Teaching*, US Department of Health, Education and Welfare, Office of Education. Co-operative Research Project No. 1640 Bureau of Educational Research, University of Illinois, Urbana.

SMITH, B. O., and MEUX, M. O. (1967), 'A Study of the Logic of Teaching' in Simon, A., and Boyer, E. G. (eds.) *Mirrors for Behaviour: an anthology of classroom observation instruments*, Research for Better Schools, Philadelphia.

SMITH, E., *et al.*, (1970), *Language and Thinking in the Elementary School*, Holt, Rinehart and Winston, New York.

SMITH, K. J., and TRUBY, H. M. (1968), *Dialectal Variance Interferes with Reading Instructions* ED 026 199 (available from EDRS).

SMITH, N. (1973), *The Acquisition of Phonology*, C.U.P., Cambridge.

SMOTHERGILL, N. L., OLSON, F., and MOORE, S. G. (1971), 'The Effects of Manipulation of Teacher Communication Style in the Preschool', *Child Development* **42,** p. 1229.

SNOW, C. E. (1971), *Language Acquisition and Mothers' Speech to Children*, doctoral dissertation, McGill University.

SNOW, C. E. (1972), 'Mother's Speech to Children Learning Language', *Child Development* **43,** pp. 549–65.

SNOW, R. (1969), 'Review of "Pygmalion in the Classroom" ', *Contemporary Psychology* **14,** p. 197.

SOUTH WEST COUNCIL OF FOREIGN LANGUAGE TEACHERS (1965), *Our Bilinguals—Social and Psychological Barriers, Linguistic and Pedagogical Barriers* ED 019 899 (available from EDRS).

SPEITEL, H. H., 'Dialect' in Davies, A. (ed.), *Problems of Language and Learning*, Heinemann, London, 1975.

SPOLSKY, B., and HOLM, W. (1971), *Bilingualism in the Six-year-old Navajo Child* ED 060 747 (available from EDRS).

STERN, C., and FRITH, S. (1970), *Classroom Language of Teachers of Young Children* ED 053 108 (available from EDRS).

STEWART, W. A. (1969), 'On the Use of Negro Dialect in the Teaching of Reading' in Baratz, J. C., and Shuy, R. W. (eds.), *Teaching Black Children to Read*, Centre for Applied Linguistics, Washington D.C.

STRICKLAND, D. S. (1971), *A Program for Linguistically Different Black Children* ED 049 355 (available from EDRS).

STRICKLAND, R. G. (1962), 'The Language of Elementary School Children', *Bulletin of the School of Education*, Indiana University 38/4.

STRONGMAN, K., and WOOZLEY, J. (1967), 'Stereotyped Reactions to Regional Accents', *British Journal of Social and Clinical Psychology* **6,** p. 164.

SUPPES, P. (1970), 'Probabilistic Grammars for Natural Language', *Synthese* **22,** 95–116.

SUPPES, P., SMITH, R., and LEVEILLE, M. (1972), *The French Syntax and Semantics of Philippe*, Part 1: *Noun Phrases*. Technical Report No. 195,

Psychology and Education Series, Institute for Mathematical Studies in the Social Sciences, Stanford University.

SWAIN, M. (1971), *Bilingualism, Monolingualism, and Code Acquisitions* ED 060 748 (available from EDRS).

TABA, H., LEVINE, S., and ELZEY, F. F., *Thinking in Elementary School-children*, U.S. Office of Education Cooperative Research Project, No. 1574, San Francisco, San Francisco State College, 1964, ED 003 285.

TAFT, J., and TENNIS, M. (1968), *The Development of a Test to Assess the Occurrence of Selected Features of Non-standard English of Disadvantaged Primary Children* ED 015 790 (available from EDRS).

TATHAM, S. M. (1970), 'Reading Comprehension of Materials Written with Select Oral Language Patterns: a Study at Grades 2 and 4', *Reading Research Quarterly* **5,** p. 402.

THOMPSON, D. L., and NESSELROAD, E. M. (1971), *Teacher Verbalization and the Verbal Development of Head Start Children* ED 053 180 (available from EDRS).

THORNDIKE, R. L. (1968), 'Review of "Pygmalion in the Classroom" ', *American Educational Research Journal* **5**/4 p. 708.

TIZARD, B., COOPERMAN, O., JOSEPH, A., and TIZARD, J., 'Environmental Effects on Language Development: a Study of Young Children in Long-stay Residential Nurseries',*Child Development*,1972,**43**,pp.337–58.

TOLAR, R. L. (1971), 'An Analysis of Thought and Language in Video-taped Kindergarten Lessons' ED 067 674 (available from University Microfilms, Dissertation Copies, Post Office Box 1764, Ann Arbor, Michigan 48106).

TORREY, J. (1969), *Teaching Standard English to Speakers of Other Dialects*, paper presented at Second AILA Conference, Cambridge.

TOSH, J., *et al.*, (1969), *English in the Primary School*, Edinburgh CITE, Moray House College of Education.

TOUGH, JOAN, (1970), *Language and Environment: An Interim Report* (circulated paper).

TOUGH, J. (1973a), 'Children's Use of Language', *Educational Review*, Birmingham, November.

TOUGH, J. (1973b), *Focus on Meaning: Talking to Some Purpose with Young Children*, Allen & Unwin, London.

TOUGH, J. (1973c), 'The Language of Young Children: the Implications for the Education of the Young Disadvantaged Child' in Chazan, M. (ed.), *Education in the Early Years*, University College of Swansea, Faculty of Education.

TOUGH, J. (1976), 'The Development of Meaning'.

TRAILL, A. (1967), unpublished M.Litt. Thesis, Dept. of Linguistics, University of Edinburgh.

TREVARTHEN, C., HUBLEY, P., and SHEEREN, L. (forthcoming), Psychological Actions in Early Infancy (to appear in *La Recherche*).

TRIGG, S. (1973), 'The Mother Tongue and Thinking in the Junior School', *Education for Development* **2**/4, p. 15.

TURNER, G. J. (1973), 'Social Class and Children's Language of Control at Age five and Age seven' in Bernstein, G. (ed.), *Class, Codes and Control*, Vol. 2, Routledge and Kegan Paul, London, 1973.

TURNER, G. J., and MOHAN, B. A. (1970), *A Linguistic Description and Computer Program for Children's Speech*, Routledge and Kegan Paul, London.

TURNER, G. J., and PICKVANCE, R. E. (1971), 'Social Class Differences in the Expression of Uncertainty in Five-Year-Old Children' in Bernstein, B. (ed.) *Class, Codes and Control*, Vol. 2, Routledge and Kegan Paul, London, 1973.

TURNER, R. (1974), *Ethnomethodology*, Penguin, Harmondsworth.

VELTEN, H. (1943), 'The growth of Phonemic and Lexical Patterns in Infant Language', *Language* **19**, 281–92.

VICK, M. L., and JOHNSON, J. L. (1969) *A Study of the Relationships between Primary Grade Pupils Labelled as either Culturally Disadvantaged or Culturally Advantaged and Their Development of Certain Language Skills* ED 028 038 (available from EDRS).

VYGOTSKY, L. S. (1962), *Thought and Language*, The M.I.T. Press, Cambridge, Mass.

WALES, R. (1968), 'Theories of Learning in Relation to Language' in R. Meetham (ed.), *Encyclopaedia of Linguistics, Information and Control*, Pergamon, Oxford.

WALES, R. (1971), 'Comparing and Contrasting' in J. Morton (ed.) *Biological and Social Factors in Psycholinguistics*, Logos, London.

WALES, R. (1971), 'The Child's Sentences Make Sense of the World', presented at the Psycholinguistics Conference, Paris.

WALES, R., and CAMPBELL, R. (1970), 'The Development of Comparison and the Comparison of Development' in G. Flores d'Arcais and W. Levelt (eds.) *Advances in Psycholinguistics*, North-Holland, Amsterdam.

WARD, M. C. (1971), *Them Children: a Study of Language Learning*. Case Studies in Education and Culture Series, Holt, Rinehart and Winston, New York.

WEENER, P. D. (1969), 'Social Dialect Differences and the Recall of Verbal Message', *Journal of Educational Psychology* **60**/3, p. 194.

WEENER, P. (1971), 'Language Structure and Free Recall of Verbal Messages by Children', *Develop. Psychol.* **5**, pp. 237–43.

WEICK, K. E. (1968), 'Systematic Observational Methods' in Lindzey, G., and Aronson, E. (eds.), *Handbook of Social Psychology*, Vol. 2, Addison-Wesley, Reading, Mass.

WEIKART, D. P. (1967), *Results of Preschool Intervention Programs*, Ypsilanti, Michigan.

WEIKART, D. P. (1972), 'Relationship of Curriculum, Teaching and Learning in Preschool Education in *Preschool Programs for the Disadvantaged*, Stanley, J. C. (ed.), The Johns Hopkins University Press, Baltimore, Maryland.

WELLS, C. G. (1974), *Language Development in Pre-school Children,* School of Education, University of Bristol, (not published).

WELLS, C. G., and FERRIER L. (1972), *A Framework for the Semantic Description of Child Speech in its Conversational Context:* Proceedings of the International Syposium on First Language Acquisition, September, 1972.

WHITE, BURTON C., *et al.,* (1973), *Experience and Environment: Major Influences on the Development of the Young Child,* Vol. 1, Prentice-Hall, Englewood Cliffs, New Jersey.

WHITE, S. (1969), *Some General Outlines of the Matrix of Developmental Changes between five and seven years,* Paper read at International Congress of Psychology, London.

WILKINSON, A. (1969), 'The Quality of Language Experience in Younger Children', *Journal of Curriculum Studies* **1**/3.

WILKINSON, A. (1971), *The Foundations of Language,* Oxford University Press, Oxford.

WILKINSON, A., and STRATTA, L. (1969), 'The Evaluation of Spoken Language', *Educational Review* (Birmingham) **21**, p. 183.

WILKINSON, A., STRATTA, L., and DUDLEY, P. (1974), *The Quality of Listening,* Macmillan for the Schools Council, London.

WILLIAMS, F. (1968), *Social Class Differences in how Children Talk about Television,* Mimeo, Institute for Research on Poverty, University of Wisconsin.

WILLIAMS, F. (1970), 'The Psychological Correlates of Speech Characteristics: on Sounding "disadvantaged" ', *Journal of Speech and Hearing Research* **13**, p. 472.

WILLIAMS, F. (ed.), (1970), *Language and Poverty: Perspectives on a Theme,* Markham, Chicago.

WILLIAMS, F., and NAREMORE, R. C. (1969a), 'On the Functional Analysis of Social Class Differences in Modes of Speech', *Speech Monographs* **36**, p. 77.

WITHALL, J. (1962), 'A Symposium on Conceptual Frameworks for Analysis of Classroom Interaction: Introductory Comment', *J. exp. Educ.,* 1962, 30, pp. 307–8.

List of Participants and Observers
at Leeds Seminar, January 1974

D. Bennett, Communication Skills in Early Childhood Project, Institute of Education, University of Leeds

M. Beveridge, Hester Adrian Research Centre, University of Manchester

Miss C. L. Boyle, Her Majesty's Inspectorate, Scottish Education Department

Tom Brown, Moray House College of Education

J. S. Bruner, Department of Experimental Psychology, University of Oxford

Courtney Cazden, Harvard Graduate School of Education

Maurice Chazan, University College of Swansea

Margaret Clark, Department of Psychology, University of Strathclyde

Alan Davies, Department of Linguistics, University of Edinburgh

Ruth Day, Department of Psychology, University of Yale

June Derrick, Language Centre, University of York

W. B. Dockrell, Scottish Council for Research in Education

W. Donachy, Department of Psychology, University of Strathclyde

Hazel Francis, Department of Education, University of Leeds

Caroline Garland, Bedford College, London

W. A. Gatherer, Educational Development Branch, Edinburgh Corporation

Carol M. Lomax, Department of Psychology, University of Strathclyde

K. Lovell, Institute of Education, University of Leeds

Miss E. McDougall, Department of Education and Science

W. R. O'Donnell, Department of Linguistics, University of Leeds

M. A. Poulton, Western Australia Pre-School Education Board

John Powell, Scottish Council for Research in Education

John Rankin, Her Majesty's Inspectorate, Scottish Education Department

Elisabeth Sestini, Communication Skills in Early Childhood Project, Institute of Education, University of Leeds

Maureen A. Shields, Department of Child Development, University of London Institute of Education

K. Sylva, Department of Psychology and Social Relations, University of Harvard

J. Solomon, Western Australia Pre-School Education Board

P. M. Stratton, Department of Psychology, University of Leeds

K. G. Stukát, Department of Educational Research, Gothenburg
Joan Tough, Communication Skills in Early Childhood Project,
    Institute of Education, University of Leeds
Roger Wales, Department of Psychology, University of St. Andrews
Joyce Watt, Department of Education, University of Aberdeen
Gordon Wells, School of Education, University of Bristol
H. L. Williams, National Foundation for Educational Research

(Affiliations are as of January 1974)

List of Participants and Observers at Bristol Seminar, January 1975

Paul Berry, Hester Adrian Research Centre, University of Manchester
Marion Blank, c/o Thomas Coram Research Unit, Institute of Education University of London
Allayne Bridges, School of Education, University of Bristol
James Britton, Goldsmiths College, London
Thomas Brown, Moray House College of Education, Edinburgh
Asher Cashdan, Open University, Walton Hall, Milton Keynes
Maurice Chazan, Department of Education, University College of Swansea
Richard Choat, Social Science Research Council, London
Ruth Clark, Edinburgh School of Speech Therapy, 7 Buccleuch Place, Edinburgh 8
Alan Davies, Department of Linguistics, University of Edinburgh
Bryan Dockrell, Scottish Council for Research in Education, Edinburgh
Margaret Donaldson, Department of Psychology, University of Edinburgh
Linda Ferrier, School of Education, University of Bristol
Hazel Francis, Department of Education, University of Leeds
Colin Fraser, Social and Political Sciences, University of Cambridge
William Gatherer, Edinburgh Education Authority
Anne Kauder, Social Science Research Council, London
Ewan Klein, Unit for Research on Medical Applications of Psychology, University of Cambridge
David Mitchell, Hester Adrian Research Centre, University of Manchester
Keith Nettle, Heinemann Educational Books, London
David Olson, c/o Department of Experimental Psychology, Oxford
John Powell, Scottish Council for Research in Education, Edinburgh
Bridie Raban, Reading Centre, Bristol
Ken Reeder, School of Education, University of Birmingham
Sinclair Rogers, Department of Communication, Sheffield Polytechnic
Maureen Shields, Institute of Education, University of London
Chris Sinha, School of Education, University of Bristol
Barbara Tizard, Thomas Coram Research Unit, Institute of Education, University of London
Geoffrey Turner, Sociological Research Unit, Institute of Education, University of London
Gordon Wells, School of Education, University of Bristol
Bencie Woll, School of Education, University of Bristol

(Affiliations are as of January 1975)

Index